Declutter Your Mind and Your Life

3 Books in 1

Stop Overthinking, Digital Minimalism in Everyday Life, and Beginning Zen Buddhism

PUBLISHED BY: Amy White
©Copyright 2021 - All rights reserved.

All rights reserved. No part of this publication may be reproduced, distributed, or transmitted in any form or by any means, including photocopying, recording, or other electronic or mechanical methods, without the prior written permission of the publisher, except in the case of brief quotations embodied in critical reviews and certain other noncommercial uses permitted by copyright law.

Under no circumstances will any blame or legal responsibility be held against the publisher, or author, for any damages, reparation, or monetary loss due to the information contained within this book, either directly or indirectly.

Legal Notice:

This book is copyright protected. It is only for personal use. You cannot amend, distribute, sell, use, quote or paraphrase any part, or the content within this book, without the consent of the author or publisher.

Disclaimer Notice:

Please note the information contained within this document is for educational and entertainment purposes only. All effort has been executed to present accurate, up to date, reliable, complete information. No warranties of any kind are declared or implied. Readers acknowledge that the author is not engaged in the rendering of legal, financial, medical or professional advice. The content within this book has been derived from various sources. Please consult a licensed professional before attempting any techniques outlined in this book.

By reading this document, the reader agrees that under no circumstances is the author responsible for any losses, direct or indirect, that are incurred as a result of the use of the information contained within this document, including, but not limited to, errors, omissions, or inaccuracies.

Table of Contents

Your Free Gift 1

Book #1: How to Declutter Your Mind 3

Introduction 5

Chapter 1: What Is Mental Clutter? 7

Chapter 2: How Mental Clutter Works Against You 12

Chapter 3: The Benefits of Decluttering Your Mind 16

Chapter 4: Decluttering Your Brain 21

Chapter 5: Decluttering Your Life and Responsibilities 32

Chapter 6: Decluttering Your Personal Life and Relationships 39

Chapter 7: Decluttering Your Home 45

Chapter 8: Decluttering Your Workspace 52

Chapter 9: Decluttering Your Time Spent Online 57

Conclusion 61

Book #2: Digital Minimalism in Everyday Life 63

Introduction 65

Section 1: Defining and Understanding Concepts 66

Chapter 1: What Is Digital Minimalism? 67

Chapter 2: The Trap of Technology Addiction 76

Section 2: Digital Minimalism in Everyday Practice 83

Chapter 3: How to Do a Digital Inventory and Declutter 84

Chapter 4: The Why and How of a Digital Detox 99

Chapter 5: Digital Mindfulness 109

Chapter 6: More Tips and Life Hacks to Break Free of Technology Addiction ... 129

Chapter 7: Preventing a Relapse 138

Conclusion 140

Book #3: Beginning Zen Buddhism 141

Introduction 143

Chapter One: The Origin and Evolution of Zen Buddhism 145

Chapter Two: Buddhism: Karma, Suffering, Nirvana, and Reincarnation................ 148

Chapter Three: Zen Buddhism: Benefits and Techniques 160

Chapter Four: Buddhism and Mindfulness 165

Chapter Five: Experiencing Zen in our Everyday Life 171

Chapter Six: Transforming Your State of Mind through Kindness and Compassion...... 181

Chapter Seven: Center Your Life and Awaken Inner Peace with Zen Buddhism 187

Chapter Eight: Zen Is for Everybody.. 193

Chapter Nine: Center Your Life and Attain Inner Peace with Zen Buddhism........... 196

Chapter Ten: A Beginner's Guide to Daily Zen Mindfulness 200

Conclusion.. 207

Thank you... 209

Your Free Gift

As a way of saying thanks for your purchase, I want to offer you a free bonus e-Book called *7 Essential Mindfulness Habits* exclusive to the readers of this book.

To get instant access, just go to:

https://theartofmastery.com/mindfulness

Inside the book, you will discover:

- What is mindfulness meditation?
- Why mindfulness is so effective in reducing stress and increasing joy, composure, and serenity
- Various mindfulness techniques that you can do anytime, anywhere
- 7 essential mindfulness habits to implement starting today
- Tips and fun activities to teach your kids to be more mindful

Book #1
How to Declutter Your Mind

Secrets to Stop Overthinking, Relieve Anxiety, and Achieve Calmness and Inner Peace

Introduction

Our modern lives are as cluttered as they are hectic. There are so many different things demanding our attention at a time. Whether in school or the workforce, there's always someone expecting us to complete an assignment and follow their instructions. We are constantly bombarded with tasks and responsibilities to the point that it can feel like the only rest we get is when we go to sleep at the end of the day. Our personal lives can be just as frantic as our professional ones. Maintaining relationships often cuts into the little free time that we have, and while we may love our friends and family, sometimes keeping up with all of the plans and trying to be available for all of their needs can be as exhausting as work. Our calendars end up packed, and we're often left racing around trying to balance everything on our plates and desperately hoping we don't drop anything.

As a mother of two, I am intimately familiar with just how frantic life can be. I used to feel incredibly overwhelmed at the start of every day just thinking of all I needed to do by the end of it. I had all of my personal and professional responsibilities, and I also had to worry about my kids. I would race around in the mornings getting them ready and packing their lunches, all while running through a mental list of everything I needed to get done as soon as they were out the door. This left me with next to no time to unwind, which led me to feel anxious a great deal of the time. I was a compulsive overthinker, and my anxieties about my busy, cluttered life would play on repeat behind my eyelids as I tried to get some sleep at night. That doesn't even include how physically cluttered the house was. It wasn't uncommon to walk into a room and trip over some scattered blocks, and both my husband and I had made impulse purchases that ended up sitting on a shelf collecting dust. With so much clutter in my life, I knew I was creating a lot of stress for myself, and I needed to find a way to get things under control.

When our lives and our surroundings are cluttered, our minds are too. Our environment has an impact on our mental state. For example, certain colors can influence us based on their associations. Red is usually associated with passion and movement, so it often makes us feel more active. A small change in the colors of a room or building can affect how we feel at that location.

The same theory is true of the level of clutter in our environments. A neat and tidy room helps us feel more relaxed and allows us to focus on the task at hand because there is nothing to distract ourselves with. On the other hand, a busier environment full of distractions makes it harder for us to focus because it gives us too many different things for our brains to latch onto.

Imagine you're at work, and you have a TV playing in the room. It becomes nearly impossible to concentrate because even if you try to tune it out, the noise and visuals from the TV add to the amount of mental clutter you're experiencing. Even your phone can become a significant distraction due to the high level of clutter in the digital world. A busy schedule and relationships that require a lot of upkeep can impact you in the same way. Too much clutter for too long makes our brains buzz with activity, even when we're trying to focus or rest. If this state persists for too long, we can end up with numerous negative effects such as overthinking, anxiety, tension, and an inability to concentrate.

Knowing all of this, you might be wondering to yourself: What is the solution to reducing overthinking and decreasing anxiety? If environmental and lifestyle clutter create mental clutter, then decluttering our lives will help us declutter our minds.

The idea of reducing clutter takes a page out of the minimalism book. In minimalism, having a cleaner, more organized environment is more than just aesthetically pleasing. It is a more streamlined way to interact with our environment that reduces the number of distractions we encounter in our everyday life. A minimalist environment promotes greater mindfulness by taking the focus away from our surroundings and bringing it back toward ourselves. It becomes easier to navigate our surroundings more purposefully so we can spend less time on distractions and more time on what really matters. Living in a clutter-free household or workspace can help combat procrastination and overthinking as a result.

The concept of minimalism can be extended to the rest of your life. True minimalism means reducing the amount of unnecessary clutter in all aspects of your life, not just in your house. Deal with excessive clutter at work, and reduce the number of unnecessary responsibilities you have so you can focus on the most important ones. Limit the constant influx of non-essential information you receive from social media and other aspects of the digital world. Eliminate toxic relationships that give you anxiety, just like pruning old, misshapen branches from a tree so the tree can continue to grow. You can even start to rewire your brain, improving your mentality and letting go of harmful thoughts that take up space and hold you back. Declutter each area of your life by throwing out the stressful obligations and distractions that are ultimately unnecessary and bring you anxiety. When you live a more minimalist lifestyle and declutter your mind, you can achieve more mental clarity, focus, productivity, and peace.

With *How to Declutter Your Mind*, you will learn the secrets to living a more stress-free and tranquil life even as our modern world becomes busier and busier. You will learn useful strategies for decluttering various aspects of your life, including both your physical surroundings and your lifestyle. Applying these strategies will allow you to make more time for the parts of life that matter most. You will also have more personal time, which will help you relax and reduce any anxiety you might be feeling over deadlines and a crowded schedule.

It is so easy to fall into the trap of going with the flow of the constant hustle and bustle around us. So many people run themselves ragged every day without knowing there's a way out of this exhausting rat race. You can make time for your family and your close friends, all with time left over to pursue a professional life that aligns with your goals and eliminates busywork. Decluttering your life helps you add hours to your day and gives you a healthier, tidier mental state free of intrusive thoughts and worries. Don't waste any more time on pointless tasks and toxic relationships. Start decluttering your mind today so you can have a calmer life and experience true inner peace.

Chapter 1: What Is Mental Clutter?

"Clutter is anything that does not support your better self."—Eleanor Brownn

When a room is cluttered, it's hard to navigate. Things get lost in all of the junk lying around in unorganized piles. There are plenty of items that could be better used somewhere else in the house or thrown away entirely. These items make it difficult to find whatever we're looking for in the room, and they distract us from our intended purpose. Cluttered rooms directly impact our ability to function in the room. We might think about doing some spring cleaning every once in a while, but when we realize just how much work cleaning the room out would be, we tend to shrug and decide it's a task for another day.

A cluttered mind is similar to a cluttered room. Mental clutter is a term used to describe an overabundance of thoughts in our heads that makes it hard to think clearly. These might include thoughts of responsibilities we've given ourselves or taken on for someone else, multiple tasks we try to complete at the same time, feelings we're having trouble working through, trouble with our relationships, too much stimulation from TV or games, or anything else that only serves to distract us from more important thoughts. Like physical clutter, these thoughts pile up and effectively block out more relevant information. We might have trouble remembering important dates or tasks that we were supposed to get done instead of a bunch of small, meaningless tasks that distracted us.

Trying to stay focused on something when our minds are cluttered can feel the same as digging through a huge pile of junk trying to find the one thing we're looking for. It can cause us to feel just as overwhelmed as we would be in a crowded room or while staring at a huge pile of paperwork we have to complete by the end of the day. We have so much to think about that it all becomes too much. This can cause us to feel overworked, stressed, tired, and anxious.

In order to push back against these distracting and destructive feelings, we must target the root of the problem, not its symptoms. A relaxing spa day or a day off from work might relieve some of your stress at the moment, but as soon as you leave the spa or head back to your job the next morning, all of the stress is going to come right back. Instead, we must address the cause of the stress if we want to banish it for good. We need to reduce our mental clutter. To do this, we have to first examine why mental clutter occurs and find the sources of hyperactive thoughts in our lives.

Why Our Brains Become Cluttered

Mental clutter can come from a wide variety of sources. Some people may have a lot of stress from work, but their relationships are fairly relaxing, while others may find that keeping up relationships is more stressful than any job. Most will find at least a small amount of stress from multiple sources. When stress comes at us from many different angles, it is harder for us to deal with it since it feels like everything in our lives is introducing more mental clutter all at once. It's easy to feel overwhelmed, especially if we lack the right coping methods that might otherwise help us sort through and deal with all of the sources of stress.

Mental clutter looks a little different for everyone, but there are a few sources that are frequent offenders for most of us. If it feels like everything is slipping out of our control, we should take a look at these common causes of stress and mental clutter first. Key problems that can lead to mental clutter include a lack of prioritization of tasks, too many insignificant choices, and an equally cluttered environment. We will learn how to manage these problems throughout the book. For now, we will just take a look at how each of them can impact our lives and minds.

An Inability to Prioritize

Imagine that you have a laundry list of tasks to complete by the end of the day. Some have deadlines, and missing those deadlines will have a negative impact on your job performance, relationships with others, or sense of fulfillment. Others have deadlines further into the future, or they have no real consequences for not getting them done, but they are easier tasks. How do you work through your schedule? Do you just start at the top and work your way down? Do you begin with the hardest tasks or those with the nearest deadlines? Or do you pick off the easy tasks first and then find yourself with a mountain of work to rush through at the end of the day?

When there is too much for us to do in one day, we need to learn how to prioritize. Even though every task on our list is there for a reason, not every task has to be finished at the same time, and not every task is as important as the others. If we cannot separate the critical tasks from those that can wait a day or two, or if we choose to do what's easy instead of what's necessary, we will always find ourselves with far too much work and far too little time.

As the world around us places greater demands on our time and attention, mental clutter is becoming more and more common. We are expected to hold a lot of information in our brains at a time, but as we keep piling on responsibilities and distractions, we only increase the chances of sending the whole pile crashing to the ground. Too many responsibilities can cause us to lose sight of those that matter most. If we fail to prioritize the important tasks, we end up performing the easier, less important ones just to relieve mental clutter. This is just a short-term fix, and it only adds to the amount of clutter in the long run as we scramble to finish the tasks we didn't prioritize.

Too Many Decisions

We are inundated with countless decisions every day. These range from meaningless and benign choices to decisions that can change the direction of our lives. Unfortunately, there is little we can do to alleviate the stress of big decisions. Choosing something like your career path or where you want to live takes a lot of thought and care, and while this kind of decision can also be a source of circling thoughts and overthinking, it's not one that can be so easily set aside. However, there are many decisions we make that aren't nearly as important. An overabundance of these smaller, less significant decisions can compound our stress levels and tax our brains.

Think about the small choices you make every day. When you look in your closet in the morning, how long do you spend trying to pick out an outfit? You might try on a few shirts before you find one that looks right, or you might stand in front of your closet like you're waiting for something new to jump out at you. Staring into the fridge when you're looking for a snack is another all-too-common example of indecision. You probably have a few different things you could eat, but you might still feel like none of them really appeal to you. When you're at the grocery store, there are hundreds of products and dozens of brands for each product. Something as simple as choosing a cereal can take you 10 or 15 minutes as you weigh all of the different options, even though you know that if you had any of the boxes at home, you would eat them without complaint. Any decision would be fine, but it becomes all too easy to agonize over choices that ultimately matter little.

Too many choices can even interfere with relaxation time. You might turn on the TV only to flip through channels for half an hour, your eyes glazing over at the sheer number of options available, ensuring that you never settle on something. Rather than feeling relaxed, making a choice can feel less like finally finding something you're excited to watch and more like giving up and settling.

We desire choice, but too many choices can stress us out. We agonize over whether or not we picked the right thing or if there was a better option we passed over. Psychologist Barry Schwartz calls this the "paradox of choice," finding that "increased choice leads to greater anxiety, indecision, paralysis, and dissatisfaction" (Scott & Davenport, 2016, para. 8). More choices should make us happier, but instead, we spend more time worrying, and our thoughts become even more cluttered. We are distracted by thoughts of what could have been if we'd made a different choice, even if little would have changed in the long run. Even worse, too many of these smaller decisions can make it harder to focus on the big ones. The distraction they pose could keep us from taking the time we need to make the right choice when it matters. If we allow ourselves to get too bogged down in the details of less important choices, we will be unable to give the important choices the gravitas they deserve. Instead, they will be shoved to the backs of our minds, buried under mountains of mental clutter.

Cluttered Surroundings

Our environments have a significant impact on our mental states. You can experience the effect for yourself by just imagining yourself in different places. First, picture yourself at work, complete with all of the stresses of your job. Then, picture yourself laying on the beach, the sun beating down on you, and the waves lapping against the shore. Could you feel your shoulders relax a little bit as you went from work to the beach? Did you notice yourself breathing a little easier? If the effect of simply picturing yourself in different locations is this strong, then it is easy to see how being in one location or another can drastically change how tense you are. After all, you probably feel a lot more relaxed at home than you do at work—unless your home environment is just as chaotic and cluttered as your job.

The home should be somewhere safe and relaxing for us. When we allow it to get cluttered, we subconsciously increase our mental clutter as well until we can hardly find peace in our beds. This is true for any overly crowded location we might find ourselves in throughout the day. Clutter affects our brains and bodies, and that's not just because we might stub our toes or trip on a stray object. In fact, "clutter can affect our anxiety levels, sleep, and ability to focus," and it can also "make us less productive, triggering coping and avoidance strategies that make us more likely to snack on junk and watch TV shows" instead of dealing with the actual problem of having too much stuff (Sander, 2019, para. 4-5). When our environments are not conducive to productivity and focus, we have a hard time settling our thoughts long enough to get any work done. We also have trouble feeling fully relaxed when there are so many distractions around us.

Sometimes, it may feel more convenient to have more stuff in our homes, but the comfort that it affords us on the surface is a double-edged sword. Having too many possessions can make us less likely to exert effort. We get comfortable with our lives as they are, and while we may dream of something better, we lack the drive to achieve it because of how convenient our lives already are. We use impulse purchases as sources of temporary happiness instead of working to build a life that is truly fulfilling. This might mean we avoid anything that could jeopardize our comfort, including opportunities to build a better life. Having too much stuff isn't just a financial or physical issue; it is a problem that can completely take over our mindsets and keep us from pursuing what we really care about.

The issue of environmental clutter is something that minimalists have been aware of for a long time. They have frequently preached the benefits of decluttering your environment in order to declutter your thoughts. This same concept can be applied to all of the previous sources of mental clutter. By reducing the amount of time-wasting junk in all areas of our lives, we can slow down our racing thoughts and get rid of mental clutter.

What Does It Mean to Declutter Your Thoughts?

You can declutter your thoughts the same way you might tidy up physically. Think of your mind as a house and each area of your life as a room within that house. If there is too much junk in any one room, that room has to be cleaned up. If all of the rooms have too much clutter, then all of the rooms have to be cleaned, but you can't clean every room at once. Instead, start by examining a single room, or area of your life, and work your way through each area from there.

Sometimes, decluttering means throwing things away. When you're decluttering your thoughts, this might include lowering the number of tasks you burden yourself with each day. "Throw away" any tasks that aren't necessary and don't bring you any sense of enjoyment or fulfillment. You may also need to throw away certain relationships that have grown toxic and harmful to one or both parties. Both of these things are hard, just like throwing out items you've been hoarding, but once you clear your life of unnecessary worries, it will all be worth it.

At other times, decluttering can just mean tidying up and reorganizing. For example, creating a schedule for yourself can help you complete activities on time and stick to priority tasks above all else. Adjusting your schedule can also help you free up more time for family and friends. Reorganizing physically can help too, whether you're rearranging your closet or completely revamping the furniture arrangement in your living room. You aren't throwing anything away, but by packing things into organized boxes and lists, you're still opening up your schedule and living a more relaxed lifestyle.

As we continue through the book, you will learn how to systematically clean out each room of your mental house. As you do, you will learn what really matters and what you can live without. You will start to prioritize your responsibilities, cut back on unnecessary decision-making, and declutter your physical environment alongside your thoughts. This process will allow you to avoid the detrimental effects of too much mental clutter, helping you lead a focused, committed life full of only the things that matter most to you.

Chapter Takeaways

This chapter dealt with basic information about the idea of mental clutter. In this chapter, you learned:

- The term "mental clutter" refers to the idea of cleaning out unnecessary sources of strife and stress from your life.
- There are several common causes of mental clutter, including trouble prioritizing responsibilities, stressing over small decisions, and crowded surroundings.
- To declutter your thoughts is to remove or lessen the sources of mental clutter you encounter every day.

In the next chapter, we'll take a look at all of the ways mental clutter holds you back.

Chapter 2: How Mental Clutter Works Against You

"You can't reach for anything new if your hands are full of yesterday's junk."—Louise Smith

You now understand what mental clutter is, but you might not yet be sold on the idea of reducing it. After all, it involves rehauling a great deal of your life, and this can take a lot of effort. You might be asking yourself: Is all of this really necessary? How bad can mental clutter really be?

Though it may seem harmless in small amounts, mental clutter is surprisingly counterproductive to living a fulfilling life. If you allow clutter to persist, you invite a whole host of physical and mental effects that could otherwise be avoided.

It's no secret that clutter is troublesome, but is it really dangerous? When it comes to mental clutter, the effects can be more worrying than you would first think. Clutter works against us because it changes the way our brains process the world around us. We tend to gravitate toward organization. We function best when our environments are suited for our goals. When we work, we want a clean environment free of anything that would pull our attention away from our task. It's much easier to get some work done if we're at a desk that is free of clutter than it is if the TV remote is within our reach and there are scattered stacks of papers everywhere. The same is also true of mental clutter. If we're thinking about a conversation that we had yesterday that didn't go as planned or we're worried about completing all of the tasks on our mental list for the day, our thoughts may drift from our work more often than they should.

An inability to focus on anything for long ensures that we can't reach our full potential. It takes patience and care to work toward our long-term goals, neither of which we can achieve if we can't concentrate. When we allow clutter to distract us, we effectively sabotage ourselves. Of course, a lack of focus is a more obvious symptom of the mental clutter issue, but it's not the only one. There are many other effects of living a cluttered life that can be just as if not more damaging.

Effects of a Cluttered Life

Distraction is just one part of the burden of clutter. Living and working in cluttered environments, either physically or in terms of our lifestyle, is more likely to make us stressed and anxious. We feel trapped and restless, which can trick us into believing that we're in danger. This kind of prolonged stress can have serious results.

Another issue comes from the tension between instant gratification and delayed gratification. If we fill our lives with clutter in the form of impulse purchases or endlessly scrolling through social media instead of putting our phones down and doing something more constructive with our time, we give in to the pull of instant gratification. We choose an easy, simple task over a more complex one. This subconsciously trains us to repeat the same behavior, which can seriously get in the way of our ability to achieve long-term success.

These two impacts, stress and instant gratification, show us just how detrimental mental clutter can be to our mental and physical health. By understanding how each of these impacts works against us, we can start to understand the value of decluttering our lives.

Clutter and Stress

Stress has often been referred to as "the silent killer." Some people only experience stress briefly and periodically. This is not so bad. Our bodies are designed to manage brief bursts of stress by entering into what is commonly known as fight-or-flight mode. In this mode, our reflexes are heightened, our blood pressure and heart rate increase, and we're ready to act. In small doses, like when we're staying up late to work on a big project or if we have to run from a dangerous animal, we can process this stress without a problem. The danger eventually goes away, and our fight-or-flight response goes away with it.

Chronic stress is a much greater problem. We get stuck in the mentality that we should be running or hiding from something, even if we're not facing life-threatening circumstances. If our lives are hectic and we're always on edge, the 'threat' our minds are perceiving doesn't go away. It sticks around, leaving us saddled with high stress. Without good coping strategies or any way to decrease the amount of stress in our life, we constantly feel a low-level threat that we can't do anything about. This chronic stress can lead to serious health issues.

Stress leaves you feeling on edge and tense. Excessive tension for a long time can leave you with persistent soreness. Try flexing the muscles in your arm, then hold them that way for a few seconds. When you relax, you'll feel a minor ache that should go away quickly. Now, imagine you carry low-level tension around with you all of the time. That minor ache becomes a major one, and it doesn't go away nearly as quickly because you are never able to fully relax.

Long-term stress can also lead to high blood pressure, which increases your risk of a heart attack, stroke, or heart disease. Your heart works double or triple as hard as it usually does, which puts a lot of strain on your body. Stress can also interfere with your digestive system. It has been linked to higher rates of diabetes, eating disorders, and obesity, as well as conditions such as Crohn's disease, ulcerative colitis, and irritable bowel syndrome (American Brain Society, 2019, para. 10). These conditions range from uncomfortable to quite dangerous to your health.

But what does all of this have to do with clutter? Surely a busy schedule and a messy room can't be connected to these serious consequences, can they? Unfortunately, many studies have found that clutter can indeed act as a stressor that creates chronic, persistent stress in our lives. A research study on mothers found "the levels of the stress hormone cortisol were higher in mothers whose home environment was cluttered" (Sander, 2019, para. 11). The more clutter that surrounds us, the higher our cortisol levels, and the more likely we are to experience the damaging effects of chronic stress. To fix this problem, we must go further than temporary solutions like taking a day off. We must deal with the issue at its roots, meaning we have to reduce the number of sources of stress we are exposed to every day. If we don't, we could be facing serious health issues.

How Clutter Holds You Back

Think about the most cluttered room in your house. What kind of objects are in it? When you bought these objects, were you thinking about how they would help you in the long term, or were you just trying to fulfill a short-term need? Were they carefully thought-out purchases, or were they impulse buys? Chances are that if you had taken the time to really consider if you needed each item or not, you wouldn't have ended up with such a cluttered room in the first place. Clutter comes from the accumulation of things we don't need, which are often things we only bought to solve a short-term problem and haven't gotten around to throwing away yet.

Now think about a cluttered aspect of your life, whether it's part of your professional or personal life. Did you really think through all of the decisions you made that brought you to this point? When you chose your job, were you thinking about how it would help you achieve your future career goals, or did you just need something to pay the bills, even if the job wasn't particularly fulfilling? When you decided not to talk about the elephant in the room with someone you're close to, did you consider the future ramifications, or were you only trying to avoid the temporary discomfort?

Many of the greatest mistakes we make in life come from a place of trying to avoid pain and only looking for what is the most enjoyable. We may think that this causes the least amount of harm in the short term, but when you look at the long-term effects, these kinds of choices often end up doing more harm than good. For example, when you chose not to talk about that difficult subject with a friend, family member, or partner, you probably did it to spare their feelings. However, if the situation persists, the relationship might grow stilted and distant as the two of you dance around the topic, or you might become more frustrated because of something they don't even know is bothering you. Maybe you chose your current job for no other reason than the payment, not thinking about how it would fit into your plans for the future. If your job is draining and isn't in the field you want to pursue, it could be contributing to your mental clutter and exhaustion. As the clutter builds up from short-sighted decisions, it could become harder to recognize that there's another way.

Pursuing instant gratification and making impulsive decisions interfere with your ability to think critically about your choices. Skipping a healthy lunch and grabbing fast food might taste good at the moment, but it does no favors for your health. The longer you repeat the behavior, the harder it becomes to change your ways. This is true for all habits that work against you instead of helping you pursue your goals. Building up clutter from poor decision-making just reinforces the bad decisions. It's harder to make your lunch if you're used to getting fast food and haven't cooked in a while. It's harder to find a job that's personally fulfilling if you've convinced yourself your current one is safer, and it's harder to finally broach that uncomfortable topic with a friend if it's been tainting the relationship for months.

When you start shifting your focus toward your future rather than settling for whatever causes the least amount of discomfort at the moment, your fear of discomfort starts to fade. Cluttered surroundings and a cluttered life might keep you comfortable on the surface, but stress and anxiety sit just underneath the surface level of comfort. Additionally, this sense of paper-thin comfort keeps you just complacent enough that you don't really feel motivated enough to make the necessary changes in your life. If you can learn to let go of the things that make your life so cluttered, even when it's hard or the results are uncertain, you will live a more fulfilling life overall. Reducing the clutter lets you start seeing the forest for the trees. It becomes easier to let go of the things you're keeping around that serve no purpose, giving you greater peace of mind.

Chapter Takeaways

In this chapter, you learned about the damaging effects that too much clutter can have on your mind and your life. The lessons you learned in this chapter include:

- A life full of clutter can distract you from what's important.
- Being in cluttered environments can create higher levels of cortisol, a stress hormone, in your body.
- Stress can lead to significant health problems like gastrointestinal issues, aches and pains, and heart disease.
- Continued clutter makes it harder to focus on achieving your goals and gets you into the habit of thinking short-term instead of long-term.

Next, we'll compare these negative effects to all of the positive effects that you can enjoy if you rid your life of clutter.

Chapter 3: The Benefits of Decluttering Your Mind

"When we throw out the physical clutter, we clear our minds. When we throw out the mental clutter, we clear our souls."—Gail Blanke

As we learned in the previous chapter, distraction, stress, and caving to instant gratification are some of the negative impacts of clutter. The more stressed we are, the more likely we are to experience anxiety and overthinking. If we want to eliminate these troublesome and sometimes dangerous side effects, we need to declutter our minds.

Decluttering your mind isn't easy. It can take a lot of work, and it may require you to make some difficult choices. You are going to have to choose the hard road over the easy road sometimes. But when you know the benefits that await you when you rid your life of clutter, it becomes so much easier to make the right choice.

Mental clutter undermines you at every turn. As long as your lifestyle is cluttered, filling your daily schedule with busywork and tasks that don't align with your goals, you will experience the negative effects. Trying to achieve success, whatever success means to you, is difficult when you spend your time in a cluttered house or cluttered workspace dealing with a cluttered mind. To declutter your mind is to lessen the impact of these negative effects and, ultimately, to remove their power over you altogether. Decluttering helps you deal with the problem at its source. You reduce the number of things in your life that contribute to stress and stop using impulse purchases to manage your moods. Through this, you are able to free up time that you would have otherwise spent either completing meaningless tasks or worrying about these sources of stress. Decluttering your mind gives you more time for rest, and it can significantly improve your mentality. These are positive effects that are well worth any amount of effort required to achieve them.

How Decluttering Your Mind Supports Your Continued Growth

If you've ever done spring cleaning, you know what it feels like to transform a mess of old junk, piles of clothes, and other clutter into a neat and tidy room. The work is a little tiring, and you're sure to get a good workout from it. You might spend an entire day throwing things out and rearranging what's left, or you might break it up and tackle the work over multiple days or weeks. No matter how you tackle it, there's a sense of satisfaction that comes from a job well done. When you look around you and see everything in its place, free of anything that had only been gathering dust while it went unused, you feel good about what you've accomplished. It's like you're giving yourself an opportunity to start over, and as long as you keep things clean and avoid buying things you don't need again, you won't have to repeat the process next spring.

Since mental decluttering follows the same principles as minimalistic interior design, it can bring us similar results. When we declutter our minds, we give ourselves a greater sense of freedom. Our schedules open up, our thoughts are free of distractions, and the restless buzzing of our thoughts at the back of our head is quieted. Without mental clutter, we can feel more at peace than we have for years. Alongside all of these benefits, we also make it easier for ourselves to focus on the future rather than lingering in the past. As we begin thinking about what's next for us, we can start to clear out any responsibilities that don't help us achieve our goals, making us more efficient and more relaxed at the same time.

Free Up Your Schedule

A cluttered schedule full of assignments and deadlines isn't conducive to a good work-life balance or good mental health. We can only deal with so many tasks at a time. If we are constantly running around without any downtime, we're only going to grow more exhausted each day. Eventually, we start to feel burned out. Even doing small tasks becomes almost impossible, and everything takes much more effort than it ever did before. Burnout can decimate our ability to be productive and lead us into the trap of procrastination. When we already have a busy schedule, procrastinating makes things even worse. Mental clutter mounts as we think of all of the things we need to do, but we lack the motivation necessary to get any of them done.

When we begin decluttering our schedules, the wave of work that threatens to overwhelm us grows smaller by the day. Instead of a mountain of tasks waiting for us each day, we start doing only those that really need to get done. This allows us to manage our time better and gives us more free time. Decompression is just as important as getting work done. If we are constantly stressed, the quality of our work will suffer. Freeing up our schedules and giving ourselves breaks lets us feel relaxed and rejuvenated. Rather than making us 'lazy,' this encourages us to get more work done. We are no longer distracted by small tasks, nor do we constantly feel burned out. Because of this, we have the energy and motivation we need to tackle the important things we've been putting off. The quality of our work improves, and we have more time available to share with family and friends.

Decluttering can help us improve our mentalities about work too. When you're constantly busy, every bit of new work feels like a chore. You dread getting new assignments and responsibilities because you have to find a way to fit them in with everything that's already on your to-do list. When you drop some of the unimportant tasks and give yourself less to do each day, any new task feels less like a burden and more like an opportunity. We start feeling excited by work and other activities again because we feel like we're making a choice of whether or not to take them on, rather than having them forced upon us. When we are in greater control of our lives and our daily schedules, even the hard tasks become something we're doing because we're passionate about the outcome. We have made the deliberate choice to commit to the task knowing that it really matters to us whether or not it gets done. This feeling of self-empowerment makes difficult activities a lot more bearable.

Eliminate Circling Thoughts

When our minds are cluttered, we give ourselves a lot to think about. Whether we ruminate on the busy day we just had, think about what awaits us tomorrow, or simply get distracted by our environment, our thoughts may grow to be loud and disruptive. It's hard to focus on anything when these thoughts clutter our minds. We might find ourselves drifting and hardly paying attention to what's in front of us. This ensures we can't focus our full concentration on anything, whether we're trying to work on something or relax. We end up doing everything by half measures, sabotaging ourselves with the thoughts that won't stop circling in our heads. If we're working, our train of thought falters periodically, and the quality of our work may suffer. If we're trying to relax, reminders of the responsibilities we're avoiding keep intruding upon what should be a leisurely activity, causing stress to return full-force.

Circling thoughts are especially troublesome when they follow you to bed. If you're someone who frequently finds yourself overthinking, you've probably kept yourself up with your worries before. Every time you try to close your eyes and clear your mind, another source of anxiety intrudes upon your thoughts. You think about something that happened earlier in the day that didn't go as planned or something you need to do tomorrow that's giving you stress already. Thoughts bounce around in your skull, ensuring that every time you nearly fall asleep, you are jolted awake again. This may even become a nightly occurrence if things in your life don't slow down. Overthinking can lead to chronic insomnia, which limits the amount of sleep you get each night and leaves you feeling almost perpetually tired. You don't want to float through the next day in a barely-there haze, especially if you've got a schedule that's as cluttered as your thoughts.

Decluttering your mind helps you calm these circling thoughts so you can focus during the day and get better rest at night. When your mind isn't constantly jumping from one thing to another, always reminding you of all your sources of worry, it is much easier to settle your thoughts. Instead of lying in bed all night staring up at your ceiling, you will be able to relax and fall asleep more readily. This will leave you feeling refreshed and ready to go the next day, more than capable of handling whatever life throws at you without slipping back into mental clutter.

Trade Anxiety for Peace and Calmness

Too much clutter makes us anxious. If this clutter is physical, we can feel like we're trapped, forcing our way through our homes rather than following the natural flow of each room. It's uncomfortable to pick our way around a cluttered room, and it requires us to think about where we're going more than a clean room would. On top of this, if we keep items around because we believe we will need them again at some unknown future point, we likely do so out of a form of anxiety. We worry that we will be unprepared for the future if we don't have 20 different charging cables in our desk or if we don't keep the clothes that we haven't worn in years but "might wear again someday." Maybe we feel anxious about the money we spent on items that ultimately turned out to be less useful than we thought, and we're only keeping them around out of this same sense of anxiety. Rather than keeping our minds at peace, however, living in a cluttered environment leaves us with mounting worries and fears that are often unrealistic or unnecessary.

A cluttered schedule and mind give us this same form of clutter anxiety. If we're always racing to keep up with everything we need to do today, we never give ourselves a chance to relax and unwind. If we allow our thoughts to circle and spiral into negativity at every turn, we start looking at everything through a negative lens, which only makes our anxiety worse.

Decluttering is the solution to these problems. With a cleaner living space, a less demanding schedule, and no more circling thoughts, many of the everyday sources of anxiety we encounter will vanish too. Without them, we will feel more comfortable and peaceful. Rather than bustling around, we can take our time with tasks and give them the attention they deserve. This eliminates any worries about a poorly done job. It also takes a load off our shoulders and encourages us to slow down and breathe. Less mental clutter helps us feel peaceful and dispels many different sources of worry that would otherwise hold us back.

Focus on Your Future

Many of the things that clutter our minds are relics of the past. They sit on shelves in our mind collecting dust, even as they continue to give us anxiety and stress. Think about how many items you have in your home that you just haven't used in years. Unless you've made a dedicated effort to go minimalist, you probably have plenty of things you bought with the best of intentions but never ended up using. Now, you might only keep them around out of a sense of obligation. You made an unnecessary purchase in the past, you reason, so the least you can do is keep it until it becomes useful again. However, the item in question typically never ends up becoming useful again. It only takes up space.

Past decisions in many different forms can continue to haunt us long after we make them. If we're unhappy with our job but we've had it for many years, we might rationalize it by pointing out that we've had it forever and it would be tough to get a new one. Because we have convinced ourselves we are comfortable as we are, we cling to the past, unwilling to hunt for a job that would make us happier. Old relationships can be negative forces in our lives too. Not all old friendships are bad, of course—we might have some friends we made in childhood whose company we still enjoy, and that's fine—but sometimes, we continue a friendship only because we've had it for a long time. If the relationship is draining rather than fulfilling, we should ask ourselves why we insist on maintaining it. Learning to let go of toxic relationships is a huge step toward decluttering our minds. It isn't always easy, but if we remain stuck in these harmful relationships, we will never be able to move forward with our lives.

Impulse purchases kept around for years, dead-end jobs, toxic relationships, and other sources of clutter are all things of the past. They keep us trapped in place, connecting us to our old lives and preventing us from escaping to a cleaner, less cluttered life. We have to learn to let go of these things before we can move forward. We must keep with us only those things that are positive, healthy forces in our lives and throw out everything else. Otherwise, we will always be looking backward instead of forward. By ridding our lives of clutter, we can start focusing on our future, not our past.

Is Decluttering Really Effective?

The amazing effects of decluttering might sound too good to be true. You may also be wondering to yourself: Is clutter really this powerful? Can decluttering actually help me make these changes?

It may be hard to see just how effective decluttering can be in your life if you picture it only as throwing away some old junk or if you think decluttering only happens on a mental level. You might picture decluttering as something as simple as a meditation exercise; perhaps you will clear your mind, but all of the clutter will still be there when the meditation ends. However, while meditation might be one part of your decluttering strategy, it shouldn't be the only one. Decluttering doesn't just occur in your mind. It occurs in all aspects of your life.

Clutter is present in many different areas of our lives, so we must declutter each of these areas. Decluttering is a promise you make to yourself to rid your life of everything holding you back. It doesn't stop at just donating a few piles of unworn clothes, and it's not as temporary as a vacation away from your busy life. If you declutter your life, the effects are permanent. When you experience these effects for yourself, you will have no desire to clutter your life all over again and go back to the way things were before. You will start making decisions with more forethought, and you will subconsciously make choices that keep your life free of unnecessary clutter. This will help you feel freer as well.

Decluttering is most effective because it helps you focus on the most important parts of your life. If you find yourself caught up in activities that don't benefit you, decluttering helps you let these activities go. You throw out everything that doesn't align with your desires and goals, whether this is as small of a change as finally getting rid of old clothes that no longer fit or as big of a change as pursuing a new career path. Through this process, you find out what matters to you and what you want to achieve with your life. You also have the time and desire to work toward these goals. Decluttering is so powerful because it allows you to become more in control of your life and gives you all of the tools you need to turn your life around for the better.

Chapter Takeaways

This chapter explained how decluttering your mind can help you. In this chapter, you learned:

- Too much clutter keeps you from becoming the best person you can be.
- Decluttering will help you reduce the amount of work you are expected to do each day and cut your to-do list down to only the necessary tasks.
- With less clutter, racing thoughts will slow down, and you will experience more peace and calmness.
- From this new perspective, you can start working toward goals that are truly important to you.

In the following chapter, we'll examine how our brains function and why we're seemingly predisposed to mental clutter.

Chapter 4: Decluttering Your Brain

"Keeping baggage from the past will leave no room for happiness in the future."—Wayne L. Misner

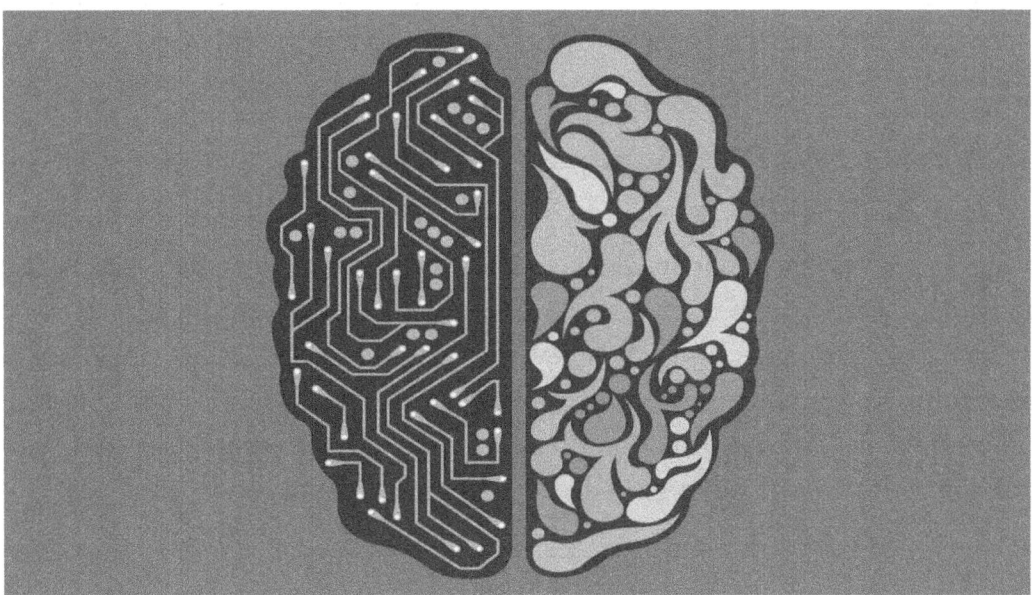

We've spent the last two chapters exploring the idea of mental decluttering and examining why it's a worthwhile endeavor. Now, we're going to start taking the necessary steps to declutter our lives, and through this process, we'll also declutter our minds. From this point on, we will focus on specific areas of our lives and take a look at some actionable advice that we can use to significantly reduce mental clutter. Since clutter affects our thoughts so severely, it only makes sense to start by decluttering our brains.

Our brains are complicated, and even scientists don't know everything about exactly how they function. Chances are you know little about the intricate processes that take place in your head every day. While it can be an intimidating topic, getting a better understanding of our brains can help us see how mental clutter becomes a problem and what we can do to stop it.

First, we'll start with a bit of background knowledge on how our brains work. Our brains control many different functions, and most of them happen without our conscious knowledge. Our brains are connected to our entire bodies. They are responsible for controlling our bodies' automatic processes, like breathing, even though we don't have to think about breathing in order to do it. Our brains are also primarily responsible for responding to stimuli that we encounter in our environments or in our bodies. What affects the mind affects the body, and vice versa; this is because the brain is so thoroughly connected to the rest of our body.

Our minds are hardwired to pick up on all stimuli in our environments. We notice and react to all kinds of things without realizing it. Thousands of years ago, we needed to have such a responsive brain to survive in our environments. Picking up on small details was a matter of life or death. Even today, we still respond somewhat similarly. We might hear a dog angrily barking in the distance and think nothing of it, but our brains pick up on the sound and label it as a potential danger. In response to the stressor, our muscles might tense a bit, and our blood pressure might increase, even though we're not in any immediate danger. These responses occur on such a minute level that you probably won't notice them unless you have a phobia of dogs, but they occur all the same. Still, this is just a minor, acute stressor, so it has little impact on our long-term behavior. The real issues appear when we experience chronic stress.

How Our Brains Process Chronic Stress

Chronic stress is different from acute stress. Our brains have much more trouble managing stress the longer it occurs. This is because our brains become almost overactive, and we have trouble "turning them off" and tuning out our automatic responses. We continue to react to stresses like clutter even if they pose little to no danger simply because that is how we are wired. A cluttered environment and lifestyle make it harder for us to focus and provide many different distractions for our brains to react to, which can overload us. If we are always moving and never get the rest we so desperately need, we can overtax our brains, causing us to experience stress and anxiety more frequently.

Think of the kind of bad mood you experience when you don't get enough sleep. This is because your brain didn't get the rest it needed to function optimally the next day. We are incredibly adaptive and reactive; filling our lives with clutter or overexerting our brains only leads to chronic stress. Over time, the effects of this stress build up and make it harder for us to react to our environments with anything other than stress.

Adaptive Thinking

The incredible adaptability of our brains allows us to react to nearly any situation with only minor hesitation. Typically, adaptability is great. It helps us survive in environments that would otherwise be inhospitable for us, whether this is because we live somewhere extremely hot or cold or because we've entered a new cultural or social environment. Our brains pick up on cues from these environments, and we learn how to react differently than we would under other circumstances. Our ancestors adapted to colder temperatures by creating and wearing clothing to insulate themselves from the cold. Now, we have socialized ourselves to almost always wear clothing in public. This, too, is an adaptation that has been passed down through the generations. A similar type of adaptation occurs if we travel to a different country and try to integrate ourselves into the culture. It takes us some time to catch on to what others are doing, but before we know it, we're acting as if we have lived there our whole lives.

It's important to note that adapting to our environments often has lifelong effects on our behaviors. For example, someone might maintain an accent from the country they grew up in for the rest of their life just because it was how everyone around them sounded when they were learning to talk. If you take a vacation to another country and don't spend long there, you will probably default to the customs of your home country in most situations unless you have been taught to act differently, and even then, it will be a conscious choice to practice the new behavior rather than an automatic response. We can learn and change our behaviors over time if we so choose, but once we have taught ourselves to think one way, it's not so easy to shake the habit.

At this point, you might be asking yourself: What exactly does all of this have to do with clutter again? Clutter is just another type of environment, which means our brains can adapt to it the same way they adapt to everything else. The circuits in our brain are 'plastic,' which means that if we experience the same situation for a while, our thought patterns will shift to accommodate it. These circuits can be "remodeled by stress to change the balance between anxiety, mood control, memory, and decision-making" (McEwen, 2012, para. 1). Changes in our thought patterns caused by clutter and stress are difficult to reverse. These changes are often maladaptive, frequently rewiring us to poorly tolerate extensive stress without developing any meaningful coping mechanisms. The longer we spend in stressful environments, the more our brains become used to this kind of pressure and the more trouble we have effectively resetting our brains.

The plasticity of our brains means that we might completely change the way we think without noticing the shift in our thoughts. When this happens, it's even harder to undo the change since we have become so swept up in our new mindsets that we forget that we have changed at all. This is most dangerous when we start developing a bias toward negative thinking.

Why We're Wired to Think Negatively

Have you ever experienced that one thing that turns a great day into an awful one? You might have had a perfectly fine morning and afternoon, but one bad experience at work or one argument with a family member could turn the whole day on its head. Rather than thinking you had an average day, you might start to believe that you had a terrible day, even though only one or two things went wrong.

This line of thinking can be expanded to your life as a whole. You've likely had both good and bad experiences, but sometimes, it's hard to see the good ones behind the bad ones. You might look back on the last year of your life and think, "That was a bad year," forgetting all of the good times you shared with friends and family along the way. There are certainly some years that are better than others, but there are always some positives to balance out the negatives. However, you have probably noticed that the bad things stand out in your mind much more than the good ones. Why is it that all of the good things that happen become discounted when we encounter minor bad things?

This phenomenon is known as negativity bias. Just like our ability to pick up on small cues in our environments that drastically affect how we interact with them, negativity bias may have developed back when our ancestors needed to avoid threats in their environments. It was more beneficial for us to always be on the lookout for the next bad thing. As psychology and neuroscience professor Barbara Fredrickson explains, "Negativity bias is nature's way of assuring that we don't get lulled into complacency and succumb to avoidable dangers" (Gould, 2019, para. 5). We might not live in environments with the same level of physical danger anymore, but our brains are still wired to fixate on sources of negativity. Everyday sources of stress can make our attitudes much worse and increase the otherwise minor effects of stressful experiences. We elevate them above the everyday positive events until all we can see is negativity.

As you might imagine, this does no favors for our mentalities. If we're always looking for the next thing to aggravate us or always thinking about the last frustrating encounter we had, our mindsets will suffer. Over time, we start to convince ourselves that this persistent negativity is normal and even beneficial. We become increasingly pessimistic, ready to rule everything as a potentially bad experience before we've even tried it. This makes us more set in our ways and can interfere with trying to make a positive change in our lives because we're not willing to take a risk, having already decided it will end badly for us. There are ways to push back against this negativity bias, like mentally reframing a negative event and recognizing that it is only a small part of an otherwise good day, but it takes some time to train our brains away from this thought pattern.

Thanks to negativity bias, our brains multiply the stressful effects of clutter far past what they would otherwise be. A busy schedule or an argument with a friend takes up space in our minds. Even if we try to distract ourselves and forget our worries, the ever-present clutter finds its way into our thoughts. With every new, unfortunate event, the clutter in our minds grows. Eventually, mental clutter itself becomes a source of negativity that interferes with our ability to destress and calm our minds. Negativity from mental clutter overwhelms any positive experiences we might have that day, and we start thinking of every day as a bad day, even if nothing particularly upsetting happened. Our minds are full of negative thoughts, and we start to lose sight of the sources of positivity and optimism in our lives.

In order to reverse the effects of negativity bias, we must work to undermine the clutter that causes our brains to overreact. By doing so, we give our brains fewer sources of negativity to latch onto, which means our thoughts become less cluttered. We must also look at other aspects of our lives that might be affecting our psyche and cluttering our brains and take proactive steps to address these issues.

Other Factors That Affect Our Psyches

Negativity bias is just one of the many factors that can have a detrimental impact on our psyches and increase clutter in our brains. If we want to effectively reduce clutter, we need to address all possible sources. These include things you may have experienced in the past, your current living situation, and events in your life that may cause stress levels that are higher than usual. By considering and addressing each of these factors, you can start to declutter your brain in a comprehensive, full-body way.

Low Self-Esteem

Many self-help books are full of advice about loving yourself. This is for a good reason; having high self-esteem makes it a lot easier to make sweeping changes to your life. Believing that you can do something is the first step to getting it done. If you look at all of the amazing things others are doing and decide you'll never be as successful as they are, you aren't going to be nearly as committed to making and sticking with a positive change. On the other hand, if you wholeheartedly believe that you are a confident and capable person who can and will succeed, you will keep looking for different solutions to every problem that you come across until you find one that works.

People with high self-esteem tend to take failure and misfortune better than those who lack self-confidence. Rather than feeling completely defeated, their confidence in themselves and their abilities allows them to bounce back and start looking for a solution to their problems rather than wallowing in their regrets. If you lack self-esteem, you are more likely to spend time blaming yourself for the unfortunate situation instead of spending that time trying to rebound from it. The more negative thoughts you direct toward yourself, the more your mental clutter grows. You may also find it hard to make significant changes in your life because you don't believe in your own ability to improve your current situation. Without self-esteem, you can easily trap yourself in a lifestyle that breeds mental clutter simply because you are too afraid to take the steps necessary to reduce the clutter.

Improving your self-esteem is tricky, and not every method will work for everyone. Some general guidelines include making an effort to try new things and spending time with people who care about you. Both of these can help you internalize the belief that you are capable and loved. Trying new things shows you that you can grow and that even if you aren't great at something at first, you can improve your skills, which pushes back against the self-defeating attitude. Spending time with loved ones reminds you that others care about you and that you are worthy of their friendship. If you catch yourself thinking negatively about yourself, adding to your mental clutter, reframe these thoughts and counter them with things you like about yourself. Improving your self-esteem gradually removes negative thoughts that are only taking up space in your mind. As your self-esteem grows, your anxiety and erratic thoughts will often calm down as well, letting you live a more peaceful and positive life.

Past Traumas

Traumatic events can follow us long after the cause of our trauma is gone from our lives. Even though we are no longer in the dangerous or stressful situation, we still feel its lasting impression on our psyches from time to time. We might be reminded of the event while doing something completely benign, or we might find ourselves unable to do certain things that remind us of our trauma. This is nothing to be ashamed of, but it can still be a source of frustration and mental clutter if we don't have sufficient coping mechanisms in place.

If left unresolved, past traumatic experiences can continue to interfere with our lives in unexpected ways. Trauma can affect our mental health, making low self-esteem and self-critical thoughts more common. These thoughts may circle and multiply in our heads, especially if we fall prey to our negativity bias. The more our traumas interfere with our lives, the more mental clutter we experience.

Trauma can also affect your behavior patterns. If you are used to people in your life criticizing you, you may put up with a toxic relationship for longer than you should. You might always be willing to give the other person the benefit of the doubt, even if you know deep down that they don't deserve it. Alternatively, if you experienced poverty, you might become more likely to hoard because you are reluctant to throw anything away. It can feel like you are wasting things, even when keeping them around and letting them clutter your house is doing you more harm than good. Financial troubles can also keep you stuck in a job you don't enjoy, even if you now have enough money to live comfortably, just because you remember what it was like to have little to your name. There are many other kinds of traumas that might contribute to clutter in their own way. If you feel like your traumatic experience is creating clutter and standing in the way of a better life for yourself and your family, you may need to seriously consider addressing and working through the trauma before proceeding with the decluttering process.

Managing trauma is not a one-size-fits-all process. Sometimes, you may need to seek professional help from a licensed therapist or psychiatrist. Other times, you may only need the support and reassurance of your friends and family. Choose the method that best helps you develop coping strategies for your trauma. Keep in mind that trauma may reappear over time, and you may not ever completely stop thinking about past events. But if you can find ways to calm your thoughts and reduce the mental clutter that you would otherwise experience, you will be able to avoid a great deal of overthinking and stress.

Current Life Events

Big life events can be incredibly disruptive. We are often completely unprepared for these unusual situations, and they tend to take up a lot of space in our minds. This is especially true if we experience a hardship or misfortune that causes our thoughts to spiral and creates clutter in our brains. Events like the passing of a loved one, the end of a relationship, a health scare, or the unexpected loss of a job or other source of financial security can leave you mentally reeling. It's hard to focus on much of anything when you are in the middle of a crisis. The grieving period that follows these events can be incredibly difficult. You may have difficulty processing your emotional reaction to these events. Your thoughts may constantly circle back to the event, distracting you from whatever you were trying to focus on and forcing your brain to work overtime. This creates a significant amount of mental clutter.

Even positive events can be the source of a lot of clutter. For example, if you're getting married, you're going to have a lot to think about all of the time. You'll need to choose a date, create the guest list, pick out a dress or suit, decide on the venue, arrange for catering, and complete a hundred other tasks before the big day. Anxieties about each of these tasks getting done can create a ton of mental clutter, and if you don't know how to clear your mind and get some rest, the clutter can distract you day and night. Other events like getting a new job, moving, and welcoming a new member into the family can also be sources of clutter, even though they are also happy events.

Dealing with these kinds of stressful events is largely dependent on finding ways to cope with the fallout. Make sure you have an opportunity to breathe and adjust and allow yourself to feel whatever emotions you are feeling because suppressing them only leads to more mental clutter. Sometimes, it's necessary to give yourself time to either heal from an especially unexpected loss or readjust to a new situation. Keep trying to ground yourself whenever you feel your thoughts spiraling, and seek out professional help when necessary.

A Chaotic Lifestyle

Our daily habits and lifestyles can influence our mindsets. If we are used to leading busy lives with no downtime, we start to develop a mindset that prioritizes constant work and doesn't leave any time for proper relaxation. As a result, we only end up running around more, convinced that staying busy is better than getting meaningful work done. We end up leading cluttered lives that create clutter in our brains.

Throughout the rest of the book, we will discuss methods for removing clutter in our lives. These methods include managing our responsibilities, eliminating unnecessary tasks from our daily schedules, reducing sources of distraction in the home and workplace, ridding our lives of detrimental relationships, and changing the way we approach the digital world. Making alterations in each of these areas will help us transform the chaos in our lives into something more orderly, which will allow us to live a life free from mental clutter.

How to Rewire Your Brain, Declutter, and Be Happier

Making changes to our lifestyles and avoiding unnecessary stressful events is only one part of the puzzle that is decluttering our minds. Sometimes, we are able to change the situation we are in. Other times, we are unable to leave a job we hate, cannot let go of a stressful responsibility, or have no way to avoid an event that brings us a lot of stress. In these situations, if we cannot control the source of our stress, then we must focus on the only thing we can control: our response to it.

When we react poorly to a difficult event in our lives, we give it more power over us. It is normal to feel upset, exhausted, and frustrated, but if we allow negativity to consume our thoughts, then we will only add to the amount of mental clutter that the event creates. If we can learn to change our reactions to situations and reframe them in our minds, we can change their impact on our minds. Here are some methods you can use to prevent the buildup of mental clutter and respond to tough situations in more constructive ways.

Start Journaling

If we have trouble dealing with and expressing our emotions, they can build up inside of us. We might try to quietly manage them without letting anyone else know how we feel, or we might try to communicate our feelings but lack the ability to put them into words. Either of these two options leaves us with tons of clutter since the thoughts we can't express build up in our minds and ensure that we are never over difficult events we experience.

A journal is a great way to take all of the clutter in our minds and put it somewhere else. When we write out our thoughts, we transfer them from our minds to the page. Rather than allowing our thoughts to spiral in our heads, we find a way to express them that reduces the burden in our brains while still allowing us to deal with problems privately if we so choose.

Additionally, journaling can help you process everything you're feeling. When your emotions only exist in your head, it can be tough to identify exactly how you feel and why you feel that way. When you get into the habit of writing these thoughts down, you become better at detangling your feelings from one another and uncovering the reason behind each strong emotion. This can help you decide how you should deal with the situation, and it usually provides results much faster than turning the same thoughts over in your head again and again throughout the day.

Writing things down is a great exercise for mental decluttering even outside of journaling. It follows the same idea, which is that getting things down on paper frees up space in our heads. Write down grocery lists, keep a calendar for important dates, and jot down the last episode you watched of the TV show you're currently binging. All of these things add unnecessary clutter to your mind and pull your focus away from the things that are actually worth memorizing.

Practice Thought Exercises

As mentioned previously, meditating isn't enough to completely rid your mind of clutter. That's still true, but it's also true that meditating and similar thought exercises can be a part of your decluttering journey. Meditation isn't just for people who love yoga. It can be a powerful tool for calming your thoughts when they get to be too much to handle. When practiced routinely, meditation can help you settle your mind and reorganize your thoughts, helping you assess any problems from a calmer vantage point.

Another thought exercise that can help you reduce clutter is mindfulness. Like journaling, mindfulness is especially useful for managing out-of-control emotions. Practicing mindfulness means that you shift your focus away from the past and the future and only focus on the present moment. Instead of worrying about everything that went wrong yesterday or that could go wrong tomorrow, you only consider how you feel right now. How does the current situation make you feel, and why do you feel that way? If you feel angry, distraught, or worried, that is okay since another big part of mindfulness is not blaming or judging yourself for negative feelings. Accept how you feel, take the time to process it, and then let the worst of these feelings go once you have come to terms with them. They will no longer take up nearly as much space in your mind. The chaos brought about by worrying about your future and past will subside as you start recentering your thoughts on the present moment and improving your ability to focus.

Ensure You're Getting Good Sleep

Exhaustion makes it harder for us to deal with difficulties in our lives. If we're tired, we're much more likely to snap at someone for a minor annoyance. We may turn a relatively minor event into a major crisis, if only in our perception of the event. Exhaustion can also interfere with our ability to learn, retain, and react to new information. We won't be able to put any of our decluttering strategies to use if we're not getting proper rest at night.

A busy schedule can sometimes make it hard to get the full eight hours that are recommended for adults. We might end up working late into the night or rising bright and early in the morning. We might be kept awake by buzzing energy because we had no opportunity to calm ourselves down after the business of the day. Cluttered thoughts might chase each other in our heads all night, leaving us lying awake and staring up at the ceiling as the clock ticks on. Reducing clutter in our lives can help us get the rest we need to reduce clutter in our heads.

Other strategies for combating insomnia include setting and sticking to a routine sleep schedule, avoiding activities right before bed, and doing something calming like gentle stretches or reading prior to laying down. Set aside dedicated time for relaxation so that you wake feeling refreshed rather than exhausted.

Talk to Loved Ones

Journaling and practicing mindfulness are good strategies for dealing with your emotions on your own, but sometimes, we need help from others. We aren't built to carry the weight of our burdens on our own.

We are social creatures, and we need to feel connected to others in order to truly thrive. Our friends and families can provide support for us when we are going through a difficult time in our lives or if we just need to vent for a while. This is another way to transfer the clutter away from our minds. This time, by explaining how we are feeling out loud, we release the clutter into the air like we're shaking out a dusty rug. Through this process, we see that there are people in our lives who want to help us and who want to see us enjoying our lives rather than letting clutter take over.

Finally, discussing your problems with others can sometimes mean that they are able to help you find a solution. Maybe they cannot solve the problem entirely, but a friend or family member may be able to help you shoulder a responsibility until you can declutter your schedule, support you as you deal with a difficult life event, or provide assistance decluttering another part of your life. It's not always easy to open up to others, but when you do, you are often able to better manage your mental clutter.

Stick to the Essentials

If you were to look at all of the things you do in an average day and sort them into columns based on whether or not they were essential, how would you sort them? What would be essential, and what could be tossed aside? Try to identify the things that are most important to living a life that's fulfilling, not just a life that is comfortable. Next, make another list based on what's most important in the current moment.

Now, think about all of the things that you do that aren't essential to your well-being and happiness. What kinds of tasks are these? Are there any you can let go of completely, or will you have to replace them with more essential versions of those tasks? Where you can, try to eliminate the most unnecessary sources of mental clutter in your life. Look for responsibilities and habits that take more out of you than you get in return for doing them. Consider what kind of reward you get from completing each task, and if it's not something that you find valuable, see if you can find ways to drop it from your schedule.

After dropping the "dead weight" from your life, your thoughts should only be concerned with things that are important, primarily things that are important right now. Eliminating all of the unnecessary sources of stress in your life will help you reduce the rate at which mental clutter piles up. Unnecessary worries are removed from your mind, and you are free to focus on only things that matter.

Often, unnecessary tasks come from responsibilities we take on not for our sake but for the sake of others, even when we are already incredibly stressed and busy. They can also come from lifestyle choices that don't bring us any benefit but instead waste our time and energy. In order to truly free

our minds of clutter, we must get better at managing our daily schedules and deciding what is important enough to include in them.

Chapter Takeaways

In this chapter, we took a look at how our brains become cluttered and what we can do to reduce the clutter. We learned:

- Our brains are great at adaptation, but sometimes, their plasticity can work against us and increase our stress levels.
- We are predisposed to think negatively because we tend to take more notice of negative events than positive ones.
- We can declutter our brains by taking steps like venting our thoughts, using meditation and other mental exercises, improving our sleeping habits, and reducing clutter in our lives.

Now that we've taken a look at the ways clutter can manifest mentally, let's see what it looks like when it appears in your responsibilities.

Chapter 5: Decluttering Your Life and Responsibilities

"Don't count the things you do, do the things that count."—Zig Ziglar

Keeping busy is one thing, but packing our schedules full of unnecessary appointments, jobs, and other responsibilities is another. We need to stay active, but we don't need to fill our days with busywork that won't help us achieve important goals. If we accept too many responsibilities, especially ones that don't benefit us, we end up exhausting ourselves and ultimately missing out on the opportunities that would make a big difference in our lives.

Excessive responsibilities are a huge source of clutter in our lives. The problem may start innocently enough. Maybe we choose to take on some extra work at our jobs, not thinking much about the extra hour we're now spending working. Maybe we agree to do a favor for a friend that starts as a one-time offer and evolves into a recurring event. Perhaps we feel bad about taking time to relax while we have so many things on our plates, so we decide to combine our relaxation time with work in some way. Each of these situations is a trap that is surprisingly easy for us to fall into. Before we know it, they evolve into either a few time-demanding tasks or many tiny, insignificant tasks that waste a lot of effort when they are added together. The presence of any useless tasks in our schedules leaves us exhausted at the end of each day, and as we repeat the process for months or years at a time, we only grow more and more tired. We start to feel burned out all of the time, and thoughts of everything we have to do only pile on the anxiety and stress. A cluttered schedule is a guaranteed pathway to a cluttered mind.

One of the biggest problems that contribute to a cluttered lifestyle is when we prioritize simply being busy over making a positive impact on our lives. You've probably been given busywork at one point or another in your life, whether it was assigned by a teacher who didn't have a lesson planned for the day or a boss who didn't know how to maximize employee efficiency. If you've ever held a job in the service industry, you have probably been told you should try to look busy at all times regardless of whether or not the task you occupy yourself with is necessary. The reinforcement of these kinds of ideas worms its way into our heads until we are convinced that trying to do as many things as possible is the best way to work. But is this true?

Think of the phrase, "Work smarter, not harder." If you can accomplish a task just as well in a shorter time, or if the task in question is only wasting your time without providing significant benefits, you are better off taking the more efficient path. In fact, many studies have shown that when we follow the advice of the old phrase, giving ourselves time to rest in between periods of work, we accomplish more. We are able to focus on the tasks that are more important instead of wasting our time on things that merely keep us occupied. One study that examined employees who were assigned busywork even found that "unnecessary work tasks were prospectively associated with a decreased level of mental health" (Madsen et al., 2014, para. 3). These tasks drain our energy and our enthusiasm. Worse, they subtly convince us that our efforts don't matter. This mindset extends far past the unnecessary tasks until we start believing that even the critical tasks are as unimportant as the rest. What we end up with is a confused sense of which responsibilities are important, little to no downtime, and an incredibly cluttered mind.

Decluttering our schedules can be a complicated process since it's not always easy to tell which tasks are important and which aren't. We may be tempted to decide certain activities are important merely because we have been doing them for a long time, and we don't want to think of that time as wasted effort. We might assume a task is useful, but when we sit down and think about whether or not it has helped us throughout the years, we see that it has had little effect on our level of success. It's not always easy to accept that we're burning energy on things that don't matter, but if we choose to leap to being defensive, we will only continue to waste this energy. By intervening and putting a stop to these tasks when we can, we reduce the amount of clutter in our schedules, thereby significantly reducing the clutter in our minds.

There are two main problems to address when decluttering our schedules. The first is the issue of multitasking, which is a much bigger detriment than we may initially believe. The second is a lack of prioritization. If we can learn to leave multitasking behind and start prioritizing the tasks that matter, ditching all the rest, we can significantly limit how hectic and cluttered our lives are.

The Trouble With Multitasking

Multitasking was once a very popular recommendation for people who had busy schedules. Instead of doing just one task at a time, you could do two or even three. Surely this would save a lot of time in the long run, or at least, that was what people believed. Recently, multitasking has started to fall out of fashion as the flaws in the system have been exposed. More and more often, suggestions on how to free up more time in your schedule include "eliminate multitasking," even if these same people were espousing the glory of multitasking only a few years ago. What happened to change the public perception of multitasking? Is it as bad as some people say it is, and if so, why?

Theoretically, multitasking should let you get work done faster. Perhaps in some situations, it does. You might be able to perform small tasks that don't require a lot of your concentration at the same time. For example, you could wash dishes and watch an episode of a TV show, and you probably wouldn't miss much from either task. However, problems arise when you try to combine two intricate tasks or if you are trying to complete two tasks with very different goals in mind.

First, let's start with the latter of the two problems. If your main goal is washing the dishes and you merely turn on the TV to keep you company as you wash, you probably won't have any issues. You might miss a line here or there, but if you're not that invested in what's happening, it's no big deal. You might wash dishes a little slower if you pause to watch something, but if you're not trying to finish the task quickly, this isn't such an issue either. However, if you are trying to use TV time as a way to relax, adding a task like washing dishes into the mix could take away the value you would otherwise receive. Now, you're not fully relaxing; you're working. Instead of completing two tasks at the same time, you've effectively rendered one of the tasks worthless.

This might be a reason why you think you're getting enough free time in your day when you're really not. If you tend to interrupt your free time with small busywork tasks, you diminish the relaxing aspect, which means you never rest.

Now, we'll take a look at what happens if you're trying to do two complex tasks that both demand your attention. If you try to deal with both things at once, your brain is going to get confused. We're not built to flip between tasks rapidly, and we're not built to keep two different things in our minds at the same time.

Imagine you're a student trying to finish your math and history homework at the same time. If you complete a few math problems, switch to your history essay, and then switch back, your brain has to shift modes each time. It's not easy to remember your multiplication tables when you're wrapped up in historical dates. You could confuse the two, or it might take you some "processing time" each time you switch tasks. You will lose your train of thought as ideas for one topic intrude upon the other. You will likely end up taking much longer to complete the work than you would have if you'd just finished your math before you moved on to history. The danger of compulsive multitasking is that we don't realize that we're wasting time by working this way. We believe we're saving time when, in reality, all we're doing is splitting our attention, decreasing the quality of our work, and confusing ourselves.

Splitting Your Attention

You've probably heard the phrase "in the zone" before. It refers to a state of mind where you are completely focused on the task at hand. Ideas come easily, and you operate at a near-expert level. If you're exercising, you move faster and more confidently than ever before. If you're typing something, your fingers fly across the keys without hesitation. If you're reading, you finish a chapter in a matter of minutes, completely engrossed in the text. In each of these examples, a heightened ability is a direct result of remaining focused on one task without any distractions.

If being "in the zone" and focusing exclusively on one task is the height of productivity, then anything that distracts you from your current task must get in the way of your focus. Trying to multitask divides your attention between two or more tasks, effectively resulting in neither of them getting the attention they need to be completed efficiently. Without focus, you spend much longer on each task than it would otherwise require. This only adds to an already busy schedule. Instead of cutting your work in half, you may have inadvertently increased it simply because you've made it impossible to focus.

This lack of focus adds additional clutter to your mind because your brain tries to jump between different topics. When you don't let your thoughts settle into one activity at a time, thoughts of both tasks take up space, doubling the amount of mental clutter you experience. Without proper focus, overthinking takes control. This is just another of the many ways in which multitasking adds more work to your schedule, ultimately adding more clutter.

Declining Work Quality

The more we try to do at once, the harder it is to maintain high standards for our work. When we split our focus, the quality of our work may suffer as a result. Additionally, having a packed schedule already has us feeling rushed to complete each task on our to-do list. This can lead to mistakes and poor quality as well. As our work quality suffers, we may start to doubt our ability to produce great work, even if we aren't multitasking or rushing. This is fueled, in part, by the negativity bias. We tend to only see the times we have fallen short in our work or responsibilities and not the times where we have succeeded. We start to believe that our average work quality is the same as the kind of work we produce when we are under pressure. This can all culminate in a lot of self-doubt about our abilities.

Self-doubt only adds to the amount of clutter in our lives. Feelings of inadequacy, low self-esteem, and uncertainty generate a lot of mental clutter. Our minds buzz with activity, reminding us that we've fallen short and making us believe that we will continue to do so. Negative thoughts abound, and it becomes hard to calm our minds.

Are You Trying to Do Too Many Things at Once?

Self-esteem issues, exhaustion, and a lack of focus are all products of trying to do too much at once. When we multitask to the point that we overwhelm ourselves, we end up far more tired than we would be if we just took tasks one at a time. By trying to complete many different tasks at the same time, we only succeed in filling our minds with extra noise.

Of course, this desire to multitask stems from having an incredibly busy schedule in the first place. When we are constantly working on one task or another, we feel the urge to try to get them done faster, unknowingly accomplishing the exact opposite. While no longer multitasking can help us free up some time in our schedules, it doesn't take away any tasks. We are left with the same amount of work. If we don't make significant changes to the way we approach work, including cutting down on the sheer number of tasks and only doing activities that provide value, we will always be stuck in the same mentality that caused us to multitask in the first place.

How to Prioritize What Really Matters

We want to feel like everything we're doing is worth the time and effort we spend on it, but often, this just isn't true. Sometimes, we do certain tasks for very little reward or a reward that isn't proportional to the amount of time we spend on the task. If the task in question doesn't matter to us, we need to ask ourselves why we're doing it and whether or not it is worth continuing to do. Eliminating the unnecessary tasks from our schedules allows us to spend more time doing things that benefit us. We waste less time, and we provide ourselves with ample time for rest.

The most effective way to reduce clutter in your schedule is to learn how to prioritize your tasks. Ideally, every task on your to-do list should be ordered by its priority. This means that tasks that are very low priority may not get completed each day, or you may end up removing them from your schedule altogether. This is much better than having important tasks get pushed aside and put off even when you know you need to complete them. When you pare down your schedule to the bare essentials, performing only those tasks that help you feel fulfilled and accomplished at the end of the day instead of run-down, you make a lot more of the limited amount of time you have available to you each day. You can start taking on bigger projects that may provide more of a reward, and you can drop anything that isn't helping you be your best self. Prioritizing helps you declutter your schedule and lighten your workload every day.

Identify Your Core Values

What things matter the most to you in your life? If you had nothing at all, what would you most desire? If you had every possession you could ever want, what would you still look for in your life in order to make it fulfilling? The beliefs, values, and traits that are most important to you make up your core values. They represent the things that you can't live without and the things that you should always strive to achieve.

However, sometimes our lives don't line up with our core values. We waste time on things that don't hold any personal value for us, cluttering our lives with busywork and never feeling like we are making any progress on our goals. This is a reductive way to live that gets in the way of our growth and ability to feel fulfilled.

One exercise that can help you identify your core values is visualizing your dream life. Think about what your life would look like if you could make it anything you wanted. What kind of job would you have? Would you be well-off financially, or would you be fine with a comfortable amount of wealth? What would your house look like, and where would you live? What about your family? Would you weigh work a little higher than your personal life, or do your family and other personal relationships come before all else? Try to answer these questions as you think about what each aspect of your ideal future would look like.

Once you know what you want to achieve and what really matters the most to you, you can start looking at ways to achieve this life for yourself or at least come as close as possible. Eventually, you will start to remove tasks from your schedule that don't fit your goals and keep only the ones that help you make progress toward your dream life. For now, it is enough to just identify the things that matter to you personally.

Look at the choices you made when you visualized your future. Where did you assign value? Did you prioritize your career and wealth, or did you immediately start thinking about your future family? What kind of person are you in your dream life? Are you determined, driven, courteous, kind, and motivated?

Are you good at maintaining relationships and listening to others? Do you provide value to your community? When you think about your future house, what does the interior look like? Do you value having a lot of stuff with plenty of clutter, or do you value a lack of clutter and a minimalist lifestyle? These core values are what make you an individual. They reflect what you care about most. You owe it to yourself to shape your life in a way that prioritizes these values so you can live the life you've always wanted.

Determine If Your Responsibilities Align With These Values

Now that you know what your core values are, you can decide if the tasks you occupy your day with support your efforts to live up to these values. The responsibilities you take on should reflect what you care about most. If not, why do them? You are just expending time and energy on tasks that don't matter to you. When your schedule is already cluttered, these kinds of tasks create unnecessary stress and anxiety. Reducing their presence in your life can bring you greater peace of mind.

You might wonder: How do I know if a responsibility aligns with my core values? After all, it's not like the tasks we take on come with a specific label of what kind of values they promote. However, you can figure this out by thinking critically about both the type of task you're doing and its results.

First, consider the benefits of completing a task. What, if any, kinds of rewards do you get from it? Is there a financial incentive, like there might be with a job or a favor you get compensated for? Do you get access to something you wouldn't otherwise, or is it something you do so you can maintain a good relationship with someone? Could you replace the task with something less time consuming or more beneficial to you and still get the same reward? If the reward that comes from a given responsibility isn't worth the effort you put in, or if the rewards don't align with the things you value, the task may be a good candidate to strike off your list.

Next, consider the risks of not completing the task. You know what you stand to gain, but what do you have to lose if you stop doing the task? There are some responsibilities that you cannot afford to give up. For example, you may not be able to leave a job you hate without securing a new one because you wouldn't be able to support yourself without it. On the other hand, there are many responsibilities that aren't very important to you at all. If you could stop doing something right now and face no negative repercussions, it's probably not something you need to continue doing. Sometimes, you might face minor discomfort or a brief period of uncertainty when you stop a task, but it ultimately wouldn't make too many waves in your life. These kinds of responsibilities are good contenders for ones you can safely drop from your schedule too.

Finally, consider if a task provides you with any inherent rewards. Some tasks are beneficial because of the work itself rather than any sort of reward others give you for completing it. A task may help you cultivate a valuable trait like focus, discipline, or persistence. These are worth learning and practicing as a form of self-investment. You might also spend your time improving your skills by engaging in a creative hobby. Alternatively, you may simply do something because you enjoy doing it. Playing a game may not come with any concrete rewards, and there may be no consequences for no longer playing, but that doesn't mean you should drop all games from your schedule. If it brings you enjoyment, you are still benefiting from the task in some way, as long as you don't allow it to take up all of your time.

Responsibilities that fit into any of these categories are worth keeping around. If something doesn't give you rewards relevant to your goals, there are no consequences for dropping it, and you don't enjoy doing it, then stop doing it. All it is doing is adding clutter.

Eliminate Any Unnecessary Responsibilities

After determining which responsibilities are necessary and which are unnecessary, you can rid your schedule of all of the unnecessary responsibilities. You may be able to stop some of them right away, or you may need to make alternative arrangements. Either way, try to plan on stopping this unnecessary work within the next month or so when possible. As you start to drop responsibilities from your schedule, you will be able to enjoy free time once again. You will find it easier to relax without the burden of more work looming over your shoulder, and you will spend less of your day dealing with responsibilities you don't care about or benefit from.

The additional advantage of cutting down your responsibilities to only those that benefit you is that now, everything you do will help you achieve your goals. Before, so much of the clutter in your life was purposeless. It didn't help you get where you wanted to be in life. After throwing out all of the clutter, you are left with only the important things. These will help you accomplish your goals without wasting your time, helping you become a more goal-driven and successful person. This is the hidden power of decluttering your life. It's not just about what you throw away; it's also about what is left and how it reshapes your life.

Chapter Takeaways

This chapter took a look at how your lifestyle and how busy you are can negatively impact your level of mental clutter. Some of the things you learned include:

- A cluttered life where you give yourself no opportunity to rest leads to burnout and frustration.
- Multitasking may seem like a good idea, but it usually ends up adding to the amount of time you spend on tasks rather than helping them go by faster.
- Prioritizing your tasks and eliminating those that don't help you achieve your personal goals will allow you to live a less cluttered life.

In the next chapter, we'll look at how your relationships can put a similar strain on your mentality and what you can do to fix this problem.

Chapter 6: Decluttering Your Personal Life and Relationships

"Avoid popularity; it has many snares and no real benefit."—William Penn

When we think of staying busy, we tend to think of things like our jobs and other professional responsibilities. Of course, these are not the only things in our lives that place burdens on our time. Our relationships can also eat up a significant amount of time, whether that time is spent socializing or doing various favors for friends and family members. This contributes to having a busier schedule with no time for relaxation since we make plans with others irrespective of how much free time we have available. Just like when we crowd our lives with work and other tasks, we end up working ourselves to exhaustion, except this time, it is even harder to recognize this as work. We might continue to offer our time to our friends because we think it's the right thing to do, but if we are hurting ourselves, we aren't helping anyone, least of all the people in our lives who would want us to be happy.

Additionally, if we have too many people to keep up with in our personal lives, this can add to mental clutter. We end up spreading ourselves thin, sacrificing time that could be better spent elsewhere. We also offer more of our mental space as the number of friends and acquaintances we have grows. The more important dates we have to remember at any given time and the more time we devote to socializing, the more cluttered we make our lives and our minds, especially if we aren't particularly invested in these relationships.

We want to think of all of our relationships as valuable, but many of them only exist to add clutter to our lives. Of course, this is not true of all of our relationships. We may have very close relationships with friends and family we care about a lot. As long as these relationships remain positive for both parties, they are worth any additional effort we make to maintain these relationships. However, the problem comes when we take great pains to maintain relationships that aren't especially valuable to us. These could be people who we know as a friend of a friend or those who we are just barely acquaintances with, or they could be relationships that started positive but have since faded over time. They may even include relationships that have become toxic and detrimental to one or both parties over time. If you are putting in a lot of effort to keep up relationships with people you barely know, or if you feel that you are trapped in a toxic relationship that is generating strife and mental clutter, it's time to make a change in the way you approach relationships.

The Myth of Popularity

Many people strive to have relationships with as many people as possible. Rather than trying to build a close-knit group of good friends, they seek out dozens of casual acquaintances, never able to spend enough time with any one person to make the relationship more meaningful. If you find that this is something you do, consider why you might be doing it. Are you just trying to meet and engage with new people, or do you find that with every new person who enters your life, someone else falls by the wayside?

Are you trying to form these relationships because you genuinely care about everyone you spend time with, or are you prioritizing quantity over quality in an attempt to chase popularity?

Unlike what we might have been led to believe in high school, popularity doesn't do us any favors. In fact, we have trouble dealing with too many people in our lives at once. Our brains aren't built to keep up with so many different relationships on a personal level. As originally proposed by anthropologist Robin Dunbar and popularized by Malcolm Gladwell's book *The Tipping Point*, the maximum number of relationships we can deal with at any given time is 150. This is the "'point beyond which members of any social group lose their ability to function effectively in social relationships" (Sugihto, 2016, para. 2). Once we start dividing our time even more than this, we lose track of many of the people in our lives, and our relationships become more distant. All of the extra noise just turns into clutter in our minds rather than becoming something meaningful.

Ideally, we should try to keep the number of relationships in our lives at no more than 150, although even less than that is better if we can manage it. This helps to ensure that we are forging relationships for the right reasons and alleviates the burden of trying to remain in contact with hundreds of people.

Dealing With Toxic Relationships

Sometimes, relationships drain us for reasons other than simply being too numerous. A toxic relationship is one that is full of conflict, unhealthy competition, and a lack of support. Our friends and families should empower us just as much as we return the favor, but when there is an imbalance in a relationship or one party actively seeks to harm the other, these relationships can turn toxic.

Toxic relationships can come from many different areas of our lives. Someone we once thought of as a friend may become someone who takes advantage of us, routinely puts us down, or keeps us from achieving our full potential. A relationship with a spouse or other partner could become an abusive one, either verbally or physically. We might have a toxic relationship with our coworkers or bosses where we feel overworked and underappreciated, especially if we are expected to do things outside of our job description. Even our family members can be sources of toxicity in our lives.

As much as we might love these people, toxic relationships are especially draining. They introduce a lot of stress into our lives and put much more pressure on us than we would otherwise experience. We might go out of our way to appease these people with little if any reciprocity on their end. We end up sacrificing our time for people who don't help us grow. We may turn our frustration at these relationships inward, or we may internalize the negative things said about us in toxic relationships. All of these are forms of mental clutter that distract and harm us. It's not always easy to let a toxic relationship go, even when we recognize it for what it is. But when we do, we declutter our minds and start the healing process.

How to Identify Toxic Relationships

Recognizing that you are in a toxic relationship is not always as easy as it might seem. Many people who experience all of the signs of a toxic relationship don't even think to consider the relationship in that way, or they might make excuses for other peoples' behaviors. Without recognizing the problem, it is impossible to fix it. You will only end up hurting yourself more if you blind yourself to the possibility that a relationship is more detrimental than it might seem on the surface. Learning to recognize the warning signs can help you identify these relationships before they can do further harm.

Some warning signs are more immediately apparent than others. Any relationship that involves physical abuse, the threat of violence, or harassment is not just toxic but also highly abusive. These kinds of relationships put your well-being in danger. You may be tempted to rationalize and excuse your abuse, but at the end of the day, there is no justification for physical violence in a relationship, especially if the violence is used to manipulate you. Recognizing the danger these kinds of relationships pose to you can give you the strength you need to remove yourself from them and keep yourself safe.

Other warning signs are far more insidious and difficult to notice. Some relationships may involve subtle but persistent demands on your time and energy, or the other person may try to undermine your happiness. While these relationships don't necessarily pose a physical threat to you, this doesn't mean they're harmless. Far from it, in fact; if you fail to recognize these relationships as abusive, you may remain in them for much longer than you would remain in a physically abusive one. A common red flag is simply a feeling of unhappiness when you spend time with the person. If someone is constantly demanding your time and making you unhappy, then they are introducing toxicity and clutter into your life. If you experience a negative shift in your mentality, self-esteem, or mental health, consider if your relationships are contributing to this problem.

One more thing to look out for is a significant change in how you spend your free time or how often you spend time with other people. If you find yourself withdrawing from positive relationships in favor of ones that make you feel stressed and overwhelmed, you may be experiencing manipulation. Toxic people may try to keep you away from those who would otherwise help you recognize how harmful the relationship is. You should also keep an eye out for significant shifts in your personality, as red flags may be raised "when you're not your individual self anymore and you're giving everything to your partner" (Ducharme, 2018, para. 15) rather than finding happiness on your own terms. If you don't feel like yourself anymore, you will likely feel more distressed and experience more mental clutter as a result.

How to Let Go of Toxic People

Now that you have a good idea of the kinds of people who are adding toxicity to your life, you can work on either trying to correct the toxicity or separating yourself from these people. First, determine whether or not the relationship can be repaired. When toxic traits come from trauma or mental health issues, you may be able to encourage the other person to seek professional help to work through these problems. This is a possibility, but don't feel like it's the only option, nor should you feel like you're responsible for a friend or partner's mental health. If they are unwilling to seek help, the abuse doesn't stop, or you are simply unable to continue having a relationship with a person who has hurt you in this way, you are well within your right to end the relationship. Don't harm yourself by forcing yourself to forgive and forget. If what happened was unforgivable, or if you give someone a second chance and they don't improve, put your health first, and make the decision to leave.

Ending a toxic relationship can be difficult and sometimes dangerous, especially if there has been physical abuse or threats of violence. If you are worried about your safety and afraid to leave because of the risk of retribution, you may need to get the authorities involved. Even if you choose not to press charges against an abuser, contacting professionals in the domestic violence prevention field or in Child Protective Services can provide you with valuable resources and keep you safe as you separate yourself from a toxic household.

Of course, letting go of toxic people in your life can be difficult even if there is no physical abuse involved. There may still be mental and emotional manipulation that makes you reluctant to leave. Keep an eye out for relationships where you've given three, four, five, or more chances—these people aren't likely to change, and every time you give them another chance, your mental health suffers. If you find it intimidating to leave these relationships through your own willpower, rely on the support of genuine friends and family members who you have a positive relationship with. These people care about you, and they can help you break off the relationship in a way that prioritizes your safety and happiness.

Forming Healthy Relationships

It's hard for many people who have been in toxic relationships for a long time to form healthy relationships instead. We may always feel like we're waiting for the other shoe to drop, which interferes with our ability to communicate and relax around others. We may unknowingly engage in new toxic relationships instead of replacing them with healthy ones. To defeat the mental clutter caused by unhealthy relationships, we must create a social circle full of loving, supportive people who are understanding of our needs and desires. It is only through forging these positive relationships that we can start to undo some of the damage of the old, negative ones.

Communication is a key part of any healthy relationship. If we can't communicate with our family, friends, and partners, we will bottle our emotions up inside and fill our heads with emotional clutter we can't express. We should strive to be open and honest in our relationships whenever possible. This doesn't mean that you have to immediately discuss past trauma or other sensitive personal information with near-strangers; you should only talk about these things when you feel comfortable. But if you find that you are holding yourself back out of fear of punishment or having this information manipulated and used against you, stop and consider if this gut reaction makes sense. Do you think this person would do that based on their past behaviors, or are you projecting your old friend or partner's behaviors onto them? Try to rationalize these thoughts when you notice them. If you need personal space, be honest about this too. People who care about your well-being will understand, and they will be there to support you when you are ready to let them in.

Healthy relationships also require boundaries. It's not fair to either party if one person is constantly demanding the time and attention of the other. It's also not healthy to allow friends to cross lines you're not comfortable with. First, determine what your boundaries are. Figure out what you're okay with and what you're not okay with. It's okay if some of your boundaries are a little stricter than others if you feel you need them to be right now. Then, take the most important step: Communicate your boundaries to the people in your life. Make sure they understand what's acceptable behavior and what's not, and listen to what their boundaries are in return. Once you've explained your boundaries to the other person, they have no excuse for crossing them. If you know they are aware of the boundaries but continue to demand your time, take up your energy, and trivialize your desires, these should be huge red flags. Anyone who repeatedly doesn't respect your boundaries is not a good candidate for a healthy relationship. Walk away from these toxic relationships before they can get any worse.

If you struggle with honesty or boundaries because of past negative experiences, you may find it helpful to talk to a mental health professional. Speaking to a therapist, counselor, or psychologist can give you a better understanding of what you experienced and the ways it affects your behavior. They can also provide you with helpful coping strategies you can use to clear your head of harmful, spiraling thoughts.

Once you've established the basic foundations of healthy relationships, you can begin expanding these relationships past the surface level.

Building Deeper Relationships

We are heavily social creatures. The number and quality of our relationships impact all areas of our physical and mental health. If we withdraw from relationships entirely, we harm ourselves. If our relationships are all very shallow and we don't make any deeper connections, we don't benefit much more than if we had no relationships at all. Research has found that "good relationships help people live longer, deal with stress better, have healthier habits," and may even offer "improved lifespans" (Brickel, n.d., para. 3). Deep, supportive relationships reduce mental clutter and improve our lives, so they are more than worth investing in.

Not all of your relationships need to be deep. You can have some casual friends and acquaintances, but you should have at least a few people you can be completely honest and genuine with and who you can always rely on to help you out of a dark place. You can identify good candidates for these roles by considering who motivates you to become a better person just by being around them and who you naturally enjoy spending time with. Look for people who make any task fun just because you're in their company. Invest in people who build you up. Take an active role in the friendship to encourage its development. This means reaching out when you haven't seen each other in a while, making plans, and being emotionally available. If you focus your energy on the relationships that matter instead of those that are purely superficial or toxic, you will get the social support you need without all of the mental clutter.

Most importantly, remember that you deserve to be happy. You deserve relationships that make you feel good about yourself. You deserve people in your life who will support you and who want you to succeed. When you devote time or mental energy to spending time with someone who genuinely cares about you and who you care about in return, it won't feel like a sacrifice, and it won't add clutter to your life. It will be a source of stress relief rather than a source of stress. As you forge more of these healthy, positive relationships, your mental clutter will decrease significantly, and you'll feel so much better about yourself and your life.

Chapter Takeaways

In this chapter, we took a look at our social lives and discussed ways we can remove the more stressful aspects. You learned:

- Overextending yourself and trying to keep up too many relationships at a time is exhausting and adds to mental clutter.

- Removing toxic people from your life can get you all of the benefits of a good relationship without any of the stress of the unhealthy ones.

- Making new, healthy relationships and forming meaningful connections with others helps you push back against clutter from previous negative experiences and stay motivated through all of the ups and downs of life.

In the following chapter, we will discuss ways to declutter your home just like you've decluttered your schedule and relationships.

Chapter 7: Decluttering Your Home

"Instead of thinking I am losing something when I clear clutter, I dwell on what I might gain."—Lisa J. Shultz

Clutter in the home is almost omnipresent. Every time we turn a corner, we're all but assaulted with visual information. Trying to retrieve something from a cluttered closet turns a five-second activity into a half-hour excursion, if you even end up finding what you're looking for. It's frustrating, it wastes our time, and it makes it impossible to truly relax, especially if we want to clean up but never seem to get around to it. This is the last thing you want your home to be. The home should be a space for relaxation, but instead, it becomes a place just as chaotic and hectic as much of the outside world.

Clutter isn't just bad because it's unappealing or because you're more likely to lose something. It has a real, measurable impact on our minds and our ability to focus. Minimalists routinely preach about the dangers of living in a messy environment, and their arguments are backed up by science. In a 2011 experiment, "neuroscience researchers using fMRI (functional magnetic resonance imaging) and other physiological measurements found clearing clutter from the home and work environment resulted in a better ability to focus and process information, as well as increased productivity" (Sander, 2019, para. 10). If our living spaces are cluttered, we lose our ability to maintain focus. Our minds jump from one thing to another, and our thoughts become endlessly restless. Physical clutter in the house is also referred to as visual noise. Just like regular noise, the louder the visual noise is in an environment, the harder we find it to work, let alone to relax.

The good news is that reducing clutter in your home doesn't have to be a painful process. You can apply the basic concepts of minimalism to sort through your belongings, keeping those that provide value and getting rid of those that don't. It's not always easy to agree to let go of things that you've been keeping around for years, especially if you tend to be a bit of a pack rat, but if you can learn to reject the superficial trappings of an overly material world, you will find that decluttering your home follows naturally.

Making Your Living Space Livable

Cleaning out your living space can feel like a mountain of a task, but it's much simpler than it might seem. You just need to use a few tricks to your advantage. The first is to be more aware of how you interact with your environment. Pay attention to what you use, and more importantly, pay attention to what you don't use. You can even start marking things or otherwise flagging them when they get used. If you look back on everything you've flagged over a week, the things you left untouched are probably good candidates for things you can get rid of. If you extend this experiment to a month, are there any non-seasonal items you still haven't used? Chances are that if you haven't used them within a month, you probably don't need them as much as you think you do.

Another good tip is breaking the work down into more manageable chunks. Decluttering your whole house is going to sound like way too much work. You couldn't possibly do it all in one day or even one week. You see it as such a colossal task that you subconsciously start to push it to the back of your mind.

Before you know it, months have gone by, and you've made no decluttering progress. Instead of worrying about the whole house, start by focusing on a single room. You can even begin with just one area of a room, like your bedroom closet or your kitchen pantry. Start with something easy to get into the rhythm of decluttering. Then you can expand your radius, steadily progressing through each room. When you break the work up into smaller pieces, it is suddenly a much more manageable task.

Finally, having a good routine for how you declutter will save you a lot of time spent hemming and hawing over what really matters and what really doesn't. Develop a system for figuring out if something should stay or go, and follow the same system for every room you declutter. As you practice the habit, it will get easier to get rid of the unnecessary things every time. You can use the following four-step method for effective decluttering every time.

Judge the Worth of Your Possessions

The first step to decluttering any space is figuring out what's clutter and what's not. You don't need to empty a room to declutter it. You only need to get rid of the things that you don't use and that don't provide any value. To do that, you have to learn how to assign value to your possessions.

One reliable way to decide if something is still worth keeping around or not is to consider when you last used it. Chances are that if it's been months or years since you touched something, you probably don't need it. Whatever emergency you're keeping it around for isn't nearly as likely to happen as you think. If something has been sitting under your bed or at the back of a closet for multiple years, it's not providing any value. Think of your home as an apartment building with you as the landlord and your items as your tenants. Your tenants have to pay 'rent,' which is a measure of how useful they are. If a tenant fails to pay rent for multiple months in a row, landlords generally kick them out because they're not holding up their end of the bargain. Don't let junk stay in your house rent-free either.

Be sure to check any items that have expiration dates when you're decluttering. This includes food, medications, makeup, personal hygiene products, and cleaning products. All of these things can go bad if you don't use them up in time. Chances are that if you let something expire, you probably had little intention of using it in the first place, or it didn't live up to your initial expectations. Toss anything that's expired automatically, and try to avoid purchasing it again in the future. Alternatively, if it's something you use only occasionally, try to buy a smaller size so less goes to waste.

There are some valid reasons to keep things around even if they're not constantly in use. Some items may not be used frequently, but they still serve a purpose. For example, just because you haven't set the kitchen on fire yet doesn't mean you should throw the fire extinguisher out. Still, you should probably check to make sure your fire extinguisher has been serviced recently so that it still functions. Keep similar items only for as long as they are good for, then replace them when necessary. A good rule is to use common sense when decluttering. Don't throw out things that could keep you safe in a dangerous situation; focus on the things with little to no purpose that pose no threat to you if you were to remove them.

Another reason you might want to keep something that gets little to no use is sentimental value. It is okay to keep things around because they are personally meaningful, but be careful when applying this label, and try to keep the number of purely sentimental items in your home as low as possible. More often than not, we claim something is sentimental as an excuse to keep it around, not because it is. Be honest about how much an item means to you. If you would be devastated to see it go, then it's okay to keep; otherwise, it's probably not particularly sentimental.

Ask these questions about each item you come across in your cleaning process. Decide if the item serves a purpose, if that purpose is useful, and what that purpose is. If something doesn't meet these criteria, it's not valuable after all.

Sort Everything Into Piles by Usefulness

Now that you know how valuable everything is, you can figure out whether or not you should keep it. Separate the things you deemed useful from the things you decided served little if any purpose. You can technically do this by making a list, but I prefer to do it by physically sorting the items. Clear space for three distinct piles. The first pile is for the things you're definitely keeping. The next is for the things you might or might not keep. The final pile is for everything you've decided doesn't add value to your life.

Let's start with the first pile, which includes everything that you're confident about keeping. Try to keep this pile as small as possible. Reserve it for only those items that serve a significant purpose and get plenty of use. This pile should be primarily everyday items that you use at least once a week on average. It can also include a few important items that still see occasional use.

We'll skip the second pile for now and look at the pile full of things you want to get rid of. These are the items you've decided hold little value, the things you bought impulsively, or the things that have worn out their welcome. They will probably be a mix of things that are well-worn and things that are completely pristine. This is perfectly normal. Sometimes, we don't use the things we buy, even if we thought we would when we bought them. We might be tempted to keep these things just because we feel like we didn't get our money's worth out of them, but this doesn't do us any favors. We're better off reducing the clutter and tossing these items when they no longer have worth for us. In the next step, we'll take a look at ways we can repurpose or gift these items so that they're still serving a purpose for someone else.

If you can't decide whether to sort something into the first or third pile, put it in the second. This is the pile for anything you're not sure about keeping. If you're trying to decide how often you use something, leave it in this pile for a bit. Transfer these items to a bin or another container so that they're out of the way but also easily accessible. You can leave them here for about a week, depending on the kinds of items and the frequency at which they would normally be used. If you need to use an item, take it out of the bin and use it, but don't put it back in the bin. Instead, return it to its original location. After a week or so, look back at the bin. The items that are still there are those that you never used. At this point, you can pretty safely label these items as ones to be tossed.

Toss, Donate, or Keep

You've got your piles, and you know what you're doing with each one. Take all the things you've decided to keep and set them off to the side. We'll come back to this pile in the next step. For now, we want to focus on the things we're getting rid of.

You've probably realized by now that if you were to just throw out all of the clutter in your house, you'd generate a lot of garbage. On top of that, you would be throwing away a lot of things that aren't necessarily ready for the trash. Just because something isn't useful to us doesn't mean it's not useful to anyone. We can do a lot of good by donating and gifting things that are still in good condition and may hold value for other people. This can encourage us to declutter too since we don't feel like we're just generating trash. We feel like we're having a positive impact on our community and making a difference, which inspires us to be more liberal with the things we decide to release from our lives.

First, look through your pile for anything that can be repurposed. These items might not hold much value in their original forms, but they can be recycled into something more beneficial. For example, a stray sock missing the other half of its pair could become an easy way to wipe dust off of surfaces. The jar from a used-up candle could become a storage container for small items or a pot for a tiny plant. Clothing that's well-worn and full of holes can be torn up further and turned into rags for cleaning. By transforming items in this way, you give them new value without being wasteful.

One word of caution on repurposing: Only keep something around with the intention to repurpose it if you are planning on using it soon. Try not to save these things for "a rainy day" since they often end up sitting and waiting to be used. This turns them back into clutter, which is the last thing you want to do. If you do keep things around to repurpose, don't put them back where they were before. Move them so they're grouped with other items that share their new purpose. This means that in the case of the stray sock, you should move it out of the sock drawer and store it with your cleaning supplies instead. This increases the chances you'll remember to use it. Keep only the things that you can repurpose and use in the near future, and disregard any DIY materials that are more likely to sit and gather dust.

Next, see if you can identify any items that would make good gifts for people in your life. Maybe you have a purse you like but rarely use anymore. If you think someone else would enjoy it, set it aside as a way to brighten their day sometime soon. Old books are great gifts too, especially if you know someone who would enjoy the story as much as you did.

Depending on the types of items you are left with, you may be able to donate them. Clothing and canned goods are some of the most commonly donated items, but they're far from the only ones. Most shelters are also in need of spare toiletries and personal hygiene products, and donating any unopened packages you have can be a big help. Pet shelters are often in need of spare towels and pillows, and they rarely care about the quality of the items. Some libraries will accept donations of books and other media like movies, CDs, and records. Some charities accept toys and sporting goods. Occasionally, you can donate furniture that is still in good shape to certain organizations. Check with local donation collection centers near you to see what they accept and what they're most in need of. Also, make sure to check the expiration dates on anything that you're planning to donate so that you don't end up sending expired goods.

Once you've exhausted all other options, use the trash as your last resort. This helps you minimize the amount of waste you create while still leaving you with a home free from clutter. While the trash is usually a good catch-all for items that can't be disposed of or repurposed in another way, watch out for items that shouldn't get thrown away. Some electronic devices, corrosive materials, and medications have specific disposal methods that you should follow. Additionally, recycle anything you can to avoid plastic and glass pollution.

At the end of this step, you will finally be free of the clutter that has taken over your living space for so long. From this new, clutter-free vantage point, the amount of storage space you have available may seem larger than ever before. All that's left is for you to return to the pile of items that you've decided to keep and organize everything that's left.

Organize What's Left

A good organization system helps prevent future clutter. If you know where everything is and everything has its place, you can find what you need quickly, and you're more likely to put it right back where you got it. Gone are the days of endlessly hunting around for that one thing you need in a huge pile of things you don't need. When you get organized, you'll save yourself time and hassle, and you'll also make it less likely that you'll fall back into your old habits.

The period right after a big clean-out is the perfect time to organize what you have. There is a lot more space available to you, so make good use of it! When you put things away, try to group them in ways that make sense and help you find what you're looking for easier. Instead of throwing books and movies haphazardly back on your shelf, organize them in alphabetical order. Rather than putting all of your clothes back in your closet, hang up the clothes that are currently in season, and store the rest until you're going to wear them again. Know where everything is, and pack away anything you're not currently using.

You also want to arrange each room in a way that looks tidy visually. Just because everything's organized doesn't mean it's not still visually loud. A library might follow the Dewey decimal system religiously, but most libraries aren't exactly minimalist. The best way to do this is to find storage solutions that are 'hidden' or otherwise out of sight. Make use of space under the bed, in drawers, and in closets, so long as you can keep these areas organized and the things inside them easily accessible. Put things away in storage bins, jars, baskets, and other containers to group similar items. This will give each room a clean, open look with minimal distractions.

Finally, move things where you tend to use them. It wouldn't make any sense to put your TV in one room and your remote control in the other, so why do we do this with so many other items? Keep toiletries in the bathroom, laundry supplies by the washing machine (or where you pile your dirty clothes if you use a laundromat), and video games near their consoles. If you want to read more, a neat trick is to take the book you're currently reading and store it not with your other books, but instead nearby wherever you're most likely to read it. For example, if you want to start reading before bedtime, leave the book on the nightstand by your bed. This way, it's easily accessible to you, which means you're more likely to read it.

Rather than adding clutter, you improve your ability to focus on a task you might have otherwise put off or forgotten about.

What you're left with after all of this decluttering and reorganizing are the most important items. You have gotten rid of the sources of distraction and visual noise that once dominated your house. Now that all of the hard work is done, you'll likely find it easier to relax, focus, and live in your newly decluttered home.

Preventing Future Clutter

You might be asking yourself: Didn't you just say the hard work is over? Actually, the hardest part is over. When you start with a neat, organized home you've just rid of many unnecessary items, it's not hard at all to keep it that way. Still, you don't want to go back to your old bad habits. If you don't make some changes in the way you treat your home and the things inside it, you might turn around in a few months to find that all of the clutter has somehow returned. Thankfully, there are two simple rules to follow to prevent clutter from coming back. The first is to adjust your spending habits, something that you'll want to do anyway to save yourself money. The second is to make cleaning and decluttering something you do routinely.

Stop Buying Things You Don't Need

Impulse purchases account for a lot of the clutter we generate over the years. When we don't think hard about what we're buying, we don't get a chance to decide whether or not the item is worth having around. We might use shopping as a pick-me-up when we're experiencing a hardship, which makes the tendency to spend money on unnecessary things even worse. The more we spend compulsively, the more clutter we accumulate over time, and we end up hardly touching half the things we buy.

We can train ourselves out of this behavior by stopping to consider the value of everything we buy. We might think that a pair of heels would be cute, but how often would we wear them? Maybe it's better to invest in a comfortable and cute pair of sneakers, which we would wear far more often. When we pause before making a purchase, we give ourselves time to analyze the value said purchase would bring to our lives. If it's not going to bring any value, it will only end up as clutter.

Make Decluttering Part of Your Routine

Here's a fun fact you might have heard before: The cells in your body are constantly growing, dividing, and dying. New cells are made as quickly as the old ones die off, and the lifespan of a cell is not nearly as long as that of a human. Because of this, it's estimated that the human body completely replaces all of its cells about every seven years (Opfer, n.d., para. 3). Of course, this process doesn't happen all at once. It would be incredibly difficult for your body to generate enough energy to replace all of its cells at the same time, and you'd probably stop being able to function during this process. Instead, your body makes these changes gradually over the seven years. A relatively small number of cells are replaced every day, which eventually culminates in a much larger effect.

This is the same way you should treat the decluttering process. Despite your best efforts, you might still make a few impulse purchases here and there that can reintroduce junk into your household. If you wait years at a time to declutter, you're going to have a lot of work ahead of you. Breaking it down room by room helps to ease the difficulty a bit, but there's still a lot to do if you let the problem get worse and worse until it gets out of hand. Instead of waiting until the clutter is almost unbearable, start turning decluttering into routine maintenance, which is much better for your mind and much easier on you. If you do a little bit of decluttering every few months, you can get the same amount of work done with much less energy expended. Even better, this helps you maintain a good standard for how cluttered you allow your house to be, which reduces the risk of developing mental clutter once again.

Ideally, you want decluttering to become something you do routinely. Try to set specific dates because this helps you hold yourself accountable for getting it done in a timely manner. Every two or three months, you should go around your house and get rid of any clutter that's built up over this time. You probably won't have to do much work. You might be able to get everything done in an afternoon, which is a lot faster than taking weeks to get rid of several years' worth of clutter. As long as you hold yourself to a high standard and address clutter when it initially appears, not when it's been given time to build up, keeping your home decluttered should be a breeze.

Chapter Takeaways

This chapter took a look at some of the reasons why a clutter-free home is necessary and supplied you with tips for decluttering your home. Some of these tips include:

- Be more mindful of how you interact with everything in your house, and pay attention to the things that rarely get used.

- Weigh the value of every item in your home. If it's not providing you any value, it's just taking up space.

- Don't give clutter problems the opportunity to get worse. Manage them early, and you'll save yourself a lot of work in the long run.

Next, we'll learn how to declutter what often feels like our home away from home: our workspaces.

Chapter 8: Decluttering Your Workspace

"Minimalism is not subtraction for the sake of subtraction. Minimalism is subtraction for the sake of focus."—Anonymous

Imagine you're working in a cubicle at an office. You have plenty of work to do but not so much that you can't goof off a little, you figure, and there are plenty of distractions on your desk that all seem more fun than your actual work. Maybe you waste a little time with these distractions, but you're ready to get back to work soon enough. But as soon as you do, one of your coworkers pulls your attention away again, pulling you into a discussion about some TV show or something equally trivial. Before you know it, an hour has gone by, and you haven't done any work at all. When you try to work, now keenly aware of how much time you've lost and how hard it has become to focus, your boss comes by and assigns you an additional project. Suddenly, it feels like your attention is being split a hundred different ways, and you can't keep up with everyone's requests. How can you possibly focus with all of this clutter?

As it turns out, you can't. The more distractions and diversions from your responsibilities that litter your workspace, the harder it becomes to focus on anything at all. Your mind fills up with unrelated, unimportant thoughts, and it becomes impossible to think clearly. This is especially bad if your job requires you to do a lot of critical thinking and problem-solving. Distracted thinking probably isn't going to get you great results, at least not compared to the results you would usually have. All of these distractions create clutter, and that's the last thing you want when you're trying to focus.

Decluttering your workspace is well worth the initial energy and time investment. It becomes much harder to locate important papers when you have a cluttered, disorganized desk or filing system. It's also much harder to put your head down and get your work done when dozens of things are vying for your attention at all times. Clutter leads to wasted time and diminished returns on the time you spend working. By decluttering your workspace, you reduce the risk of procrastination and become a more efficient worker.

Decluttering Your Desk

Whether you head into an office every day or work from home, you should have a dedicated workspace. At most jobs, this might mean a cubicle, a desk, or just an area where you're typically posted if you work a service or retail job. These kinds of spaces are specifically designed to improve workflow and sharpen your focus. Even if you share the area with your coworkers, you still get a space, whether it's a desk or another type of work area, that is exclusively for work. Of course, it's your responsibility to keep it this way, but we'll return to this in a moment.

If your home is your office, it's even more important to designate a specific area as your workspace. It's difficult to get into a working mentality if you're trying to do your work from your bed or your couch. Instead of focusing on your tasks and responsibilities, your thoughts will start to drift to the other things you usually do in the same area of your house. Additionally, your brain starts to make associations between where you are and what you do there. It's harder to turn on the work mindset if your brain is stuck in the relaxation mindset. This can make a tendency for procrastination worse. It also becomes hard to turn off the work mindset, which is an especially big problem if you try to work in your bed. This breaks down the association between your bed and sleeping, replacing it with working associations and making it harder to quiet your thoughts for long enough to fall asleep at night. The best way to remedy this issue is to set aside one part of your house as your home office. Get all of your work done there, and avoid bringing anything unrelated to work into that space.

Now that you have a specific area that you use for work, it's time to declutter it just like you decluttered your living space. Eliminate all possible sources of distraction, and try to keep only the things that help you complete your work. If you successfully keep your desk clear of distractions and time sinks, you'll find the amount of work you're able to complete each day will increase drastically.

Be Wary of Common Sources of Distraction

While anything can become a distraction in the right context, there are some items that are more effective at pulling our attention away from our work than others. These tend to be things that are more fun and interesting than our work. Our brains crave the little energy and mood boost we get from doing fun things, especially when we're working and craving something more enjoyable. Be on the lookout for anything in your workspace that isn't helping you get your work done, and try to remove these things before they can sabotage your progress.

Two of the biggest offenders are TV and video games. These are usually more of a problem for home offices, but your place of business might also have a TV set up. Games and TV are designed to hook us in. They're often meant to be pure fun, and we build up a lot of positive associations with them. This means that when we're offered a choice between work and play, we're going to pick play just about every time, regardless of whether or not we have the time to waste. The best way to deal with these distractions is to get them out of our sight when we need to buckle down and work. When we're not directly looking at something, it's easier for us to forget it's there. If you can, move the TV or video game console out of the room you're working in. If you can't, turning them off is your next best option. Just be sure to hide the remote or controller, ideally leaving it somewhere out of your reach. Sometimes, the simple barrier of having to get up to turn on the TV will remind you that you're not supposed to be watching TV right now. This brief pause is enough for your critical thinking skills to kick in and return your focus to your work. If your boss won't allow you to turn the TV off—for example, if you work in a doctor's office's reception area and the TV is on for patients—ask if you can at least mute the noise and turn on closed captions. This doesn't remove the problem entirely, but it will still drastically cut down on the amount of distraction the TV can create.

Not every distraction can be managed by simply getting it out of your sight. Sometimes, the source of distraction is part of your work. This is often the case with computers and cell phones. You might need your computer for your job, but it also gives you direct access to hundreds of distracting, clutter-inducing sites. With a few clicks, you can end up procrastinating hours of your time away. The same is true for your cell phone. You may be able to shut your phone off and leave it in your pocket or a bag in some situations, but dealing with the distraction becomes a lot harder when you need your phone for important work-related calls.

Luckily, as much as technology has the power to distract us, it has the power to help us reduce the risk of distraction too. There are many different software programs designed to help you be more productive, and a great deal of them work to eliminate the temptations that your phone and computer pose. You can install programs and extensions on your computer that will restrict your access to certain sites, some of which allow you to set a time limit and make it fairly difficult to bypass these restrictions. Similar apps exist for your phone that disable notifications for everything outside of calls and texts. This cuts down on the amount of buzzing your phone does every five minutes and ensures that every time you stop and check your phone, you're only looking at things relevant to work.

No matter what form distraction takes in your workplace, you can protect yourself from it by doing one of three things. You can remove yourself from the presence of the distracting thing if possible, you can move the distracting thing away from you so that you're not constantly reminded of it, or you can use creative solutions to diminish the risk of falling prey to distraction. Each of these solutions lets you keep your focus on your work so you can get it done.

Organize Your Workspace

Poor organization wastes your time. The longer you spend hunting down a file that's not where it's supposed to be, precariously balancing new clutter on top of all of the existing clutter on your desk, or combing through your emails looking for a specific one, the less time you have for work. As you eat away at your time, you end up having to rush through assignments to meet deadlines and expectations, which leaves you stressed and can bring self-critical thoughts to the surface. To avoid all of this, all you need to do is get organized.

Organizing your desk or another workspace isn't that different from organizing your home. You can follow the same basic principles of giving everything a dedicated home and returning things to this home after you've used them. This means you don't have to spend any time or mental energy trying to figure out where you left something; you'll always know right where it is. It's also a good idea to come up with a system for organizing new files or other resources. You can order them alphabetically, group them by their purpose, arrange them by their relevant dates, or use any other strategy that helps you find what you're looking for on the first try. Fruitlessly hunting for something is as frustrating as it is distracting, so the small amount of time you spend revamping your organizational system is worth the decrease in your mental clutter.

Finally, keep the surface of your desk clean. You might have to flip back and forth between different documents as you work, but as soon as you're done with them, you should return these files to their proper place in your organizational system. Try not to leave old drink bottles or food wrappers on your desk after you're done with them. Clear away sources of clutter like pens and pencils, keeping them in a cup or in a drawer instead. These are small changes, but they'll make a huge difference in keeping your workspace neat and organized.

Dealing With Clutter From Bosses and Coworkers

We tend to think of sources of distraction as inanimate objects, but people can be distracting too. As we discussed in the chapter about decluttering your relationships, other people can be a source of mental clutter. This is especially true at work, where too many conversations with coworkers or getting assigned too much work at the same time can make it significantly harder to focus our efforts where they're most needed. It's hard to get work done with someone always staring over our shoulder or even if they're just popping in and out, always seeming to appear at the most inconvenient times.

The worst thing about distraction that comes from our coworkers or bosses is that they often don't even realize they're adding to our mental clutter. A chatty coworker may just be trying to make friends at the office. A boss who tends to micromanage may honestly believe they're being helpful. This makes us reluctant to correct them because we don't want to hurt their feelings, but tolerating constant disruption and distraction isn't good for our mental health or our productivity. Again, as in all good relationships, honesty is key. Whenever the urge arises to sweep your concerns under the rug, counter it with an attempt to speak up for yourself. Otherwise, nothing's going to change.

Setting boundaries is equally important in the workplace. You need enough time to focus on your work if you want to get it done. When people interrupt you or make demands on the time you've set aside for yourself, they interfere with your ability to do your job. If you're a people pleaser, you'll probably be tempted to drop everything and give others your attention, but resist this urge. Instead, gently but firmly let them know you're busy and that you'll get back to them when you can. This isn't an unreasonable request, and most people will have no trouble granting it. If coworkers continue to bother you after you've made your boundaries clear, discuss the issue with your HR department, boss, or whoever is responsible for managing employee conflicts in your company. If your boss doesn't respect your boundaries and keeps adding to your mental clutter, it may be time to look for a new line of work. It's a tough decision to make, and you should give it a lot of thought, but you need to feel respected and valued in your job. If you're constantly overworked and overwhelmed by work-related stress, your job is creating too much mental clutter, and your talents may be better suited elsewhere.

Chapter Takeaways

In this chapter, we took a look at how your job can contribute to clutter and what you can do about it. We discussed many tips for managing workplace clutter, including:

- Remove distractions from your work environment to improve your focus.
- Create and stick to an organization system that you can navigate easily. This cuts down on wasted time.
- Set boundaries at work so you can concentrate on important tasks and get them done.

In the final chapter, we will learn how we can declutter not just the physical world but the digital world too.

Chapter 9: Decluttering Your Time Spent Online

"Your worth is not measured in likes, comments, notes, or followers, but in your ability to love, be kind and keep negative comments to yourself, take notes, and lead by example."—Mariah McHenry

Clutter in the digital world isn't always as easy to recognize as clutter in the physical world. You could certainly say that having multiple pages' worth of apps you don't use counts as clutter, but this is a minor annoyance at best. Digital clutter can be much more insidious and damaging than this, and it all has to do with the power technology has over us.

If you're an avid user of social media, the last thing you want to hear is how technology is bad for you. It can get exhausting to hear people talk about how everyone is so obsessed with their phones, to the point that you might roll your eyes whenever you hear the idea. After all, as you've probably said to yourself multiple times, technology is a great resource that connects us all to information at the touch of a button. Shouldn't we use this resource to our advantage?

While technology certainly has its positive uses, it also has the potential to be a source of negativity, overthinking, and mental health issues. Nowhere is this more apparent than on social media where the constant scramble for likes and followers and the need to constantly compare yourself to others can drive you to prioritize your digital persona over your real life.

Tech also poses the danger of getting you hooked, which can cause you to spend hours mindlessly scrolling and consuming meaningless content that clutters your brain. Websites and apps employ different motivation techniques to guarantee you keep returning to them, including "'scarcity' (a snap or status is only temporarily available, encouraging you to get online quickly); 'social proof' (20,000 users retweeted an article so you should go online and read it); 'personalization' (your news feed is designed to filter and display news based on your interest); and 'reciprocity' (invite more friends to get extra points, and once your friends are part of the network it becomes much more difficult for you or them to leave)" (Ali et al., 2018, para. 3). These are all incredibly effective ways to grab your attention and get you checking your phone every 10 minutes.

It's important to remember, however, that it's not the technology itself that is inherently dangerous; it's how we use it that poses a risk. If we declutter our digital spaces and reduce the risk of harm, we can maximize the positive results of technology and avoid all of the negative ones. When we consume digital content in reasonable amounts and don't allow it to take over our lives, we forge a much healthier relationship with technology.

Decluttering Your Feed

The people you follow and the posts you interact with on social media have a huge impact on what kind of experience you have with technology. As you know, the content you interact with on your social media accounts is different from the content your parents might interact with. Everyone is able to personalize their experience by following and unfollowing whoever they want. This is one of the most underutilized tools in the digital world. Curating your experience can help you avoid all of the worst parts of social media, including the toxic competitive nature, the endless negativity, and the subtle and persistent encouragement to always be online. By making changes to who you follow, you can vastly improve your experiences and cut down on clutter.

Unfollow Excessive Negativity

It's easy to get swept up in the more toxic, negative parts of the internet. A few complaints here and there won't give you much trouble, but certain people only ever seem to post about things that make us angry and upset. When we follow these people, we get a direct line to all of their negativity until we start to internalize it ourselves. Their frustration rubs off on us, and our mentalities suffer because of it. Worse, we may not even realize that we're doing this due to the whiplash-like nature of the tone of the posts on our feeds. A typical scroll through your timeline might include a joke, an incredibly negative post, and then another joke. The negativity flies past us so quickly that we hardly have time to recognize it, but our brains pick up on it thanks to our negativity bias. When we let depressing and aggravating posts sneak their way into our feeds on a regular basis, we allow this same negativity to invade our thoughts.

Luckily, you get to control the content on your timeline. You can decide whether or not you want to expose yourself to so much negativity. If you want to cut down on mental clutter and relieve social media-induced anxiety and overthinking, unfollow the people who repeatedly make you a more negative person. Sometimes, these will be strangers. Other times, you may need to unfollow someone you know in real life, even if you still enjoy their company in person. It's okay to unfollow anyone who is turning your feed into a cluttered, gloomy mess, and you shouldn't feel guilty no matter who it is. Prioritize your mental health first and foremost.

Limit Your Screen Time

The other big danger of most digital spaces is that they are designed to get us to keep scrolling. Most websites have implemented an auto-scroll feature, which means that instead of clicking a button to take you to the next page, posts simply appear when you hit the bottom of the current page. This is convenient, but it makes us more likely to continue consuming content. We feel like we have to like the next post or watch the next video that comes up. Auto-scroll eliminates the natural pauses in our attention that reaching the end of the page would have provided us, so we spend longer and longer on our phones and computers. If you struggle with excessive screen time, try setting a timer for 10 or 15 minutes when you open social media. Once the timer rings, put down your phone and move on to something else. This interrupts the endless flow of content and shows you just how long you're spending on social media. With this knowledge, you can decide if it's truly a good use of your time. You can also limit the time you spend scrolling by following fewer people. If there are fewer posts to read, you'll eventually run out of new content, which will force you to take a break.

You should also try to take breaks when you feel yourself getting excessively frustrated. Social media encourages interaction, but not all of that interaction is positive. You might get swept up into an argument or two, sometimes with a total stranger. While there's nothing wrong with having a discussion with someone on social media, when the discussion devolves into senseless arguing and bickering, it's time to take a break. It's not doing your mentality any favors to obsess over fights with strangers.

Stop Caving to FOMO

The fear of missing out (FOMO) is an incredibly strong motivator. We want to be a part of the action, and social media makes us feel like we're connected to others in the same position. This can give us a sense of community, but it can also be used to manipulate us into returning to the same website or app over and over again. Be wary of "limited time" offers and events because these prey on your FOMO and can lead to you spending far more time on the internet than usual. Look out for other ways that sites and content creators subtly influence your decisions, and pause to consider your actions instead of reacting impulsively. When you get a little perspective, it becomes a lot easier to recognize when someone's trying to manipulate you.

Decluttering Your Own Posts

It's not just other peoples' posts that we should be worried about. We can develop a toxic relationship with social media through our posts as well. This is especially dangerous when we start devoting more time and effort into our online presence than we do our real-life relationships. When we allow the digital world to start meaning more to us than the real world, we lose sight of the things that matter in our lives. We cave to our desires for instant gratification in the form of likes and comments, deeming them more important than our real experiences. All the while, thoughts of our posts crowd our heads. We keep thinking about posts that didn't do as well as others, wondering what we did wrong. We see the success of others, and we become jealous and frustrated. These emotions only make the clutter worse.

There is no 'winning' in the social media game. There is no amount of likes we can receive where we will feel truly happy about what we've accomplished. If all we care about is how many people click a button on our posts, then we will just keep chasing more and more likes, getting increasingly frustrated, and leveling criticisms at ourselves for something that's ultimately meaningless. The only way for us to break this cycle of negativity and clutter is to stop playing the game.

Limit How Often You Post

Just as you should limit the number of people you follow to avoid being overwhelmed with posts, so, too, should you limit the number of posts you make. Posting is addictive because it creates a positive feedback loop in your mind. As you start making more and more posts, possibly posting multiple times a day, you get more invested in the social media game. You start caring more about engagement and how well-received your posts are and less about whether or not they reflect an accurate picture of your life. As it turns out, many people who have picturesque lives on social media don't show the world their private struggles and hardships. You, too, can fall into this trap of pretending you have an ideal life instead of trying to achieve it.

Posting less frequently helps you keep your distance from this possibility. It keeps you from getting too wrapped up in the digital world and all of the clutter it creates. Enforce a hard post limit on yourself. If you usually post five or more times a day, cut it down to no more than twice per day. This way, you'll spend less time online and less time worrying about what people think of each post.

Chapter Takeaways

This chapter discussed the troubling and sometimes toxic relationships that are all too common with technology. You learned:

- The digital world, especially social media, is purposefully designed to be addictive and take up space in your thoughts.
- You can curate a more enjoyable and positive experience with social media by making changes to the ways you interact with technology.
- Improving your relationship with technology can reduce or even eliminate social media-induced mental clutter.

Conclusion

By now, you know just how harmful clutter can be. You know that it can bring you to the brink of exhaustion and cause you to become overly critical of yourself, getting in the way of your ability to grow and flourish. You also know that clutter isn't just the unread books you collect in your house or the old fast-food wrappers littering the interior of your car. It can arise from chaotic and hectic situations and experiences in all their forms. Your mind, lifestyle, friendships, home, job, and social media accounts can all be filled to the brim with clutter, ready to spill over into your life.

Even though clutter is a powerful force, you aren't powerless to stop it. In fact, you can take the steps necessary to rid your life of clutter in all of its forms. The most important takeaway from this book is that the power to shape your life is in your hands. If you allow clutter to persist, you're always going to be fighting a losing battle. You will make things harder for yourself in every area of your life you leave cluttered, and these difficulties will be reflected in your mental state. If instead, you choose to sort through everything in your life, keeping the good and tossing out the junk, you'll find that these sources of resistance will disappear like they never existed in the first place. Your thoughts will settle, and you'll finally be able to enjoy a peaceful, stress-free life.

Throughout this book, you have learned plenty of actionable steps you can take to defeat clutter. These include methods for thinking positively more often, recognizing how past events can affect your current mental state, and rewiring your brain away from negativity. They also include tips for decluttering a busy life such as cutting back on multitasking and narrowing your focus to pursue the goals that matter the most. You learned how to declutter your relationships by limiting their number and only keeping the relationships that are positive forces in your life. You also learned the basics of redesigning your living space along the lines of a minimalist aesthetic. Through this, you can get rid of the junk that is a source of distraction and stress and train yourself to avoid making useless purchases.

Next, you learned tips and tricks for decluttering your workspace, which included getting your desk organized and avoiding interruptions, even when those interruptions come from your coworkers. Last but certainly not least, you discovered actionable steps you can take to minimize clutter from the internet by spending less time on things like social media.

Every single one of these steps is integral to living a more fulfilling life. If you allow clutter to persist in one area of your life, you guarantee that you will never truly feel well-rested, and you will never fully get rid of your stress. The best and only way to declutter your life and have the effects last is to declutter all parts of it. Through this, you will finally get your mental clutter under control so that you can pursue the goals and achievements that hold personal value to you. When your time is your own, you can choose to do whatever you wish with it.

If you follow the steps and tips for decluttering every area of your life as outlined in *How to Declutter Your Mind*, you will never have to worry about clutter again. You will be able to live a calmer, more well-rested life full of peace, good mental health, and happiness.

Book #2
Digital Minimalism in Everyday Life

Overcome Technology Addiction, Declutter Your Mind, and Reclaim Your Freedom

Introduction

At its core, minimalism is all about getting more with less. It's more than just an aesthetic choice, but it is rather a philosophical decision. Digital minimalism is all about choosing reduced dependence on the internet, your smartphones, computers, and other devices, and regain control over your intentions, focus, and freedom to choose.

This book was inspired by lessons and ideas that I learned and practiced as Cal Newport presented them in his book *Digital Minimalism: Choosing a Focused Life in a Noisy World.*

I hope you don't mind if I chime in with him in saying that digital minimalism is indeed a philosophy that centers on technology use. I also think that we all should practice digital declutter, deprive ourselves of solitude from time to time, control our social media exposure (if not to remove it completely), and prioritize real-world experience over the synthetic associations in the digital world.

In this book, I only touch on the impact of digital media on adults and kids. I even present some numbers to prove the points that have been raised. However, I do not deal heavily with the subject of technology addiction in this book since Cal Newport has already done such a wonderful job at it. In other words, there is no need to reinvent the wheel.

What I would rather like to present in this work are actionable steps, tips, and tricks that you can do yourself so you can handle the challenges of technology addiction on your terms in your daily life.

This is a book for the average folks who can't always understand psychological and other technical terms. A lot of effort has been made to ensure that this book is jargon-free as much as possible. However, where jargon has been used in these pages, it is accompanied by explanations that can be understood by everyday folks.

This book focuses on how to live a digital minimalist lifestyle. I have also borrowed a few concepts from Newport to explain how digital media and technology affect us human beings. On the other hand, I depart from the theoretical base that he introduced, and emphasized on how you can apply digital minimalism for everyday situations.

For instance, section two of this book begins with doing a digital inventory and declutter. It is then followed up by strategies for doing a digital detox. You will also learn mindfulness techniques that will help you stay focused and present with your current situation.

Other techniques and strategies, to include going on a tech sabbatical, doing art therapy, creative work, and digital communication will be covered.

Remember that it takes time to form new habits and get rid of the old. That is why the strategies and techniques you will learn here are not one-time quick fixes. You need to spend time trying them and practicing them so they become a part of the new you.

Section 1

Defining and Understanding Concepts

Chapter 1: What Is Digital Minimalism?

Minimalism is a word that gets thrown around a lot these days. One version of this philosophy or way of life is called digital minimalism. But before we go into its "digital" aspects, we need to learn what minimalism really is.

Understanding the core concepts of a minimalist lifestyle will help you understand what digital minimalism is.

What Is Minimalism Anyway?

You may have heard people describe what a minimalist lifestyle is. Some say that it means you can only own around a hundred things and nothing more. Others would say that minimalism means that you will have to quit your career.

As you try to go over the myriad of descriptions, you might think that it's some kind of mystical or exotic way of living. The pictures of minimalist homes look really inviting.

However, living life by starting a blog, not having children, and not owning a phone sounds like way too far-fetched for ordinary folks like you and me. But here is one thing that I would like to emphasize:

A minimalist lifestyle isn't like that.

Those are not what minimalism is all about, frankly speaking. Some people might dismiss minimalism as some sort of home organization fad. Some people might even think that it is a lifestyle that is too restrictive.

Some people say they can't switch to a minimalist lifestyle because of the so-called rules and restrictions mentioned above. Just remember that being a minimalist isn't about any of those things. Sure, if you want to live with less clutter in your life, then practicing minimalism can help. But that isn't the point.

Think of minimalism as a tool.

If it is a tool, then what is it used for? You use it to find freedom. It is your gateway to freedom from worrying, fear, that feeling of being overwhelmed, consumer culture, and even depression.

Take note, however, that minimalism doesn't say that having material possessions is wrong. There is nothing inherently wrong about wanting to own a car (or two) or owning a house, or cell phones, or a shoe collection.

What you don't want is to make your possessions be the center of your universe. We sometimes give too much meaning to what we own and have, and forsake all the other equally important things such as your health, mental and emotional well-being, relationships, and personal growth.

Do you want to have a wonderful and successful career? Then go ahead, work towards your career goals. Do you want to raise kids and have a great family? Do you want to own a brand-new car and a million-dollar home?

Minimalism actually welcomes those things. However, what this philosophy or lifestyle choice does is to help you decide to own or work on those things deliberately and consciously.

If we were to summarize what a minimalist lifestyle is, here is a very simplified definition that anyone should be able to understand:

> *"It is a lifestyle choice where one gets rid of the excesses of life to allow you to focus on aspects of living that are equally important and contributing to freedom, fulfillment, and true happiness."*

How Minimalism Has Benefited Me Personally

Speaking from experience, a minimalist lifestyle isn't easy to start, and it is one that isn't easy to maintain. But it depends on the individual—I have friends who have switched over to a minimalist lifestyle with no problems.

Personally, it has helped me to:

- Discover my purpose in life
- Get rid of the unnecessary things in my life
- Contribute to causes and things that are beyond and larger than myself
- Reduce focus on me and help me learn to help others
- Find fulfillment in life
- Grow as a person
- Focus on my mental and physical health
- Tap into my creative side
- Consume less and help preserve the environment
- Experience real freedom (no longer living the nine-to-five life)
- Pursue different passions
- Live in the moment and enjoy what I have
- Be content and not allow greed to overcome my desires
- Reclaim time for myself
- Eliminate that feeling of discontent no matter what situation I'm in

You can say that ever since I have successfully implemented a minimalist lifestyle, I was able to discover true and lasting happiness. And I hope that is what you will achieve as well.

I have long since found that lasting happiness isn't found in my possessions. I have found happiness in life itself. The good thing is that finding your happiness is a decision that is yours and yours alone to make.

Minimalism Gone Digital

You can say that digital minimalism is minimalist living in the digital age. It has become quite popular because our modern-day lives have become centered on technology. The rise of smartphones, tablets, and other personalized technology has affected us pretty much the same way as to how our possessions and other material things have done previously.

You may think that minimalists like me are just overreacting, but if you look at our personalized technology (cellphones, etc.), you may see that we have an unhealthy relationship with it.

Someone once stated that in a world where we have made interconnectivity possible across the globe, human beings have drifted more distant with one another. Artificial digital connections now replace the human connections that we used to have, and our dependence on these things has become quite addictive.

Benefits of Minimalism in General

Before we go any further, I would just like to highlight some of the benefits of minimalist living in general. After that, we will go over what digital minimalism is specifically, what its core principles are, and how it would be like in case you try out digital minimalism right now.

Remember that minimalism is a lifestyle choice that leads you to ask what specific things really bring value to your life. This is the same fundamental rule that you will follow when you practice digital minimalism. Here are the benefits that you can expect from living a minimalist lifestyle in general:

1. You save more money because you tend to spend less

When you practice minimalism in your life, you will make a conscious choice to only spend your money on things that you need. That doesn't mean you won't allow yourself some form of luxury.

You will spend money on fun and games as well, but you will be more mindful of the things you spend money on. You will learn to avoid unplanned splurges on vacations, impulsive shopping, and other financial excesses.

Since you will tend to spend less on things that you don't really need, then you will end up reducing costs.

2. Reduce stress

Living with less means you don't have to stress about a lot of things. You don't have to keep up with the Kardashians or whoever it is that people have to catch up to. In terms of digital minimalism, you don't have to stress about how many likes your post gets, how many views your videos make, and who is paying attention to your news feed, etc.

The bottom line is that you learn to be who you are regardless of who is looking at your profile or what others think or say about you online.

3. You get a clearer and cleaner feeling

When was the last time you checked the number of icons you have on your computer? Have you seen how much clutter you have on your hard drive? What pictures and movies do you have on your folders?

The first time I tried de-cluttering, the effect was very profound. For the first time in my life, I saw my house with clear open spaces. My computer desktop screen was neat, and I can see the wallpaper picture I chose.

The same thing was true of my phone. Everything was more organized. It made me feel like I'm off to a fresh start—and it definitely was a fresh start. It was a uniquely clean slate feeling, and it made me realize that I was moving forward to better times ahead.

4. A more powerful sense of freedom

The refreshing feeling you get from clear and clean spaces at home and work gives you a sense of freedom. It kind of gives you a better sense of independence. On top of that, it also influences your productivity—there is no longer any clutter that you have to pay attention to, and so you end up becoming more productive at home and work.

5. You have an opportunity to support a cause and help others

One of the first things I ever did when I started de-cluttering was to go to a local homeless shelter. I had so much stuff like clothes, food that was in storage (food that I didn't like to eat), tools and equipment, and even old gadgets that I have never used for years.

My old computer screen went to charity as well as a bunch of keyboards and other computer equipment. Last time I checked, they're using it now in one of their offices.

I packed them all up and donated them to the shelter. Helping others also helped me feel good about myself.

On top of that, since I do not throw away a lot of garbage anymore, I believe I am doing my part to help preserve the environment.

6. Focus on quality, not quantity

I have noticed that people who practice any form of minimalism tend to focus more on the quality of the things that they acquire from clothing, food, and even the apps that they download.

You are no longer instinctively lining up to buy the latest phone model or gadget. You learn to practice the principle of delayed gratification. You wait until you know that the phone you are interested in is truly something of high quality.

If it doesn't meet your expectations, then keep your old phone (or whatever gadget it may be). If your gear still performs as expected, then there is no sense throwing it away for a brand spanking new item as a replacement.

You are more mindful of your choices, and therefore you focus more on the quality of the things you purchase, whether it is software or any kind of technology.

7. More time to rest

Since you don't waste time on things, you find more time to take care of yourself and rest.

8. Invest in more meaningful things

You can spend more time and effort on making your home look just the way you want it. You're not tied to the past, and you don't worry about the future, so you can focus on more meaningful things.

Digital Minimalism: Important Details

Now that we have gone over what minimalism is, the benefits we can gain, and how it applies to our digital lives, we can dig deeper into the details. Just remember that digital minimalism is the application of minimalist philosophy and way of life in our use of technology.

One of the leading figures in the world of digital minimalism, Cal Newport, is a computer science professor from Georgetown University. He defines digital minimalism using the following terms:

> *"[it is] a philosophy that helps you question what digital communication tools (and behaviors surrounding these tools) add the most value to your life."*

From Newport's definition, we see that digital minimalism doesn't only apply or refer to the digital technology that we use, but it also applies to the behaviors we have about the digital technologies that are at our disposal.

Just like physical, emotional, or psychological issues, our digital tools and products can also become an impediment to us. They make us lose our focus, worry too much, and at times cause us to overthink things. They can even stress us out or, at the opposite end of the spectrum, they can make us rely on and be addicted to technology.

In that regard, we can say that undertaking digital minimalism as a way of life can be a healthy response, especially when one is coping with potentially addictive or dependent behavior.

We do not only gauge the type of technology that we use, but we especially pay attention to the behaviors, emotions, and attitudes that we have with regard to digital technology. Practicing it means that we also need to pay attention to the tradeoffs that we make, the signs and signals of tech addiction, and our dependence on it.

Essential Principles of Digital Minimalism

When applied to our digital lives, minimalism follows some fundamental principles. Think of them as the main goals behind the practices and tips that you will read in the later chapters of this book.

People Always Come Before Technology

We live in an age when people are supposedly brought closer through the internet and social media. We are in an ever-increasingly connected world. However, despite the digital connections that have been afforded to us, we as human beings are ever more disconnected.

These technologies have rather become a force for isolation. A typical scenario pictured so many times is an entire family sitting together in a living room, but each family member has his face buried in a screen.

Where is the human interaction in that? We may be digitally connected, but it is as if we are emotionally, socially, and mindfully distant. We are, as you may call it, distracted by our screens. Our attention is sucked into the device in our hands and before our eyes that we do not realize the real relationship with the people in front of us.

So, rule number one in digital minimalism is people always come before technology. If we need to interact with someone who is in the same room, then do it the good old-fashioned way—talk.

Some people are now starting to realize that digital communication is great, but nothing can replace actual human interaction. There is something about that person-to-person interaction that we all long for, and now people realize how lacking digital communication truly is.

For instance, Antony Cauvin was featured in a BBC news report where he created what he calls a "cuddle curtain" that allowed him to hug his grandmother. The video that was uploaded on Facebook leftg netizens deeply touched.

In a similar story, a ten-year-old girl by the name of Paige had a marvelous idea—she made her own "hug curtain"

The curtain she made wasn't something medical or a product that was endorsed by the CDC. It was just made using Ziploc bags, a shower curtain, plastic plates, and a glue gun. Her hug curtain was affixed on their front doorway, and it allowed her to physically hug her family and get a cuddle from grandma and grandpa.

People long for that person-to-person connection. It's part of human nature. And science may have a pretty good explanation for that.

It's something called touch starvation. What happens when we get a supporting, loving, and emotional touch? It doesn't have to be a hug, but that can also be quite helpful too. Sometimes we just need someone to give us a friendly pat on the back, a supporting rub on the shoulder, someone to hold our hand, or at the very least someone we can literally lean on.

Dr. Katalin Gothard, a neuroscientist, speculates that this thing that we call touch starvation is a type of withdrawal that anyone can experience. Direct person-to-person contact stimulates the release of oxytocin and opioids in the brain. Without human touch—no matter how trivial—the brain will have less endogenous opioids and oxytocin.

This is part of the reason why we adopt dogs and other pets. We all want that direct interaction with another creature. This personal contact lowers our heart rate, and it boosts our immune system.

San Diego State University professor Dr. Colter Ray explains that when we are deprived of something so basic such as direct human interaction and the accompanying friendly touch, our bodies signal to us what we are missing. Sometimes, we just look beyond the mark as it were and miss the message entirely.

We become unhappy, and at times we may even get depressed. This is because the brain is no longer releasing essential hormones like serotonin.

This first fundamental rule of digital minimalism fits in perfectly to address this basic human need—that real person-to-person connection. That is why we need to learn to emphasize that *people come before technology*.

Intentional Use of Technology

Sometimes, our use of digital technology has become a matter of habit. Okay, so what's the first thing that you do when you wake up in the morning? Does it involve reaching out for your phone to turn off the alarm? Maybe you're old-fashioned, and you still reach out to an actual alarm clock to turn it off.

What's the first thing you check when you get to the office? Do you check your emails? What is the first thing you do when you get back home from work? Do you sit on the couch and watch TV? What's the latest hit show on Netflix?

It is a fact that our use of digital technology today has become habitual. Sometimes, we may not notice, but one of the first things that we habitually do is to mindlessly reach out for our phone and check social media.

Here's a fact—digital technology today has become a force to reckon with in our lives. It is both increasingly powerful and more readily available. It is relatively cheap (depending on the type of phone you're using anyway). And on top of all of that, it is very addictive.

Today, experts use multiple terms to describe this type of experience. Sometimes, they call it internet addiction, smartphone addiction, and others. However, to make things simpler, we'll just use the blanket term *technology addiction* to refer to these phenomena.

In later chapters of this book, we will address each of these conditions and provide you with signs and symptoms so you can know how to identify if you have them. We will also offer practical and actionable tips so you can reduce the symptoms and free yourself from an over-dependency on technology.

For now, just know that one of the foundational concepts or principles of digital minimalism is that your use of technology—any form of technology—should be mindful. It must be a conscious choice and not one that is borne out of an established habit.

When we are intentional about our technology use, it is easier to break free of bad use or overuse of digital technology. We can better determine what we truly value in life and make better decisions based on those values. Eventually, our use of technology will be purposeful and intentional.

Digital Technology Is a Creative Tool

Our addiction to digital technology is based on the stimuli that we gain from it. Some people have become so dependent on their gadgets that their purpose in using them is to make themselves feel better.

You can do this little self-evaluation quickly. It won't take a minute. Ask yourself, and try to answer these questions:

1. Do you get bored whenever you're not using your phone?
2. Do you feel like you need to play games on your phone when things around you aren't that interesting?
3. Do you often find yourself checking out your social media every now and then even when you're talking to someone that's right in front of you?
4. Do you feel like your day is not complete if you don't use your phone?

If you said yes to any of these questions, then there is a chance that you may have formed some kind of dependence on digital technology. It's not just your phone, your computer, your iPad, or your tablet. It can be the same comforting feeling when you watch Netflix, your web TV, or some other device—such as any Alexa-powered device like the Amazon Echo or Echo Dot.

Here is a common response that some people may be familiar with. You feel angry, sad, anxious, tired, upset, or any sort of discomfort coming your way. The first thing you do is to find relief—and where do you get it?

You can play a game on your phone, watch a video on YouTube, chat with your friends, make a short video on TikTok, take an Instagram selfie, or maybe just check your email again even though you've checked it like a hundred times already.

But why do we do it in the first place? We use it to avoid discomfort, sadness, boredom, and uncomfortable feelings. In short, it is a quick fix. But a short quick fix is not enough.

Experts believe that if we continue to do that, we are just allowing ourselves to suffer in the long term. A quick fix is nothing more than a gate to allow us to escape momentarily. The more we do it, the harder it gets to face the actual problem head-on.

The good news is that there is an alternative.

So, what's the alternative? The other option is to realize that digital technology is a creative tool, and we should use it that way. We stop using this technology as some kind of cheap relief from pain and discomfort. We should start using our technology to create meaningful, valuable, useful, and important things.

When a minimalist lifestyle and philosophy are applied to one's digital life, you gain the same benefits from minimalism in general as they were described earlier. You will get freedom, have a lot more free space on your devices, more time for yourself, fewer worries, less stress, and more opportunities for the things that matter to you.

Key Takeaways

- Minimalism is a lifestyle choice and a philosophy that centers on having less is more

- Digital minimalism has a lot of emotional and psychological benefits—one of which is regaining control over your power to choose and reducing your reliance on digital technology
- Digital minimalism doesn't mean you will stop using your phone; what you will do instead is make purposeful and well-intentioned use of your digital devices instead of impulsive usage

Chapter 2: The Trap of Technology Addiction

Important Note: we will be talking about a lot of behavioral addictions in this chapter, such as technology, smartphones, social media, internet addiction, and others. Please remember that there is advocacy towards classifying these behaviors as an established illness.

*However, they are **not yet officially** recognized as a disorder or illness, according to the DSM-IV (1995) or DSM-V (2013). Note that the Diagnostic and Statistical Manual of Mental Disorders (DSM) is the authoritative guide used by psychiatrists and mental health professionals.*

We refer to them in this book as addictions because of the addictive nature of the behavior even though they are not yet officially recognized as such. We may have to wait a while before medical experts officially recognize these behaviors as actual disorders.

And now, let us continue with the discussion.

It might take a bit of effort to finally acknowledge that we are addicted to digital technology. It comes in many forms—smartphone, social media, internet, and videogame addiction, among others.

These technologies have some things in common. They were created to be used daily and they are also specifically designed to steal people's attention. As they steal your awareness and attention, you become more addicted to them due to a variety of rewards programmed into the entire system.

What is Technology Addiction?

Technology addiction can be classed as a type of behavioral addiction. It might sound like a brutal description, but mental health professionals place it in the same category as other addictive behaviors such as sex and gambling.

Experts describe it as being similar to substance addiction. The big difference, of course, is that there is no substance (e.g., drugs, alcohol, tobacco, etc.) that the individual is dependent on.

It is rather characterized by an inability to limit, regulate, or control one's use of digital technology. This lack of control is also progressive, which means that as time goes on, you may lose that control further as you persist in this addictive behavior.

Some experts also observe that technology addiction has similar traits in common with other behaviors, such as obsessive-compulsive disorder.

Attention-Grabbing Equals Profit

In a lot of ways, you can say that attention-grabbing is the lifeblood of digital technology. The companies that produce them won't get any profit if their products are ineffective at maintaining your focus and attention. Tech giants like Netflix, Amazon, Facebook, and Google make use of this formula to amass sustained growth, increased revenues, and lots of success.

The evolution of digital technology and how they are used for profit has raised a lot of ethical questions. Are these businesses using technology to manipulate people? Aren't people supposed to have more control? Isn't the general public supposed to be made aware of how technology can be addictive?

Since time immemorial, human beings have been susceptible to different forms of behavioral addiction. What digital technology has done in our time, however, is to create an amplification of the above-mentioned human tendencies.

In many instances, our addiction to different things has made people miss out on many important life events. Most of these moments are things that you can never relive or have a chance to experience again.

Types of Technology Addiction

There are several types of technology addictions. They include the following:

- Addiction to online auctions
- Addiction to games of chance (e.g., online gambling)
- Footage or video consumption addiction (e.g., YouTube, Netflix, Hulu, etc.)
- Shopping addiction (e.g., buying things from eBay and Amazon)
- Social media addiction
- Gaming addiction

Many of these digital or tech addictions affect certain critical parts of our brain, specifically the brain's pleasure center. Some of these technological addictions have intense physical effects, while others have emotional and psychological effects.

Note, however, that our dependencies on these different digital technologies do not cause us any direct harm. However, as our dependence on them increases, their impact on us can be quite overpowering.

Why Is Digital Technology so Addicting?

Why is digital technology overpowering? It is very addictive.

Just like any other kind of addiction, digital addiction also appeals greatly to the pleasure center of the human brain. Since it is a type of behavioral addiction, it produces a short-term reward, and it entices us to repeat the same behavior.

Every time you use (or overuse) technology, you get the equivalent of dopamine and/or a serotonin release, which behavioral experts say is the same high or pleasure you get from gambling, drugs, and other things that can induce an addiction.

Note that there is an interplay of several important elements that feed technology addiction and behavioral addiction in general.

Key Elements That Feed Digital Addiction

The following are the key elements that make digital technology so addictive. And more often than not, each of these elements tends to feed off one another

They are the following:

- **Distraction**

Boredom is a great need that can be filled in so many ways. The term that marketers use is to exploit something—it's not inherently a bad thing, though. What that means is to capitalize on a need to produce profits. For instance, when a band produces a new album, the producers find ways to "exploit" the new product (i.e., find ways to make a profit from it).

They would then use the material for airplay in traditional and digital radio, album sales, individual song sales, the use of the music for commercials and movies, royalties on the lyrics or the music (they're two separate things).

The same is true with boredom—you fill a need or void when you have nothing to do. People would do anything to avoid that feeling. People will do things that will entertain them, and surprisingly, people will still do things repeatedly, even if they are unpleasant.

Social media and smartphone use is a great example of this phenomenon . Some people use it as a method of distraction. Not everyone feels great after using social media. Many Facebook users say that they feel less happy after using the platform, but they still use it anyway.

Why do people still use Facebook (or any other social media) despite its negative effects? Again, people will do anything to get distracted regardless of the means. Experts say that we do it because we would do anything to get rid of boredom.

- **Variable Rewards**

Why are gambling games and games of chance so addictive? Why do people keep playing slot machines even though there is no strategy that you can apply to win whatsoever? The reason is that these games give you variable rewards, which increase the excitement that you get in anticipation of the reward.

The same thing is true of social media. When you post a photo, video, message, comment, event, etc., you don't know how many reactions you will get. The anticipation builds up, and the reward is finally delivered once you see how many likes, reactions, shares, and other vanity metrics you get out of that post.

The number of notifications that you get from social media also varies. Since the result is different every time, it piques your interest. You begin to think, *Okay, so how many people will like this one? Is it one of my coolest pictures? I wonder how many will react to this?*

Sometimes you have none, sometimes you have ten, and sometimes you have a hundred. One photo may have three likes, but next time you post, you may get 300+, and that will feed the anticipation and excitement that you feel. You feel satisfied when someone likes your latest video or photo update, right?

The feedback you get from social media is the reward, and that makes the behavior very enticing, which is why we keep repeating it.

The reward is variable, and it is very much like gambling. It is very alluring, and you risk very little financially speaking, but you invest a lot when it comes to psychology and your attention. In short, it is very hard to beat once you get started.

- **Vanity Metrics**

In the previous section, we mentioned the term vanity metrics. This refers to the number of likes, dislikes, and other reactions we get from our social media posts. In simple terms, digital technology feeds your vanity. Five hundred people like your outfit of the day (OOTD). Two hundred people shared your post that criticized how the government handled a particular situation.

You now have a thousand people following you—a real milestone. It's a big victory, right?

These so-called victories feed your vanity. Feeding our ego is fine; we all need that from time to time. But when it becomes persistent and gets out of control, that is when it leads to social media addiction or technology addiction.

On top of that, there are metrics (i.e., numeric and tangible measurement) that validate your vanity. Getting a lot of reactions in social media is comparable to dopamine hits.

Once you become satisfied with that experience, you tend to repeat the behavior just to re-experience the reward. In other words, you look for that dopamine hit again and again and again. This is called *dopamine-driven feedback*.

But it doesn't only happen on social media alone. You get the same effect in other digital technologies. You can even get the same pleasure hits when using other forms of digital media and digital technology—like unlocking your smartphone, for instance .

There are also vanity metrics of some sort when it comes to other types of digital media and content. We check out email inboxes, play games, ask Alexa some questions, and shop (or window shop) online out of habit just to get the same pleasurable reward no matter how big or small it may be.

- **Never-Ending Content**

Back in 2012, Netflix launched its auto-play feature. It was a binge-watching revolution, so to speak. It was the first time for any video on demand or video streaming service to provide non-stop entertainment. Needless to say, it was a big hit, and it reeled in a lot of profits.

Soon enough, other digital media content providers followed suit. YouTube adopted the same feature as well as Facebook. You can now scroll through hundreds upon hundreds of content, and it never stops.

This is one of the biggest reasons why you end up spending a minimum of 30 minutes to an hour on social media when all you ever wanted to do was to see that funny cat video your best friend posted two minutes ago. The strange thing about it all is that you get so hooked you never realize what you were doing in the first place.

Causes of Digital Addiction

There are different causes of digital or technology addiction . Sometimes, the causes vary from one person to the next. Sometimes, it would take a variety of causes for a person to become dependent on certain technologies.

Here are some of the most common causes of tech addiction:

1. Depression: Sometimes, one's dependence and eventual addiction to technology can be triggered by depression. The strange thing is that our experience with our use of technology also feeds our depression, and so a cycle is made. Some people get satisfaction from their internet use and somehow forget their problems for a while. Sometimes their experience in social media can feed their depression, but they still seek out social media anyway since it is also a form of release for them.

2. The Friend and Gang Effect: Some children use gaming and social media to gain friends, and that is sometimes okay. However, when kids use digital technology too much and use it in lieu of actual interactions with real-life friends, then that eventually turns into a habit. Some kids spend hours and hours playing role-playing games online just to get stronger game characters to attract more online friends whom they have never met in real life.

3. Social Anxiety and Shyness: Some people are different when they are online. It's as if they have taken on a different personality when they're interacting with other folks online. Some people who are naturally shy or those who have social anxiety issues may turn to the internet as a way to escape their fears. Some of the shyest people can express themselves better online—as if their online avatars serve as their cover or shield.

4. Expression of Other Addictions: Sometimes, one addiction can feed into another addiction. For example, if one person tended to be a shopaholic in the past, it is possible that they can switch to internet shopping and then move on to social media addiction as another expression of their previous dependencies.

The Impact of Digital Technology and How It Affects Us

Interestingly, a lot of people don't know just how much time they spend on their digital devices. If you check out the figures, you might get alarmed at how terrible the impact of this technology is.

Researchers estimate that people, on average, check out their smartphones or mobile devices every six minutes. You can't even wait any longer to check out what's going on via the internet. We adults also check our phones an average of 150 times a day .

Impact on Cognitive Ability

Using smartphones also tends to reduce human cognitive capacity . Ultimately, dependence on digital technology affects us just like a drug does, and it inhibits our ability to think for ourselves . Experts also believe that another underlying reason why digital media and technology are so addictive is that they feed human impulses and limit our intentions .

Impact on Children

Note that this is the impact on us adults. The situation is much worse when our children are involved. For example, according to one report , the marketing of Apple was so good that 40% of US children who are under the age of nine have their own iPad.

Children in that same age group also tend to spend more time on their mobile devices. There is an 860% increase in time spent from 2011 up to 2017. They spend more time on small screens than playing with kids their own age . This reduces their social skills, and playing violent videogames limits the ability to empathize with others . If you think you're overusing your phone, you better think again. Experts say that all children under 18 years old use their smartphones almost twice as much as adults . This overtime, if you want to call it as such, on smartphones and other digital devices has now affected how people deal with their relationships . The end result is that it has made a lot of people less happy . Instead of improving connections, it has driven us into loneliness, especially in the younger generation.

Chemical Alterations and Changes to Brain Structure

Internet addiction has been found to create structural changes to the brain and also cause chemical alterations . The structural changes affect a person's ability to connect with attention, cognitive control, emotional processing, and decision-making .

Studies show that parts of the brain that deal with a person's ability to pay attention (e.g., dorsolateral prefrontal cortex and orbitofrontal cortex) tend to have reduced amounts of grey matter in individuals who exhibit internet addiction.

Studies also show that the proper connection and processing between different hemispheres of the brain gets impaired when one is addicted to the internet .

Experts have also found that dopamine transporter levels in the brain also decrease in a technology-addicted brain . What does that mean? As your addiction to technology progresses, the less satisfaction you get from such behavior. That means you tend to seek more of and different forms of that behavior to get the pleasure (or dopamine rush) that you are expecting.

For example, consuming the same type of internet porn won't be as appealing over time. The internet porn addict will tend to look for other types of porn to get that desired satisfaction from that type of digital media.

In the same vein, the same games won't be as appealing as before. The same social media posts won't be as funny or as entertaining. You will tend to seek out more variants just to get the good feelings you used to get.

To learn more about the impact and influence of digital technology on our children and us, I would like to invite you to read Cal Newport's book entitled *Digital Minimalism: Choosing a Focused Life in a Noisy World*. It is a comprehensive work that reveals just how fraught our relationship is with today's technology.

As it was mentioned earlier, this book dwells more on actionable solutions and tips that you can do right now at home so you can reduce and eventually get rid of your dependence on digital technology.

In the next section of this book, we will go over the very strategies that you can implement for yourself at home and work.

Impact of Technology Addiction to Human Life

The following is a list of the effects of technology addiction to human life:

- Obesity
- Excessive weight loss
- Neck pain
- Poor personal hygiene
- Unhealthy nutrition
- Insomnia
- Carpal tunnel syndrome
- Headaches
- Back pain
- Boredom when performing other things besides the consumption of digital media
- Loneliness and fear
- Mood swings
- Disruption and deferment of responsibilities
- Avoiding work
- A lot of time lost
- Isolation from social circles
- Euphoria when using the internet
- Anxiety
- Guilt
- Depression

Key Takeaways

- Digital addiction affects all of us, especially our children
- It is addictive because it also taps into the pleasure centers of the brain
- Digital addiction affects us in so many ways, and it feeds our anxieties, depression, and other conditions

Section 2

Digital Minimalism in Everyday Practice

Chapter 3: How to Do a Digital Inventory and Declutter

One of the key things that you should do as you practice digital minimalism is an inventory and to declutter. Remember that digital minimalism is a process. It is not a one-time event. It's something that you will have to constantly work on.

Just like physical clutter, our digital life is also prone to entropy. Notice that when you leave things by themselves—your bookcase, your kitchen, and even your bedroom—things tend to pile up without you knowing it.

Sometimes, you forget to put a cup away before leaving for work. Maybe you forgot to put yesterday's laundry in the hamper, or you may have forgotten to organize the groceries the other day. Sometimes you even forget to prep your bed before you go to sleep and after getting up in the morning.

Don't worry. Take the time to forgive yourself for these slip-ups. They're natural, and it happens from time to time.

That is what minimalist living is for. Since you own only a few things, then the clutter won't be that much, not like how things were before. In the case of digital minimalism, things also get piled up every now and then.

That may include apps that used to be essentials for work that is now no longer required by your boss. It is also possible that you temporarily downloaded files in places where they are easy to find—like your home screen or desktop screen.

All of that is forgivable.

It's Not Just You

Don't worry; you can get over this. It's a phenomenon that is happening everywhere it seems. Here are some stats that might give you some insight:

- Since 2013, the total digital media usage in the world has increased by 40%.
- The average person today will spend at least (at least!) three hours with his face on his or her phone (or another mobile device) each day.
- For every five minutes that people spend each day, they will spend one minute of that on social media—no matter which platform.
- For every two minutes that people spend nowadays, one minute will be used for online entertainment. This includes watching videos on YouTube or other video streaming services, music, games, and other forms of online entertainment.
- The total smartphone usage in the last three years has doubled.

These trends will continue unless we do something about it.

Dealing with Digital Entropy

And because everything is subject to entropy—that phenomenon where everything just ends up going back to utter chaos—then you will have to do some decluttering and inventory every once in a while.

In this chapter, we will go over the steps on how you can do an inventory and declutter your digital life. You will have to perform this periodically on your computer, your phone, your inbox, your social media accounts, your digital files, internet usage, and others.

Let's start with the easiest place to do it.

How to Do a Computer Declutter

Your desktop computer, the one you use for work or at home, is a device that easily gets cluttered. If it's the family computer, then you should expect the clutter to accumulate rather quickly, since every family member has access to it.

Remember that the goal in a desktop declutter is to remove anything that hasn't been used from your computer in a while. This will free up some space on your hard drive and clear up the visuals on your desktop screen.

Besides, there is no reason to keep files that you no longer use anyway. It will also allow you to use your device with intention. Anything that is not adding value to your life and is just taking up space should be removed.

Here are the steps:

1. **Clean up your desktop screen**

This is usually the place where you can start. It is a common practice for people to download stuff and save the said downloads on the desktop. The rationale is that it is the first thing you see when you boot up your computer, thus reminding you that you downloaded your files there.

Your files are easier to find once you see them on your desktop's wallpaper. That is if it was free of clutter, right? I got started on this habit ever since I had to call Dell tech support.

I had to download a file or app to get my computer fixed, and the tech support guy told me to save the file on my desktop. And so I did.

It was relatively easy to find at first because I only had less than ten icons on my screen back then. Eventually, it became a habit, and I also forgot to delete or move pretty much everything that I downloaded.

The day I started decluttering my files, I still found that very file on my desktop after more than two years had passed. It was just sitting there, and I never really had much use for it ever since, so it didn't make sense to keep it.

Go through all the icons on your desktop—I mean everything. If it is something that you haven't used in the last six months, then delete it. If it is a picture that has some value to you, then upload it to social media or your Google drive (or some other cloud storage). Keep it there, not on your desktop.

You can choose to reduce the number of files on your desktop to only the system icons like the Recycle Bin, Network, and control panel icons. If you have apps, folders, and programs that you use frequently, then just pin them to the taskbar or dock. And then you can auto-hide the dock/taskbar so that it is out of your way.

2. Change your wallpaper

Since you're already in the process of decluttering and changing things on your active desktop, you also need to change your wallpaper.

Yes, it might sound like something trivial, but your wallpaper is something that can either have a positive or negative impact on you. If you choose a picture that inspires you to do better at work, then that should be the photo that you use for your wallpaper.

Now, your desktop wallpaper won't make or break your day—that's for sure. But it can be a source of inspiration, which is why you should make a conscious choice about the images that you will use.

If you spend a good chunk of your day in front of your computer, then using a new picture for your wallpaper every now and then can be a source of motivation to start your day.

To maximize the benefits that you can get out of your wallpaper, here are a few wallpaper ideas that you might find useful:

- **Wallpaper pictures that organize and turn your desktop into a to-do list**: Find a wallpaper picture (or make one of your own) that divides your desktop screen into different sections.
  One section would be for icons (i.e., notes, tasks, video, etc.) that you need to get done for that day. Another section would be for reminders and other stuff that you need to read. Another section can be for things that you need to do the following workday.
  Choose a desktop picture that allows you to logically and efficiently organize the desktop icons you see on your screen. Remember that you will eventually add more icons on your desktop from time to time. You might as well have a way to organize every new download into a category or section on your screen.
  You should also have a section for icons that you can delete immediately. If you don't need a particular download or file, then put it in that section so you can delete it any time during the day.
  Here are some more ideas: you can choose workflow wallpapers, wallpapers that help you prioritize certain tasks, wallpaper organizers that will also come in handy, and to-do list wallpapers might also be your thing.

- **Calendar wallpapers:** If you're the type of person who lives and dies by your calendar, then use your wallpaper as a calendar. You can download editable calendar wallpapers. These are the ones that you can customize, like whether it should start with Monday or Sunday, highlight certain days and holidays, and a custom photo that you can choose as the background to the calendar that you will see on your screen.

I suggest using a super cleaned-up desktop when you opt for a calendar type wallpaper. That means removing as many icons as you can on your desktop or just choose the option to hide all the icons so that all you will see on your desktop screen is your calendar.

- **Inspirational quote wallpapers:** Having a quote-worthy statement on your desktop screen is like having your coach give you a much needed motivational speech. Sometimes, that quote on your screen can motivate you and make you more than willing to face the day.
  Sometimes, they can even compel you to action. Sometimes they serve as a kind of pick-me-up in the middle of the week, especially when you feel like nothing is going your way.

- **Wallpapers that calm you:** What scene brings a sense of calm to your soul? Is it a beautiful sunset at the beach, a panoramic view of the mountains, or a photo of a local garden with lots of pretty flowers?
  Any day can become an agitation—something may come up to bring you down or maybe just make you angry. To help you get over any emotional highs and lows during the day, a calming and relaxing wallpaper might just do the trick. Use colored wallpapers and choose colors that brighten up your mood. Use a desktop background that features your favorite colors.
  Applying some color theory, remember that blue color gradients can be quite relaxing. If you're looking for happy, warm fuzzy feelings, then background images that have green and yellow will do well. If you're interested in colors that can give you an energy boost in the middle of the day, then get images that feature red and violet colors as a central theme.
- **Brain-stimulating abstract images:** If you need something that will mesmerize your mind, especially when the day is getting dull, then use a desktop wallpaper that has abstract patterns. Look for ones that have fractal art, psychedelic prints, or even kaleidoscope-like patterns. They don't really represent anything, but they can have a pleasing and stimulating effect on your brain.
- **Nature scenes:** Nature visuals can have a motivating and inspirational effect on the human mind. Use a picture of your next planned weekend getaway for your wallpaper.
  Your wallpaper picture can also be something seasonal—summer at the beach, rivers at springtime, beautiful falling leaves, or even snowcapped mountains. Choose nature scenes that make you feel good instantly.
- **The minimalist wallpaper:** You should have known that this was coming—yes, there are minimalist-themed wallpapers that you can download for free. They're very simple, and the aesthetics can help to drive the goal of digital minimalism home. Some minimalist wallpapers have a single image tucked away in the corner of the screen.
  Sometimes, it's just a single word or maybe a motivational phrase right smack in the middle of the screen. These wallpapers help to keep the minimalist vibe going on. Plus, they help you spot the clutter you make on your wallpaper rather easily.

Choose the wallpaper that works for you. You can even change things up from time to time as needed. The important thing is that you keep your desktop clean. If you can maintain that for a few weeks, then you're off to a good start on your journey to digital minimalism.

3. Uninstall apps and programs

Just like files, photos, videos, and other stuff you download, apps and programs also tend to clutter things up on your computer. You may already have some programs that you haven't used in a while. Sometimes, your computer comes pre-installed with bloatware—apps that you don't need that come preinstalled with your computer when you bought it.

Go through your list of programs. On Windows operating systems, you need to go to your computer's Control Panel to add and remove programs. Be careful, though; you may uninstall something necessary for your computer system to function properly.

If you're not really that techie, then here's a simpler and safer way to do it. Click on your Start screen and then go through the list of apps and programs that you see there. Uninstall the ones that you don't need or use.

Remember to keep your malware cleaner, antivirus software, and productivity tools. You may have some games installed there, so just uninstall them, especially if you're not playing games on that computer. Most people play games on their phones anyway.

4. Use full-screen mode

Almost every app will allow you to work in full-screen mode. Don't split your screen using smaller windows. If you need to see multiple windows, then I suggest that you use multiple screens.

Connect another monitor to your computer so you can work in a multi-screen fashion. That way, you can have one document or file open on one screen and the other things you need for work on another screen. Working on the full screen allows you to focus and concentrate—and thus keep distractions away.

How to Declutter Your Files

After cleaning up your desktop and wallpaper, you're ready to move on to the next step: cleaning up your files. This will be a bit more difficult since you will have more items to sort out.

Here's an observation from someone who has been around computers for decades: as hard drives get bigger, the easier it is for people to accumulate junk. Back in the day, we worked with kilobyte-sized drives—you know those old floppy drives?

And then hard drives got installed on computers. They weren't much—just a few megabytes worth. And then the most you could get was around 80 gigabytes—and we were already celebrating back then.

And then the drives got bigger—around 500 megabytes (and we were still celebrating—yay!). Until today, we had terabytes worth of hard drive space. With smaller hard drives, people were more mindful of what they stored and saved on their computers.

You had very little space, so you needed to conserve what you had. And with the imminent increase in hard drive space, people no longer had to worry about storage space. Except now, you have a lot of clutter and digital junk. These unnecessary files slow down your computer system, and they bog down your productivity.

Let's go over the things that you can do to reduce the amount of digital junk on your hard drives.

1. Learn to delete the unnecessary

Remember that you can do all of these declutter steps at any time. You will also be doing them regularly, so it would be best to get started now. If you have a computer or laptop, then you can start with that. Take note of how much space you have recovered and how good your wallpaper looks.

You can then move on to your emails, your phone, and other devices. It will be a painful process for some, especially for those who have been hanging on to certain files for quite a while. However, do take note that it will be worth it in the long run.

2. Upload files to cloud storage

There will be files on your hard drive that will have a bit of sentimental value. This could be photos of your kids while they were still infants, pictures of loved ones, documents, and files that were shared to you that have some personal significance.

So, why use cloud storage?

Cloud storage allows you to store your files in a remote location that is accessible through the internet. That means you can access your files using any device that has an internet connection.

You don't have to rely on a single physical hard drive, external storage, phone, or computer to store your videos, pictures, and other files. Cloud storage improves your productivity and efficiency.

Using this type of service also saves you from the hassle of maintaining your storage device. Remember that even external backup drives also have a usable life—around five years or so.

After five years, you will need to transfer your files from one backup drive to another. But what if you forget when you should do that, and then your backup expires? One day it fails, and you can no longer access your files.

With the help of cloud storage, the service providers will maintain your data and have backups of backups, so in case one of their drives goes down the drain, they still have backups that you can use to retrieve your files.

Of course, not all cloud storage options are the same. Some are better suited for certain people's needs. Here are my recommendations according to specific needs that you may have.

- **Dropbox**: I think this is the best cloud storage option for light data users. It's great for personal use, small teams (for the free option), but they also have service plans for large businesses too. Storage options start at 2 GB, which is pretty small, but you can upgrade it. Storage plans start at $8.25, which makes it one of the most affordable options.

- **Google Drive**: This is the most affordable cloud-storage option today. It is free for the first 15 GB that you upload. However, you can choose from larger storage space plans starting at 100 GB up to unlimited data storage. Note that the 200 GB storage space plan is only $2.99 a month, which is pretty affordable. Google Drive is best suited for collaborating with your team at work or for families who want to share files with one another.

- **Microsoft OneDrive**: If you're a Microsoft Windows user, then this might be the most compatible cloud storage option for your device. They provide free storage for the first 5 GB of files you want to upload. The paid storage plan starts at 50 GB for $1.99, which makes it one of the more affordable options on this list. Note that OneDrive also works great for iOS and Android devices.

- **pCloud**: If you're looking to store really large files, then this might be the cloud storage service for you. They provide free storage for the first 10 GB of data that you upload. You pay $3.99 per month for 500 GB of storage. They also have lifetime plans where you only pay a one-time fee—no recurring monthly charges.

- **iCloud**: This may be the best storage option for iOS users—it's already integrated into your iPhone or iPad or other Apple device. It's a great option for private users—you know, if you don't want to share your files with anyone. The first 5 GB of storage is free, and the paid storage plans start at 99 cents per month for the first 50 GB you use. You can also opt for the maximum 2 TB of storage for $9.99 a month.

What you should do at this point is to decide which cloud storage solution is best for you, depending on the particular needs you may have. Before signing up for any cloud storage service, you should check out what their basic plans will give you, the allowed upload limit, and any terms and conditions as well.

3. **Make your folders and files easier to search**

Tell me, which of these two folder names will be easier to understand and remember:

- CB1HQ6HALH
- Work Files 2020

You will have to admit that option number one above would make a really good password, right? It's pretty random, and it will be very difficult to guess. On the other hand, option number two will be easier to decipher. The name is rather easy to recall, and it already hints at the contents of the folder.

The next step is to scan all your folders and files and rename the ones that don't make any sense, like the first option in the example above. Make the names as descriptive as you can, and make them easier to remember.

4. Reduce the number of folders

You don't need to clutter your drive with very specific folders. The search capabilities of today's operating systems have been made more efficient, thus making files easier to find. You don't have to create different folders that contain very few things.

For instance, you can group all pictures into Photos 2020 or Photos 2019 (arranging things by year). Don't worry about what time of the year each photo was taken since each photograph that you take with your device will have a timestamp and you can arrange your pictures in chronological order, which makes them easier to find.

In my case, I organize things by year, but you don't have to do that too. How you simplify your file organization is up to you. The point here is that you don't need a thousand folders on your computer. You can just use Work, Fun Stuff, and Personal Stuff to help you identify where each file should go.

5. Shut down and give your device a clean start

Tell me if this is one of your habits—you're done using your computer, and you just close it and go to sleep? Do you leave your computer in sleep mode? When was the last time you turned off your phone or took it off the internet?

Here's a new habit that you might want to start:
  a. Close all the tabs, apps, and programs that you have running at the end of the day or before going to bed at night.
  b. Move all the files that are in your Downloads folder to their designated folders. If there are files there that don't belong anywhere and won't be used anyway, then just delete them.
  c. Make sure to empty the Trash/Recycle bin.
  d. Finally, shut down/turn off your computer/phone

This way, you're giving yourself a fresh start each time you restart your device. If you're using your phone as an alarm clock, then just do a power cycle.

6. Don't buy your digital media—rent it as much as possible

Here's a little confession that I would like to make—I still have movies and videos that I have downloaded since the late '90s. I even have the movie *12 Monkeys* (starring Bruce Willis).

But I now have them all in a USB backup drive. I have more than a decade's worth of videos and movies stored in backup drives. Some of the ones I downloaded were movie bombs but hey, I remember the people I enjoyed watching them with back then, so it's not always about the film.

Going back to the present moment, notice that your computer or mobile device will usually have a lot of digital media in the form of eBooks, videos, documents, pdf files, and whatnot.

Here's something that I did—I stopped buying and downloading them. Unless you're downloading it for your collection, then just rent it. Let's say you fancy a new eBook on Amazon; don't buy it if you're unsure if it's a keeper—rent it.

If it doesn't pan out, then at least you're not filling up your Kindle library with books you have never even read or ones that you have only casually read (around five or so pages). The same is true with video. Don't download videos unless you intend to watch them sometime soon.

If you're just curious about whether it's a great movie or video, then just rent it instead so it won't clutter up your device. Use the same rule for your music and other digital media. Stream it as much as possible; rent it if that option is available.

Decluttering Your Phone

At this point, you have already started decluttering your computer, your phone, Kindle, and other devices. You should have completely decluttered your laptop or computer by now.

Now, we will be moving on to something a bit more difficult—your phone. Our phones right now play a big part in our lives. Ten to 20 years ago, no one needed a smartphone, much less an iPhone. Maybe 20 or so years ago, especially when Lawrence Fishbourne and Keanu Reeves played their big roles in *The Matrix* movies, cell phones had their limelight.

Nokia was the big brand back then, and flip phones were some of the most high-tech gadgets we had. So, even before smartphones and iPhones took to the shelves, people already manifested some kind of dependence on mobile devices—they're just not as high tech as we have them today.

Fast forward into the future; we're pretty much in the same situation. We still love our mobile devices, but we only have more high-tech ones with hundreds of other features than before.

Here are the steps on how you can declutter your phone:

1. **Delete apps that you never use**

If you've had your phone for a while, then it is likely that you have apps and games on your mobile device that you no longer use. That can include games that you used to play, that alarm clock app (in my case, I have this fart sound app that I use to prank my friends—it's some kind of a whoopee cushion), and other apps.

2. **Use the web/mobile version for apps you don't use frequently**

Let's say you don't use Facebook that much. Maybe you use it just to check on your friends or maybe just pitch ideas in a group that you participate in. You don't need to install the Facebook app since you can still access Facebook using your phone's browser.

That will be one less icon on your phone's screen and one less app on your phone's storage. Go over all the apps on your phone and delete the ones that you rarely use and just settle for the mobile version through your browser.

3. Dock 'em and group 'em

Choose three or four of your most-used apps. It can be your camera, YouTube, text messaging, or maybe your dialer app. After selecting your most-used apps, you should place them in your dock at the bottom of your phone's screen.

So, what about the other apps? The other remaining apps on your phone should be grouped together and placed inside a folder. Put all your social media in one folder, your work and productivity apps in another, your games and entertainment apps in another, etc.

4. Reduce the number of social media apps

Trust me. You don't need to have some kind of presence on all social media platforms. You will still live a happy life, even if you only have a few social media apps on your device. We'll go over how to stop the dependence on social media in a later chapter of this book.

5. Clean up your list of contacts

Next, go over your contact list. Go through each of the numbers listed there, and delete the ones that you don't ever call or send messages to. Any phone number that you don't intend to call again should also be removed as well.

If you have music, videos, or even podcasts you can still find in your folders and you don't use them or need them at all, then you should delete them too.

6. Turn off or remove any notifications

Chances are your apps will have notifications. Turn them off or remove them. Delete any alarms you have set up.

7. Set up a do not disturb time

Setting up a do not disturb time, say 8 pm to 6 am, will allow you to rest for the night. That means no phone calls, messages, notifications, etc. Putting that on your schedule will allow you to focus on yourself.

Declutter Your Internet Usage

Now, here's another big step that you can take—practicing digital minimalism with regards to your internet usage. When it comes to the internet, you never know how deep the rabbit hole can be. You might end up chasing the latest trends to no end. In a later chapter of this book, we will go over how to do an information diet and a social media sabbatical.

For now, here are a few tips that you can use to reduce the clutter that you experience through your internet usage.

1. Reduce the number of tabs on your browser

Back in the day, internet browsers only had one tab. If you wanted to see more than one web page, then you had to open a new window. It was only a few years later when browsers (starting with Firefox) provided the ability to open new tabs.

It was fun at first since you can open multiple tabs and such. But then as you go along with your work, you end up with a hundred tabs on your screen. Since opening new tabs has become so easy, you don't think about it and just open more tabs even if you don't really need them anyway.

Here's what you can do—limit your use to around five tabs only. The important thing here is that you choose and know what each tab contains. Don't just open tabs because you think you will read through the page later, or maybe it may have some useful info later. If it is a pop-up or pop-under tab, then just close it; you don't need to see or read what's on that tab.

2. Monitor the number of hours you spend online

Google Chrome has an extension that you can download, called Time Tracker. You can download it from the Chrome Web Store. It helps you identify which websites you visit, and monitor how much time you spend on various websites.

This is your first step in determining where you go online and identifying your time wasters. Figure out which sites you spend a lot of time on. After that, determine which of those sites are useful and which ones give value to your life.

Let's say you find out that you spend two hours on Facebook each day, and you're old school—you're still using your browser to check out your friends' posts. Let's say that you want to stop using Chrome for Facebook.

You can block Facebook in Chrome using an extension called Block Site. It is a website blocker for Google Chrome. There are other website blockers that you can use, and there are website blockers for different browsers.

There's LeechBlock for Firefox, StayFocusd for Chrome, Cold Turkey for Windows OS users, and if you're a Mac user, you can try SelfControl to block websites.

3. Unfriend and Unfollow

Consider your newsfeed as something sacred. It's not that it is something divine or worthy of worship, but it is something that you spend precious time on. If your newsfeed is full of things that distract you, then it's time to reduce and declutter.

The rule here is that if someone, something, a group, or whatever it is on social media is no longer informative, entertaining, or interesting, and it is still showing up on your newsfeed, then it's time to unfriend and unfollow.

Anything or anyone that doesn't add value to your life right now should be taken off your list.

4. Choose only one or two social media channels

I would recommend sticking to only one social media channel unless you need another channel—maybe Facebook for work since your boss wants you to do social media marketing there.

Keep only the social media channels that you like. You have the option to delete your account on certain social media sites, or if you want, you can just deactivate your account. At least you still have the option to come back to it in case you may have to—let's say a client wants you to do some marketing on Instagram as well.

5. Clean up your bookmarks

Finally, you should pay attention to your bookmarks bar. We sometimes tend to bookmark webpages or websites at will without thinking about it. I used to have more than 15 folders in my bookmarks bar, not to mention hundreds of bookmarked pages there.

It's crazy—I have everything from movies I would like to download on Amazon to Facebook posts of my friends that I wanted to comment on later (which never happens, of course).

What happens is that we bookmark pages, and we forget about them. We hope that maybe as we go through our bookmarks, we will remember what we intended to do with them. Unfortunately, when the day finally comes when you need to search your bookmarks, it will be very difficult to find the bookmarked page you wanted.

When you have a clean set of bookmarks, you will be forced to be mindful of the web pages that you will visit. For instance, if you want to open Wikipedia, you need to type the entire URL. That way, you will be mindful of which web pages you visit.

Decluttering Your Inbox

Studies show that average adults check their emails around 45 times each day. If you work with emails or use emails a lot in your job, then you tend to check your inbox more often than that.

Your emails aren't particularly life-changing. You will get some really important ones, but they won't be that frequent. However, you should take control of what gets into your inbox since going over hundreds of emails is a waste of your time.

Here are some very important tips that will be useful for you to clean up your inbox.

Opt Out of Mailing Lists

In my personal experience, I signed up for a lot of mailing lists from online courses to discount offers from different online retailers. At one time, my inbox had more than 5,000 emails—not kidding.

I spent a lot of time opting out of mailing lists, and then I spent even more time deleting emails. I had to be systematic about it. For instance, I once signed up for an email course about stock market trading. It was fun for a while, but then they sent me a lot of promotional content, from eBooks to videos. To clean up after I opted out of the service, I searched for all their emails and deleted them about a hundred at a time. Even by doing that, it took me a lot of time before I could clear out my inbox.

Turn Off Notifications

Some apps and services will send you notifications and reminders. Do you really need any of that? Turn off all notifications and then delete all email reminders of this type.

Set Up a Priority Inbox

If you're using Gmail, then you're missing out if you haven't used a priority inbox. No, you're not going to lose emails when you set it up. In fact, you will increase your productivity when you use it.

The priority inbox separates all the emails that you receive into separate categories. You have the important emails, starred, unread, and then finally everything else. I used to receive like 90 emails at the start of my day in the office.

That is like a ton of emails to sort through. After I turned the priority inbox on, I was able to spot the ten most important emails that needed my direct attention. I got more done for the day when I did that. When you turn this feature on, Gmail will sort your emails according to the sender and subject line.

To turn on your priority inbox, open your Gmail. And then, go to Menu (the hamburger icon), then Settings, your Account, Inbox Type, and then select Priority Inbox.

Allot Specific Times for Reading Emails

Treat your emails as part of your to-do list. Never prioritize going over your emails. In order for you to do that, you can set specific times when you should check your emails. As a rule of thumb, you don't want to check your inbox every hour.

You should limit the number of times you check it either once or twice a day. Some have experienced significant improvements in their productivity by simply checking their inbox at the start of the day and before leaving for home.

In the morning, they would choose one to five emails that they should respond to. The response should be quick. If an inter-office email was sent and it will take you five to ten minutes to write your response, then it would be better to walk over to your coworker's desk and talk about it.

I only view my inbox at 10 am. It isn't the first thing I do when I walk into my office. I usually have a to-do list prepared before the day ends, and that will be the first thing I would review as soon as I get to work.

I will then choose two to three tasks that would be my priority. And then I schedule them for that day. After I have allotted my time for each task, then I check my emails.

I only spend five to ten minutes and only read the most important ones. That's usually just one or two emails. If the tasks and topics under discussion in those emails can be squeezed in my schedule for that day, then I put it on my to-do list (i.e., I take a minute to compose a brief and concise response to those emails).

If there is something important, but it can't fit into my schedule for that day, then I put it on my to-do list for tomorrow. After that, I don't touch my inbox again for that day. I end up getting more things done for each day doing it that way.

Tip: Boomerang

If you're using Firefox or Google Chrome, then you might want to try the free plugin for these browsers called Boomerang. It's a useful tool that I found that helped me a lot when it comes to managing my emails.

Boomerang allows you to schedule an email that you can send a few days later, return an email into your inbox in case the person you emailed didn't reply after a few days, and set up other reminders to help you manage your email activities a lot better.

Another Tip: Use a Pomodoro Timer

We'll talk about the benefits of using a Pomodoro Timer later on. For now, just remember that you can use this timer (i.e., the tomato timer) to set a time limit for your email tasks.

This timer usually gives you 25 minutes to get everything done. After one Pomodoro is completed, you should be done with all your emails. If you're not done with one, or you still haven't gone over the rest of your emails, you should put them off for later in the afternoon.

Unsubscribe from the Majority of Email Lists

The emails from lists that you subscribed to are going to clog your inbox. You don't want to just delete them when you see them in your inbox because they will just keep coming every week.

What you should do is open one of them, scroll down, and check out the links. Find the one that unsubscribes you from that mailing list, and then follow the prompts to finally get you unsubscribed.

Do this for every email that you don't want to receive. Your mom's email doesn't count—okay? The more mailing lists that you signed up for, the longer it will take to get unlisted, but it will be worth the effort.

If you're not into the long and fun road of deleting and unsubscribing from email lists, there are apps that you can use to unsubscribe automatically. You just have to toggle the preferences and identify which emails you want to remove and retain.

Examples of these apps and tools are the following:
- Swizzle app for iOS
- Unroll.me
- Unlistr
- Unsubscriber

Remember to KISS

This is a fairly common acronym: KISS, and it stands for *keep it short and simple*. This also applies to emails that you send out. Remember to succinct when you write replies to emails.

What this means is that if you can say it in one or two sentences, then there is no point in trying to convey the same message in ten sentences. Keep your responses short. If they're asking about what time the meeting should be, you should state exactly what time. There is no need to beat around the bush.

Another thing to remember is that there is no need to ask questions of your own. If you do, you may end up replying back and forth in an email exchange, which basically wastes time. If you need to exchange emails, then call the other party instead. It makes the discussion faster and more efficient.

Don't Use Your Email as a Reminder

Some people use their emails as some sort of reminder—they send emails to themselves or ask their coworkers to send them emails to remind them of scheduled meetings and other events.

If you need reminders, then use your calendar. Use Google Calendar or other calendar software to set up reminders and other important items on your daily agenda.

If you're tired of sacrificing your productivity, wasting your time, or putting up with outrageous subject lines, the tips and tools mentioned here will be a big help. Your inbox should be treated as something sacred. It should only contain messages that are important and valuable to you.

Remember that you need to declutter your digital life from time to time. But if you follow the best practices mentioned here, everything will be made a lot easier.

Key Takeaways

- You will be doing a lot of digital inventories and decluttering
- Digital clutter tends to come up from time to time
- You need to declutter various aspects of your digital life and monitor your progress

Chapter 4: The Why and How of a Digital Detox

Detoxification is the process of removing toxic substances from the body. In cases of substance abuse, a person will have to go on a period of not taking the said substance (like alcohol, drugs, cigarettes, etc.). This period of abstention will allow the body to process the substances and clear the toxic influence.

That's basically the medical idea behind a detox. But what about a digital detox? It follows the same fundamental idea. When you do a digital detox, you will abstain from using any form of digital technology.

Does it sound scary? You're not going to use or even touch your phone for prolonged periods of time? Yes, it will be your phone, tablet, computer, TV, social media, the internet, and other forms of digital technology.

When you go through a detox of your digital life, you move your focus away from digital technology temporarily. You can then focus on real-world life from day to day. You will go through face-to-face and in-person social interactions, and you can do it without any distractions. Think of it as a kind of sabbatical but shorter—like a digital timeout from all the tech-heavy things that you do.

It can be scary for some, yes. Now, before you decide whether it is something that you can do or not, please consider the benefits that you might gain from it. But before that, you should first ask what telltale signs indicate that you need a digital detox.

Signs That You Need a Digital Detox

Here is a summary of the different signs that you need to do a digital detox. We have mentioned some of them earlier in this book.

- You can't concentrate on one task for a long time. You feel the need to check your phone even for just a minute or two.
- You have this habit of staying up late just so you can play a game on your phone. Sometimes, you wake up early just to play.
- You can't go to sleep without playing on your phone before bedtime.
- You feel like you will be missing out on something if you don't check social media.
- You always check how many likes, shares, comments, and reactions there are on your posts.
- Sometimes after checking out your social media posts, you tend to feel angry, frustrated, depressed, or have some other negative effect on your feelings.
- The reverse may also be true—after you check your social media posts, you feel like you're complete and that you're ready to take on whatever task you have in line for that day.
- Not having your phone with you for a few minutes or hours makes you feel stressed or anxious. It feels like your phone (or some other device) is an important part of your person.

The FOMO Effect

FOMO is short for *fear of missing out*. It is a fear that people feel as if they are missing out on the best part or events of the day. They feel like they're not part of the collective whole of their friends, family, and colleagues if they don't take part in the latest trend, post, or share on social media.

It is as if they need to be part of the next big trending topic, or else they don't belong to the "in-crowd." What actually happens is that they are compelled to get constant connectivity.

If they are not connected, then they experience this fear. In fact, this fear is fed by that habit of being always connected to others through digital media. Without this constant connectivity (e.g., chat, posts, voice/video calls, etc.), they feel like their lives are less exciting.

There are times when you might feel overcommitting to social events, whether they are face-to-face meet-ups or digital meet-ups via Zoom, group chat, or whatnot. The overarching fear behind it all is that feeling of being left out.

No one wants to get left out, right? And that is why some people are compelled to stay connected online through digital media.

FOMO makes people check their phones, computers, or other digital devices constantly. They don't want to miss out, and so they keep texting, direct messaging, and posting online.

A digital detox empowers you to set limits on the effects of FOMO. It doesn't mean that you are cutting yourself off completely from your digital world. What you're actually doing is giving yourself the reins as it were. You regain control over the choice when you check social media, and it's not your fear that will compel how often you need to do so.

Social Comparison in the Digital Age

Peer pressure is real in the digital age. Do you think peer pressure is only a high school thing? As it turns out, it has moved on to a wider plane of existence—the digital world. Sounds like *Dungeons and Dragons*, right? Think of it as a kind of metaphor.

Anyway, going back to the issue at hand—anyone who has spent time on social media has at least dwelled on comparing oneself to the quality of life your friends and family are showing on social media. You even compare yourself and how your life has been to strangers such as celebrities, some famous YouTuber, or some guy who is a friend of your friend whom you don't really know that is your age and maybe in the same line of work as you are.

Have you ever felt that these other guys are leading better and much more fulfilling lives than the one that you have right now? Just look at their latest picture carousel on Instagram. Look at the great vacations they have had—look at the places they've been. Look at their house, their pets, their car. They're doing better than you.

Now, before you follow that train of thought, remember this saying:

> *"Comparison is the biggest thief of your innermost joy in life."*

Doing a digital detox is a great way to take your mind off the comparison game, and focus on the life that you are currently blessed with and fortunate to have. It allows you to focus on what is important in your life without the need to compare yourself to others. In short, it allows you to be content about what you have right now and aspire for something better.

Impact on Work/Life Balance

Constant connectivity can have a strong impact on an individual's work-life balance. The level and amount of technology use play an important role in achieving that balance. Spending too much time with technology can make you feel overworked, feel job stress, and lose overall job satisfaction. This is according to a study published in the *Applied Research in Quality of Life Journal* .

Constant connectivity blurs out the boundaries between home life and work. You see, digital technology has made it very easy to check your emails, work files, text messages, and social media. A digital detox will allow you to create the necessary boundaries between work and your personal life. It can help reduce stress and allow you to focus on your family and personal life.

Mental Health Concerns

The daily heavy use of technology has been found to put people (especially young kids and adolescents) at risk for mental health issues, according to a study that was published in *Child Development Journal*.

The study suggests that the more time you spend on digital technologies, the greater is your risk for conduct disorder and ADHD symptoms. In another study , it is suggested that too much social media increases symptoms of loneliness and depression.

The same study also suggests that by reducing social media use, people can reduce these symptoms. Doing a digital detox is a great way to reduce these symptoms.

Sleep Disruption

Do you often sleep with your phone right next to you or in bed? According to one study , using your phone prior to bedtime interferes with the quantity and quality of sleep. The same study suggests that it has a significant effect on children. It is further suggested that the heavy use of technology before sleeping is, in some way, connected to a higher body mass index.

Another study says that using phones and other digital technology in bed greatly affects a person's mood. It also increases the likelihood of insomnia, anxiety, and shorter sleeping times.

Digital Technology Use and Stress

In the studies that we have cited so far, we can already see a pattern—the use of technology before bedtime and the overuse of the said technology can increase our stress levels. According to a survey published by the American Psychological Association, 18% of adults in the US indicated that one of the sources of significant stress in their lives is technology use. This includes constantly checking emails, text messaging, and social media use. The same findings were reaffirmed by a study conducted by researchers from Sweden involving young adults.

The iPhone Effect

The overuse of smartphones reduces your ability to empathize with others. Experts dub this as the "iPhone Effect." According to one study, the mere presence of an iPhone or a smartphone can reduce the quality of your conversation with other people.

This happens even if you're not even using your phone while having a conversation with another person. The mere fact of holding the phone in your hand can induce such a response.

The solution is rather simple: leave your phone behind. Leave it in your bag and go to the water cooler and talk to a coworker. It will improve the quality of your interactions and help to return your ability to show empathy to other people.

Digital Detox: How to Do It

When it comes to how to do a digital detox, you will get a lot of different opinions and suggestions. Some will tell you that you need to abstain totally from any and all forms of digital media.

That would mean no cellphones ever, no emails, no social media, no internet, no TV, etc. It would be like living as if you were stranded all alone on a deserted island with no electricity whatsoever.

Of course, living like that will be almost impossible these days. You can't always stay in touch by physically visiting loved ones. Don't get me wrong, digital technology is useful, and it helps us to keep in touch with the people we care about and work with.

That is why I propose that digital minimalism should be one that focuses on purposeful use of technology, but not total abstinence. It should be a conscious mindful and willful use of digital media. There should be self-control applied to how we use them.

By detaching from digital devices, it will benefit our mental and emotional well-being. However, that doesn't mean when you do a digital detox, you will completely separate yourself from technology.

Just think about it, what if something wrong happens and you need to call 911? How do you do that if you cut off your home phone and throw away your smartphone? I believe that a digital detox should be more about setting boundaries and making use of digital devices and media in a way that benefits us.

Step 1: Be Realistic About What You Want to Do

If you can totally abstain from digital media and technology, then that would be great. If you can do it for just one day, then you will already get some kind of benefit from such a detox.

However, if you can't do it that long, then it's fine. If you can only partially detach from digital technology, then that is great too. But for a lot of people, a total separation from digital technology is impossible. Some of us rely on it to communicate with others, thus making it a necessity.

But that doesn't mean you can't go on a digital detox. You can still do it even if you're just limiting your use of your phone and other devices. The key here is to disconnect and abstain at times when it works well for your schedule.

If you need to use digital technology in your day-to-day life—for instance, you need it in your day job—then it is okay to use technology during the day. But since you don't need it as much after office hours, you should start by limiting your tech use by not checking your emails, no more Facebook and other social media, and just limit your phone use to texts and phone calls.

Step 2: Set Up Limits to Digital Tech Use

You can use Spotify to play music while working and it is okay, even when you're doing a digital detox. As it was mentioned earlier, the important thing is to set limits to your digital use. I would recommend that you should limit your tech use to a bare minimum—only as necessary and nothing more.

One way to set limits to your use of digital media is by putting your devices on airplane mode. That way, your devices are disconnected from the internet and other wireless connections. You won't get distracted by online messages, texts, phone calls, app notifications, social media notifications, game announcements, and others.

You should also time your disconnects. As it was explained earlier, you should set what times you allow yourself to use digital media. If you do that, then you allow yourself to focus on other important matters like your personal space, health and fitness, family, hobbies, and other personal relationships.

Here are a few suggestions that you might want to try. Set limits to your digital technology use at the following times:

- Before you go to bed at night
- When you wake up in the morning
- When you're in a meeting
- When you're spending time with loved ones
- When you're catching up with friends
- When you're working on a project
- When you're spending time on your hobby
- When you're eating meals
- When you're dining with loved ones or other important people in your life

Step 3: Start Slow

You don't have to do it all in one day. Some people will find that quite difficult. You can start by reducing your social media usage by 30 minutes each day for a week. Research suggests that doing this will improve your quality of life by reducing depression symptoms and loneliness.

So, where do you find that 30 minutes of no social media time? You can start by not using your phone in bed before going to sleep. If using your phone at bedtime is a habit, you need to replace it with another habit. Instead of using your phone, read a book before going to bed.

Do all of that for about a week and try to make a habit out of it. If there were nights when you failed, then that is okay. Forgive yourself and try again the following night. You can also reschedule your 30-minute cellphone abstinence. If you missed it before bedtime, then you can do it during your morning routine—no smartphone use for 30 minutes in the morning—particularly during breakfast.

Step 4: Get Rid of Distractions

Now that you have reduced your smartphone use, you can start reducing your digital technology use a little bit more. You can continue by imposing no smartphone use during breakfast, lunch, and dinner.

You can take it up a notch by getting rid of distractions like push notifications, unnecessary alarms, and social media alerts. Turn them all off and keep only the really important ones.

Step 5: Set a Time for Social Media Use

Like I said earlier, digital technology has its uses—even social media. Social media is one way to connect and/or reconnect with friends and family—especially long lost ones. What you're trying to avoid when doing a digital detox is the overuse of social media.

Set certain times during the day when you can allow yourself to use social media. Let's say 30 minutes late in the morning and maybe 30 minutes at the end of the day when you get home. Think of it as your catch-up time with friends and family.

Step 6: Take It Up a Notch—Do a Digital Fast

Do steps 1 to 5 for several weeks. After you have gotten used to these new restrictions, you can step things up a notch by doing a complete digital fast for one whole day. You don't have to do it every day or every week. You can start by picking one day each month when you will do a digital fast—say the first day of each month—or maybe the first Sunday of each month—that way, you're not expecting any communication from work.

During your digital fast day, you're not going to touch or use any kind of digital technology. Think of it as your offline or unhooked day. It's just one day when you're totally disconnected from the internet and all kinds of digital media.

Step 7: Taking It Two Notches Up—Do a Digital Fast One Day Every Other Week

Now that you have tried to do a digital fast the previous month, it's time to move things up a little bit. This time, you're going to repeat step 6, but you're going to do it on the first and third Sunday of each month.

Step 8: Three Notches Up—Weekly Digital Fasts

This time you're going to do a digital fast one day each week. But there will be a little twist—you get to choose which day of each week you're going to do it. This will require a little more commitment.

Step 9: Fine-Tuning Things

By now, you have been doing a digital detox for quite a bit. You already know what it's like to disconnect and get more time for yourself. Now, it's time to fine-tune your efforts.

Notice that there are certain things that you do in your digital life that uses up a lot of time. Some people spend 11 hours each week on social media, which makes it a problematic habit.

It can be social media for some, but it may be *Fortnite* for others, and for others, it might be binge-watching TV shows on Netflix. It's different for everyone. To fine-tune your digital detox, determine how much time you spend on each of the digital media and technology.

Pick the one that you spend the most time on. Let's say it is *Fortnite*, and you spend four hours each night from 11 pm to 3 am playing it. Sometimes you do it on weekdays, but sometimes you do it on weekends.

What you can do is to reduce your *Fortnite* time. Let's say you make it a rule to stop playing *Fortnite* during business days (Monday to Friday). You will then restrict your use to the weekends since you don't need to report to work anyway.

Pick the app or device that you spend too much time on and reduce your usage.

Step 10: Reduce Social Media Time

People use social media all the time, even though we may be a bit shy to admit it. I'm not saying that you completely stop all forms of social media use. What I'm saying is that you should restrict your use of social media by reducing the number of social media platforms that you use to just one or two (Facebook and Twitter maybe). You can also reduce the amount of time you spend on social media using the strategies that we have discussed here.

More Digital Detox Tips

Here are some more that might be very helpful to you when you do a digital detox. Note that some people will find it easy to give up using their digital devices and tools, while others will find it a bit difficult. Sometimes, not using a smartphone even for just 24 hours can trigger anxiety in some people.

Each person is different, and sometimes people will need help and support to get it done. Try any of the following tips as you practice digital detoxes from time to time:

- Let your best friend, your spouse, other friends, and other family members know that you are doing a digital detox. This will remind them to not call, text, email, or send you online messages during your digital detox hours or days.
- Write down your progress in a journal. Someone once said that when effort is recorded, performance is increased. When your efforts are recorded and reported back to you, your success multiplies. One way to do just that is by recording your digital detox experiences in your journal and reading your journal at least once a week.
- Get out of the house—don't get stuck inside doing nothing. The idle mind is the devil's playground, as the adage goes. You will increase the level of temptation to use digital media when you're idle doing nothing, and you're all alone. Go out for a walk in the park, meet friends, have dinner with your special someone, go to the gym, take your dog out for a walk, go jogging, etc.
- Once you have opted to reduce the number of social media channels that you use, then you should make the ultimate step of deleting the apps you no longer use from your phone. For instance, you decided that you won't use Facebook anymore, then go ahead and delete the app from your phone. By doing that, you reduce the chances of getting tempted to sign in to your account.
- Try a new thing. For you to completely quit an old habit, you must replace it with a new one. For instance, you created a rule of not using your phone after 6 pm. That means your face shouldn't be buried in front of your computer screen after that time. You should find something else to do. Let's say you heard about a new sport like Brazilian Jiu-Jitsu, and it sounded interesting. What you should do is ***find a friend who will try BJJ with you*** and show up for class at 6 pm. <u>Doing it with another person and setting a time will help you form a new replacement habit a lot faster.</u>

Remember that you shouldn't rush your digital detox. Follow the tips mentioned here and take things slowly. If ever you find yourself succumbing to the temptation of using digital media for hours on end, then forgive yourself. After that, try again. Don't worry—it takes time for new habits to grow on you. The important thing is that you never give up.

Effects of Digital Detox on Your Brain

There was an experiment where entrepreneurs and neuroscientists were left in the Moroccan desert without any access to the internet. They underwent a short term digital detox, and the results were quite fascinating .

Researchers reported that study participants were better able to create deeper and more meaningful personal connections. There is also a physiological benefit when the brain is no longer too focused on a small screen in your hand.

Participants reported reduced back and body pain. Their digestion also improved. Researchers attributed this to the fact that you no longer slouch and look down and thus improve your posture.

People were able to remember things a lot better simply because they were more present when interacting with others. Study participants were also sleeping better. This can be attributed to the fact that blue light from smartphones disrupts your circadian rhythm . By just doing a 24-hour digital detox, you greatly improve your sleep pattern. With the reduced blue light emissions, the brain is better able to signal the release of melatonin, which triggers sleep.

The benefits of digital detox were also reported in a study by the World Conference on Technology, Innovation, and Entrepreneurship. In this study, students went through a short period of digital detox .

The male students reported that they felt calmer and less stressed after a short-term digital detox. This meant a reduced production of cortisol in the brain and other parts of the body. The female students reported that they were better able to empathize with other students after participating in the experiment.

Another study suggests that a digital detox may help improve one's mood. Improving one's mood is only one of the benefits of short-term abstinence from digital technology. Studies suggest that it may help reduce anxiety , better manage depression symptoms, and may help relieve eating disorders .

Ways Your Life Can Improve After Digital Minimalism

Here are some of the immediate benefits of undergoing a digital detox. Consider it as your first brush with digital minimalism.

Allow me to list some of the benefits that you can get out of such an experience.

1. You Identify Which Technology is Essential and Which Ones are Just Fluff

The very first benefit that you will get out of digital minimalism is that you will know which digital media and technology are essential. You will learn to clean up your computer and your phone, and your devices will run more efficiently. Apart from that, you will also work more effectively and get your life straightened out.

2. You Learn to Control Your Use of Digital Technology

When you have identified what pieces of technology are essential to you and your work, you will be able to focus on those tools. You choose how and when to use digital resources; you will use them to their utmost potential.

You don't need to run one hundred apps on your computer and your phone. You only need a handful or less, and you maximize the usefulness of each one. You also save money on the side because you reduce the monthly subscriptions that you have to pay.

3. You Become More Productive

This is related to the previous two points mentioned here. You become more productive because you are no longer distracted by hundreds of notifications. You don't need to pay attention to a dozen different work tools.

For example, if you're a graphic designer, you don't need to jump from GIMP to Photoshop, to Canva, to Pixlr X, and other tools. You just pick one or two, and that's it. You increase your productivity and spend less time at work and get more time for yourself.

4. You Don't Feel Overwhelmed

Do you remember the last time you cleaned up your room and organized your mess? Everything was so tranquil, peaceful, and you felt calmer, right? That's about the same thing you will get after doing a digital detox and practicing digital minimalism.

You no longer have any work backlogs, you don't have a ton of emails to respond to, you don't have a pile of reports you need to review. Everything runs smoothly, and there's no need to rush.

5. You're No Longer Distracted

One expert was on the button when he said that scrolling through endless posts, videos, pictures, and shopping items on your phone's screen is the new way we smoke cigarettes.

We have all mindlessly scrolled through our feeds. Don't worry; even I am guilty of doing that as well. You get distracted by the many notifications, and before you know it, you're halfway through your day, and you have accomplished very little.

The good news is that after doing a digital detox and practicing digital minimalism for at least a couple of weeks, you will feel less distracted, and you will have a renewed sense of purpose. You will know exactly what it is you want to do and when you need to get it all done.

Key Takeaways

- There are signs that you can use to determine whether you need a digital detox
- Digital addiction has many negative impacts, including those on our mental health
- You can reduce your stress levels, get better sleep, and get better focus when you do a digital detox
- Digital minimalism brings a lot of benefits such as better mental clarity, being less distracted, and you regain control over the technology you want to use

Chapter 5: Digital Mindfulness

Digital mindfulness is the application of mindfulness practices in your digital life. It involves the creation of structure and routines when it comes to your use of digital technology. Mindfulness is one of the tools that you can use to eliminate interruptions and distractions.

What Is Mindfulness?

Mindfulness is both a psychological process and also a state of mind when you are conscious of the present moment. You achieve it by focusing on the things that are currently happening around you. At the same time, you are also calmly and consciously accepting your thoughts, sensations, and feelings as you become aware of them.

It is something that you have done from time to time, whether you were aware of it or not. Mindfulness is also used as a therapeutic practice that allows people to relax.

At its core, mindfulness involves the acceptance of your memories, feelings, and thoughts minus any judgment on yourself or others because of those things. You will allow these experiences to come along and then just observe them. There will be no judgment whether they are good or bad thoughts, memories, and feelings.

You also do not rehearse the past as you live in the moment. In a mindful state, you also do not focus or imagine the future or its possibilities.

Origins of Mindfulness Practice

Mindfulness has deep roots in Buddhism. Buddhists have practiced it for hundreds of years. However, you don't have to believe in Buddhist teachings to enable you to practice mindfulness and mindfulness meditation.

Mindfulness as a practice (and not just the meditation part) reached the Western world through the efforts of Jon Kabat-Zinn. He was a Professor of Medicine Emeritus at the University of Massachusetts Medical School. He later founded the Mindfulness in Medicine, Health Care, and Society.

He also founded the Stress Reduction Clinic, where he introduced the Stress Reduction and Relaxation Program. In his work, he removed the Buddhist framework in his practice, taking away any religious aspects of his clinical practice. He then reformulated and renamed his stress reduction program as Mindfulness-Based Stress Reduction, or MBSR.

By distancing his practice from traditional Buddhist teachings, Kabat-Zinn was able to put mindfulness practice into mainstream clinical practice. Today, mindfulness is recognized as an effective therapeutic tool.

Studies show that meditation, specifically mindfulness meditation, induces the brain to create new gray matter and improves its plasticity. This is one of many studies that have shown how useful mindfulness meditation is.

How Mindfulness Can Help You: Two Key Points

According to Kabat-Zinn himself, mindfulness is:

> *"...a means of paying attention in a particular way; on purpose, in the present moment, and nonjudgmentally."*

Two main key points should be emphasized here when it comes to mindfulness as a practice before you can use it in digital minimalism. The first point is that you must learn to do things on purpose.

The opposite of mindfulness is mindlessness, which means you do things automatically or reactively. When something happens, you automatically follow or use a pre-programmed response.

For instance, if you have used your phone as a habitual escape from boredom and sadness, then whenever you feel bored or sad, the first thing that you will do, without thinking about it, is reach for your phone.

Some might think that this is a rather quick solution to boredom, loneliness, and all those negative feelings. But there is a problem with this automatic and technology-dependent response—what if the next time you grab your phone to check your email, social media, etc., you get a negative response—the news or posts are negative?

People don't like your posts. Someone even disliked the video or picture you posted. Someone even made a critical comment about it—and mentioned you as well. Instead of solving your problems, it caused more problems in return.

You find nothing interesting to watch on YouTube or Netflix. There is nothing to catch up on. There are no trends to follow. Instead of helping you find peace, you find more boredom and more stress.

The solution that mindfulness provides is purposeful and intentional choice. By doing things on purpose, you regain the power to choose and human agency. You do not only regain the power to choose how to get rid of boredom, loneliness, and stress, but you also are empowered to choose how to respond to the stimuli behind such feelings. You tackle the root cause of the problem and not just treat the symptoms.

The other key, according to Kabat-Zinn, is going through the experience non-judgmentally. When you feel bored, you will learn to acknowledge the experience. But you won't judge whether that experience is a bad one or a good one.

When you are mindful, you are in the zone. You are in control. You feel sadness because of a memory that came to you because of a post on social media. You feel it, and you do feel sad, but you choose not to be affected by it because you did not judge it as a negative or positive influence for you at that moment.

All you ever do in a state of mindfulness is to go through the experience and let it flow. These feelings, memories, and experiences come and go. And when, after they have passed, then you are still you. You are in control, and you no longer need to be depressed because you choose not to.

As you learn more about mindfulness and practice it in your daily life, you will become more aware of what's going on in your inner world—your inner dialogue. It's this internal monologue that pushes you to grab your digital technology (phone, Alexa speaker, TV, etc.).

According to best-selling author Stephen Covey, there is a brief time and space between stimulus and response. When something triggers a reaction from you, for a brief moment, you have a choice about what to do.

Reactive people tend to use a habitual response (e.g., use their phone, check social media, listen to sad music, etc.). But a non-reactive person (aka one who is proactive) will recognize that brief moment between stimulus and response. They will use that short moment to choose how they will respond.

Practicing mindfulness allows you not only to recognize that brief moment between stimulus and response, but you also get to expand it. By practicing mindfulness, you regain that inner strength and empowerment. You no longer have that need to check your emails every hour, hoping that you will find something interesting.

You will no longer be affected by what people post on social media. Even if people don't react to your posts and even dislike them, you do not feel sad, angry, or resentful. You choose how to respond to such things. They don't like your photo? It's okay. You move on. What's important is that you did something that you felt was important to you regardless of how people reacted to it.

You never get robbed of your satisfaction, contentment, or even your sense of hope. Remember that the ultimate goal in mindfulness practice in the digital world is to allow you to slow down and fully experience life as it happens.

We have become so acclimated to a fast-paced environment that we have failed to fully live. Digital mindfulness is not about avoiding the negative things in life. That is utterly impossible. Bad things happen all the time, and good things happen all the time too.

What you will learn through mindfulness practice is that you can live in those situations and still be okay—still in control. You regain the power to learn from these experiences and healthily cope with the negative.

Mindfulness will teach you to be aware of all your emotions. By being aware of them and understanding them, you learn to cope with the things that you used to avoid. Eventually, it teaches you how to specifically deal with the future negativity that may come into your life.

Finally, digital mindfulness brings you peace of mind in an ever-changing and increasingly connected world.

Practicing Mindfulness in the Digital Age

Some people see digital mindfulness as the antidote to digital distraction. I would rather prefer to think of it as one of many tools that you can use. It's not the secret formula or secret sauce to overcoming digital technology addiction. It's not the only thing that you need to do for digital minimalism.

Now, without diving directly into the practice of mindfulness and mindfulness meditation, here are a few things that you can do right now that will set you up for digital mindfulness.

We'll start with some tips and then cover several mindfulness meditation and practices that you can do.

Track Your Screen Time

Tech companies today like Google and Apple have acknowledged that smartphone addiction is a real thing. That is why they have introduced tools that users and subscribers can take advantage of in order to manage their screen time.

Apple has included the Screen Time app to its iOS suite, and for its part, Google has created Digital Well-Being Tools. These tools can help you monitor how much time you have spent looking at your phone's screen. They can also show you how many times you have unlocked your phone, how many notifications you have seen, what tools and pages you have viewed like Chrome, Facebook, messaging, Instagram, games, etc.

What you can do is to install these screen time apps on your phone and monitor how much time you have spent on your device. Set a limit for yourself for each day. How many times do you want to unlock your phone, how many notifications are your maximum each day, and how many hours of screen time is your limit?

Once you have reached any of these limits, then you must resolve not to touch or use your phone again until the following day.

Stop All Non-Human Notifications

Notice that a lot of the notifications that you get in your computer, phone, or other devices are automatic. That means they are pre-programmed. There is no human being that sent it to you on purpose. The AI behind these programs or apps sent them because certain conditions have been met in their programming, and thus they sent these notifications to you.

For instance, YouTubers usually tell you to like and subscribe to their channels, right? They also tell you to click the bell button. By clicking that, you get automatic notifications. It's not like the person who owned that channel intentionally sent you a notification that they have a new video uploaded.

The notification was sent to your device because the owner of that channel uploaded something new. Do you really need to view the said video right away? The answer is no, you don't need to see it right away. But you were notified, and eventually, you got distracted.

The same is true for other apps. Allowing automatic notifications by different apps will prompt you now and then. Sometimes, when a timed event in a game has started, then you will get notified.

Here's what you should do: turn off all notifications. You can keep notifications sent by actual human beings like emails from your coworkers. But turn off all the notifications from installed apps. Of course, you can keep the ones that you need, such as notifications from your calendar and the ones from your alarm clock.

Switch to Do Not Disturb Mode

Check if your phone has a do not disturb mode or quiet mode. It most likely will have that setting. When you're in work mode, when you're teaching a class, when you're talking to your spouse, having a meal with your family, playing music, having a one-on-one talk with someone, when you're sleeping, when you're doing anything important, keep your phone in another room.

That way, you can concentrate on the thing that you were doing. If that is not possible, then switch on the do not disturb mode and keep your phone in your bag—not in your pocket, not on your person. Put it in your bag and close your bag so you forget that you had your phone in there.

Charge Your Phone Outside of the Bedroom

We all put our phones on a table nightstand when we go to sleep so it will be within easy reach. Chances are your phone will need charging before you go to bed at night. So you keep on the nightstand or bedside table while it's charging.

Here's a quick tip—charge your phone outside the bedroom. That way, you won't be tempted to grab it while you're lying in bed.

But you need your phone since you use it as your alarm, right? Switch to a regular alarm clock. It performs the same task—it wakes you up with that annoying racket first thing in the morning. It even has one advantage when it comes to digital minimalism—it doesn't have internet.

The same rule applies to your smart speakers, smart assistants, and other digital tools. Alexa can still hear you even if your Echo Dot 3rd Gen is outside your door—yes, that's how powerful those new microphones are.

Do a Digital Detox Once a Week

In the previous chapter, we talked about doing a digital detox. To help you practice digital mindfulness, you should do at least one day of complete digital detox each week. Pick a day when you can and want to disconnect and live 24 hours completely off the grid. You don't need to leave your home, just disconnect everything and turn the WiFi off. If you need to review the information on how to do a digital detox, then please review the discussion in chapter 6.

Go On an Off-Grid Vacation

Plan to go on an off-grid vacation with your entire family. You can also use it to spend time with your closest friends. It can be for a week or two. If you have enough leave credits (or if your boss grants you a month-long vacation or more), then you should plan on going off-grid for a month.

You don't need to leave the country. You can even vacation somewhere else in the next town if there's a nature park or some other place where you can stay. Enjoy the outdoors and learn to do things without digital technology. If you need to make a call, use the regular landline phone or a payphone.

Use this moment to spend some quality time with the people who mean the most to you.

Take Mindful Moments before Jumping Into a Task

Before you start any task—taking calls, calling clients, sending emails, editing videos, starting a video meeting, writing a function in the program that you were writing, etc. You should take a moment to be mindful. Don't just jump into the task and hack into it like crazy.

Take a moment to remind yourself of what you're supposed to do. Take five slow deep breaths. And then go to work. Avoid the rush so that you prevent your mind from going into autopilot mode.

Mindful Waiting

In our fast-paced work environment, we tend to multitask when there is a bit of wait time in one part of our work. For instance, when a page we're trying to open starts to lag, we tend to open another tab on our browsers to check a different page for a different task.

Whenever this happens, we lose focus on the original task that we intended to do. We have our attention divided, and eventually, we get fewer things done. We think we are multitasking, but we're not.

Multitasking is a myth , and researchers and experts confirm this fact. What we human beings are actually doing is task-switching. We switch from one task to the other rather quickly. But that doesn't mean we can do both tasks efficiently.

We sort of trick our minds that we are multitasking. Research confirms that people can hardly concentrate on two tasks done at the same time. This means that if you want to get things done quickly and more efficiently, you should focus on only one task at a time.

The reason why people can't multitask is the interference between two or more tasks. The brain starts to struggle when you pay attention to two or more things at the same time.

That is why instead of going into multitasking mode when you are made to wait, take the time to do a short mindfulness exercise. We will go over several mindfulness exercises in the next section of this chapter. Just remember that whenever you hear the queue music, don't grab your phone. Use that time to meditate and practice mindfulness.

Focus on One Task at a Time

As was explained earlier, trying to focus on a task is an inefficient way to get things done. Whenever you are tempted to multitask, take a moment to decide whether you can finish one task more efficiently and then moving on to the next. This will allow your mind to remain calm and clear instead of being stressed out while trying to do a balancing act moving from one task to the next. Unit tasking is usually the better option, all things considered.

Do Mindful Moments in Transition

We usually jump from one task to the next as if we are in a hurried flight to get everything done. In the frenzy, we sometimes fail to notice the increasing amount of tension and stress because of the workload that is given to us.

To prevent this from happening, you should do mindful transitions every time you complete a task. For instance, after completing one of the items on your to-do list, instead of just moving on to the next item on that list, you should pause and perform a short mindfulness exercise.

Note that this will be the first of the different exercises that we will go over in a little bit:

1. Be still.
2. Close your eyes.
3. Take three slow and deep breaths.
4. Pay attention to how your lungs feel as you take each deep breath.
5. As you exhale, try to recall where you are and what you have just finished.
6. Pay attention to how you feel right now—do you feel cold, relieved, still tense?
7. Let all of that feeling wash away as you release each deep breath.
8. Open your eyes and move on to the next task.

Note that it only takes a few seconds to do the exercise described above. You can do this exercise quickly before you answer a client call, walk into your office, get out of the car after arriving at an appointment, and any other time when you need a few seconds of mental clarity.

Must-Know Mindfulness Exercises

The following are mindfulness exercises that everyone must know, especially if you're trying to learn how to practice digital minimalism. These exercises will teach your mind how to be in the present moment. They will help you enter into a state of calm, something that you will need to sort through any kind of chaos that might be happening in your life right now.

Body Scan Exercise

The body scan method is one of the first mindfulness exercises that will be taught to people who want to learn mindfulness meditation. In this exercise, you will learn how to systematically focus your attention.

Don't worry—it is a very simple exercise. Doing a body scan gives you that rare opportunity to become aware of your body, and experience it as it is with no judgments. No judgment will be passed on the state of your body, and you won't even have to try and change anything.

It will also teach you to be aware of possible sources of bodily tension, discomfort, and pain. The body scan exercise is designed to counteract any resentments and negative feelings you may have towards your body.

In time, you will learn to be more aware of your body's needs. You will become more present with its needs and sensations. It will help you make healthier decisions about exercise, sleep, and eating habits.

According to one study , it is suggested that people who regularly perform body scans can reduce their stress levels and improve their psychological well-being.

How to do it:

A full body scan will require up to 20 to 45 minutes. However, you can do shorter sessions that range from one minute to 15 minutes. A body scan can be done lying down, sitting on a chair, standing up, or even while walking, albeit slowly at first.

Remember that if anything should distract you while doing a body scan, you should just observe the distraction, forgive yourself for getting distracted, and then return your focus to that part of your body that you were paying attention to.

No judgments—remember that distractions like feelings, memories, sounds, and others are just passing and fleeting experiences. They have no power over you. Observe and then let them pass. Go back to your body scan.

Here's how you get started:

1. Choose a position that is most comfortable for you (i.e., sitting down, lying in bed, or standing up).
2. Start the meditation by paying attention to your entire body.
3. Close your eyes if it helps you visualize the condition of your body.
4. If you are seated, pay attention to the feeling of your body's weight on the chair. If you're lying down, pay attention to your body's weight on the surface you're lying on. In case you're standing, pay attention to the feeling of the weight of your body on your feet.
5. Take a few slow deep breaths.
6. Notice how deep the air enters your body and the tension that comes with it that you feel in your lungs.
7. Notice the relaxed feeling you get as you exhale the air emptying your lungs.
8. Now, place your attention on your feet and legs.
9. Pay attention to the feelings in your feet—is there any tension? If there is, then try to relax your feet. Take a deep breath.

10. Focus your attention on your legs, knees, and thighs. Release any tension in these parts of your body and relax them. Take a deep breath.
11. Move your attention to your hips and buttocks. Are the muscles and tissues there tense? Relax and then take a deep breath.
12. Move your focus to your stomach area next. Relax any muscles that are too tense. And then take a deep breath.
13. Do the same for your chest and back. Pay attention to the feeling of your body pressed against any surfaces, if any. Relax your muscles in these parts. Take a slow, deep breath.
14. Focus your attention on your neck and throat. Allow them to relax.
15. Move up to your jaw and soften that part of your body. Pay attention to the sensations you have on your face. Relax any facial muscles that are currently tense. There is no need to smile, frown, or have any other facial expressions at this time. Take a slow, deep breath.
16. This time, allow yourself to focus on the sensations that are being experienced by your entire body. Allow your body to experience them and then let your body relax.
17. Take several deep breaths and when you're ready, open your eyes and get on with your day.

Note that a shorter body scan session will only give you enough time to focus your attention on one or two parts of your body. You get to choose which part you want to focus on.

Mindful Breathing Exercise

This is another basic mindfulness exercise, and it is also one of the first exercises to be taught to beginners. Mindful breathing is a great way to relieve yourself of anger, stress, and anxiety. After doing this exercise, you will feel that your powers of better judgment will return, your skills and capabilities will reset, and you will regain your ability to pay attention and focus on things.

You can say that mindful breathing is a foundational exercise that will be used in pretty much every kind of mindfulness exercise. If you noticed, you were already performing mindful breathing in the previous exercise (i.e., body scan).

Mindful breathing distances you from your feelings and your thoughts. You begin to realize that your feelings and experiences may be part of you, but they do not define who you are.

This distancing from your personal experiences empowers you to tolerate the negative things that happen to you. Mindful breathing allows your mind to anchor onto something (i.e., your breathing).

You have something to focus on and thus separate yourself from emotions and thoughts. You stay present and become aware of the present moment. You do not get distracted from drastic decisions and actions that you might regret later.

In one study , researchers suggest that people who perform mindful breathing or focused breathing become better at regulating their emotions.

How to Do It

Mindful breathing can be done in two to 15 minutes, depending on how much time you have. Experts suggest that you should perform this exercise at least once a day. The more frequently you do this exercise, the better you will be at focusing your mind and remain more mindful.

Here's how you can do it:

1. Find a nice, comfortable, quiet place where you can relax and sit down. You can sit on a chair or just sit on the floor—if you're sitting on the floor, please find some kind of cushion to sit on since you may end up sitting in that area for an extended period of time. Your tongue should be placed on the roof of your mouth. You can place your hands on your lap, on the chair, or anywhere you like.
2. Give yourself a few seconds to get comfy where you're sitting. Be mindful of the feelings that you experience. Allow these feelings to come and go.
3. Now, begin your mindful breathing. Breathe in and pay attention to the feeling of the air rushing into your lungs.
4. You don't need to breathe in any way. Just breathe as you usually do. It can be a short breath, a deep breath, or even a rapid shallow breath.
5. As you breathe, notice how it feels to have the air pass your nose, mouth, throat, neck, and finally into your lungs.
6. Try to notice how one breath ends and how the next one begins. Follow the rhythmic pattern of your breathing.
7. If anything like memories, feelings, sounds, or anything that you sense tries to take your focus away from your breathing, give it a moment and allow it to pass. Forgive yourself if you got distracted and go back to focusing on your breathing.
8. Repeat steps 1 to 7 as long as you like. It's all up to you. The important point is that you are able to maintain your focus on your breathing.
9. Keep breathing, and appreciate what you have accomplished at this time. Now you can get up and go back to life in general.

Walking Meditation Exercise

Walking meditation is one of the methods that you can practice mindfulness even when you're on the go. After practicing mindful breathing and body scans several times, you can now try doing walking meditations.

When you do walking meditations, your attention and focus will be on the actual physical experience. It is something that we have taken for granted. When you go on this meditative walking exercise, you will pay attention to every movement that you make when you take every step.

According to one study , incorporating mindful walking in your daily routine can help reduce stress, improve mental conditions, fight depression, and relieve physical symptoms due to medical conditions such as heart disease.

How to Do It

For you to enjoy the full benefits of meditative walking, you should do this exercise at least ten minutes each day for an entire week. The more times you do it, the easier it will be for you to enter into a mindful state in your everyday life.

1. The first step is to find a nice quiet place where you can walk back and forth without any distractions. This is important if you haven't done mindful walking or meditative walking before.

   You don't need a very long lane to walk on, and you don't even need a specific place to go to. A quiet lane on your block that is usually free of traffic will be great. You can even do it indoors if you like to avoid a lot of distractions too. If you do it outdoors, just make sure that there won't be anyone there to stop you or grab your attention. Now, move on to the next step.

2. Take 10 to 15 steps forward on the pathway that you have chosen. After completing the required number of steps, pause for a bit, and then take a deep breath.

3. Now, turn back and then walk the other way. When you reach the other end, pause and then take a deep breath.

4. Now that you have walked back and forth at least once in both directions, the next time you walk back, pay attention to each step that you take.

5. Focus on how you lift your foot, take a step, how well your foot lands on the ground, how you move your weight forward, how your body swings as you take each step, and how your arms move while walking.

6. When you take each step, it doesn't have to be done in a very fast manner. In fact, you should take a slow walk so that you can easily observe how you take each step.

7. Don't take large steps, take small shorter steps. Make it a relaxed stroll, one that is unhurried.

8. If you want, you can clasp your hands in front of you or behind you so that you can concentrate only on the movement of your feet—which makes observing your body's motions a lot easier.

9. Notice that your mind will eventually wander as you walk back and forth. It's okay; it's very natural for all of us to do that. When your mind gets distracted, forgive yourself, and then go back to observing and focusing on the motions of your body as you take a relaxed stroll.

10. After you have felt that you have done enough walking and achieved a complete awareness of your body's movements, you can stop, take a deep breath, and then go back to whatever it was that you were doing.

Do walking meditations every day for a week. After that, you can try to do it every time you have a chance to walk.

Raisin Method

We sometimes do things automatically with no thought about what we are about to do. Many times during the day, we go into a mindless auto mode where we follow a habitual chain of reactions and do things using preconditioned responses.

For example, when you hear your phone ringing, you instinctively reach for it and answer it, giving no thought about the wonderful technology that you have in your hands. The cheeseburger you ordered has been served; you instinctively dig in, go on bite after bite, have a conversation about something with your friend, and before you know it, you are done with your meal.

Did you notice the power of your mobile device? Did you notice how well-made your sandwich was? This exercise will help you make mindfulness an automatic habit. You will learn to take notice of the little things and appreciate the little things in life.

This mindfulness exercise will require a prop—a box of raisins. What if you don't have raisins? Then you can use some other treat. Choose something small, not so filling, and healthy. This exercise also teaches you to engage your different bodily senses.

It is recommended that you take five minutes each day to do this meditative exercise. Here are the steps:
1. First step: Hold one raisin gently in the palm of your hand.
2. Look at the raisin in your hand. You can hold it in between two fingers if you want to just let you see its features.
3. Pay attention to how it feels in your hand. Is it rough, smooth, hard, or soft? Pay attention to how its folds and ridges look like. Hold it up against the light and see the kind of shadow it makes. If you look at it with the light shining behind it, can you see the silhouette of its internal parts?
4. How much do you think it weighs?
5. Turn the raisin over between your fingers and explore how it feels. How do you describe its texture? You might want to close your eyes so that you can visualize its surface texture.
6. Smell the raisin. How does it smell? Do you remember smelling that sort of scent when you eat foods that use raisins as an ingredient?
7. Close your eyes. Now place the raisin in between your lips, but don't put it in your mouth.
8. Did you notice that? Notice how your hand knows exactly where your mouth is. You don't think about it; you never estimated the exact distance your hand had to travel and the exact placement of your mouth in relation to your face. You were aware of exactly where to put that raisin so that

it will reach your lips. On top of that, your lips also know exactly how much pressure should be applied to the raisin so that it won't fall to the floor. Your spatial awareness is something that you have taken for granted, and now you are re-experiencing it all over again.

9. Next, put the raisin in your mouth. But don't swallow it. Take your time and chew it slowly. Pay attention to the flavors that you taste in your mouth. If one raisin is not enough to allow you to taste the actual flavor of a raisin, then eat another one (or two). Chew slowly and try to describe the taste in your mouth.

10. Finally, swallow the raisin. How does it feel as it slowly makes its way into your stomach?

This raisin method can actually be used as a mindful eating exercise. When you use this process to mindfully eat your meals, you should pay attention to the look of the food that was served on your plate, how it feels when you cut it into bite-size pieces, how it smells, and the effect of the flavors in your mouth.

Self-Compassion Method

Do you often relive past mistakes? Did you ever say things that you regret saying? We all have regrets—we regret wrong decisions, bad moves, wrong things we did to others, poor judgment, and a lot of other things that we may have directly or indirectly caused.

We rehash the past and fail to find joy in the present, and thus we think our futures are clouded. Yes, it sounds like something mystical or even Buddhist, but these observations have roots in our present experience even in our modern day.

This exercise will allow you to focus or center on a single tangible object. You will use it to channel your focus and come to a realization about your past experiences and your current state of awareness.

This mindfulness exercise will allow you to take a break when you tend to beat yourself up for past faults and mistakes. Instead of using harsh self-criticism, you will practice a healthier response—a compassionate response.

The following exercise will walk you through all the essential components of compassion towards self. You will learn how to be mindful, be kind to yourself, and have that feeling of common humanity (elements defined by Kristin Neff Ph.D., University of Texas).

Here's how you can do it:

This exercise requires only five minutes of your time. You can do this exercise every time you feel that stress is building up, and if your memories are starting to haunt you at any time of the day. But for starters, you can just do it once a week.

1. Find a quiet place where you can sit down and be alone with your thoughts. Get comfy, and start breathing slowly. Be mindful of each breath you take.

2. As you sit there paying attention to your breath, think of a situation that you are going through. Choose the toughest one that you are facing right now.

3. As you recall that problem or situation, try to notice if you feel any sense of emotional or actual physical discomfort. You will usually manifest a symptom like butterflies in your stomach, sweat, feeling cold, despair, or some other feeling.

4. Now, acknowledge that experience by saying, "I am suffering from this right now." There is no need to judge the situation as either good or bad for you. Tell yourself what you feel—"it hurts" or "I feel stressed," etc.

5. Next, point out to yourself that the experience of difficulty and pain is a common experience for all human beings. You can do that by saying to yourself, "This suffering is part of my human life." You can also say, "I am not alone; there are others who are also going through the same problems that I am going through."
The important thing in this step is that you acknowledge that your suffering is not unique and that other people have or are currently going through the same level or amount of suffering.

6. Place your hands close to your heart, or you can even just give yourself a tight hug. Say to yourself, "May I offer kindness to myself" or some other similar phrase. Examples of similar phrases are "May I always be forgiving to myself," "May I always be patient with myself," "May I learn to accept me for who I truly am," "May I always be strong no matter what," and others. You get to choose the phrase depending on the dilemma or situation that you are currently encountering.

You can perform this five-minute exercise of self-kindness at night before going to bed, when you wake up first thing in the morning, or any time when you find an extra five minutes during your day. The important thing is that you can find time to be compassionate to yourself.

Meditation for Extending Kindness

In the previous mindfulness exercise, you learned how to express self-compassion for five minutes. In this exercise, you will be doing it for 15 minutes. However, there is also an added twist: you will be extending kindness and compassion to others as well.

Experts say that people who are kind to others tend to be more satisfied with their lives. They also have better relationships with others. This type of mindfulness meditation is also called metta meditation, and it can increase your natural capability to be kind to other people despite the situation you find yourself in.

How you can do it:

This form of meditation will be similar to the previous mindfulness exercise. This exercise was developed originally by Stanford University's Science Director, Emma Seppala. You can learn more about its benefits and download guided meditation audio from Dr. Seppala's website .

There are two phases of this exercise. The first one is to receive kindness and compassion and be aware of all that you have received. The second one is to send it out to others so that you may bless others as well.

Receiving Loving Kindness

1. Find a nice comfortable place where you can sit down. Lean back on a chair's backrest and then close your eyes. Take several deep breaths until you are completely relaxed. You will go through several visualizations, so keep your eyes closed throughout this exercise.
2. Think of someone very close to you—someone you hold dear to your heart. It should be someone you know who loves you very much. It can be a deceased parent, the person mentoring you right now, your best friend, your spouse, your children, your grandparents who died when you were a kid, etc.
3. Select one of those people who love you and imagine that person sitting right beside you right now. Imagine that person giving you a warm, reassuring hug, a pat on the back, or other means of expressing their love to you.
4. Take note of the warm, loving feeling that you are experiencing because of that love that is extended to you.
5. Think of another person, and have that person also sit beside you on the other side. Imagine that person also extending his or her love to you. Now you have three people in your huddle.
6. Pick another person who loves you and imagine that person also expressing his or her love to you.
7. Add another person in the loving circle that you are experiencing right now. And then add another, and another, until you have several friends and loved ones who are showing you their compassion and love.
8. Focus on the loving feeling that you are experiencing at that moment.

Radiating Kindness

1. Now that you know what it feels like to receive compassion and kindness from those who truly loved you, it is time for you to return that kindness and compassion.
2. Go back to the first person you imagined or remembered. Imagine giving back that love and compassion to that person. You may say things like, "Thank you for your kindness. May you be happy and live with ease."
3. Repeat the same steps for every single person in your loving huddle.
4. After you're done reciprocating the love you have felt to everyone in your huddle, think of someone who you do not know well—maybe just an acquaintance—and then send that same love to that person. Think two more acquaintances and try to imagine how it would feel like when you express your appreciation and love for them.
5. Now, it is time to extend the reach of your compassion. Imagine people around the world who may not be as fortunate as you. Imagine extending your love to them. Say words like, "I wish

you live well, happy, and in good health." Imagine being able to help those people in your own little way.

6. Take three slow, deep breaths. And when you are ready, open your eyes.

Take note of how you feel after this exercise. Remember the state of your mind after feeling love and expressing it to others. You can always come back to this experience during the day, especially when times are rough.

How to Help Your Family Practice Digital Mindfulness

The next questions are, when will you use these mindfulness exercises, and how do you teach them to your family? If not your family, then maybe your coworkers or your team in the office; there will always be people to whom you can share the benefits of mindfulness applied in the digital age.

You can use these mindfulness exercises whenever you have idle time. Instead of grabbing your phone and playing a game or maybe scanning through social media, you can replace such activities with a mindfulness exercise.

Remember that the choice is always yours. Do you want some quick satisfaction that comes from your digital device, or do you prefer the lasting peace of mind that you can get from the practice of digital mindfulness? You can only say that practicing mindfulness is the better option after you have tried the exercises that have been described in detail above.

Here's a **big TIP**: Choose mindfulness every time you are presented with a choice between opening an email, watching a video on YouTube, checking social media, or using your phone. The long-term benefits of better focus, peace of mind, reduced stress, and mental clarity is so much better.

Tips on Practicing Digital Mindfulness in the Home

It is one thing to practice mindfulness yourself, but it is another to get your spouse and your kids to do it too. The first step to teaching mindfulness to your loved ones is to practice digital mindfulness first yourself. Once you have tried it, you can inform your family about what you're doing and ask for their support.

Talk to them about it and share your experiences. Tell them about the benefits that you have enjoyed from practicing digital mindfulness. The next person you want to get on board with the practice is your spouse.

Both of you should then set the example for your kids. You can then have a family meeting and get your kids to practice it also. Remember to relate to them the benefits, and reassure them that as parents, you are doing it for their welfare.

Now, here are a few ideas on how you can practice digital mindfulness at home and teach it to your children.

1. Set Up Family Mindfulness Challenges

Kids love challenges, and they love the rewards that come with their efforts. You may have been modeling how mindfulness is done. You may have even asked your kids to try one of the exercises described above. They may already have a bit of an idea about what mindful living is like.

You can have some family fun doing mindfulness challenges. For instance, you can teach a short mindful breathing exercise to your kids, and then reward them after the exercise.

You can also set up one of the mindful digital practices that we have described in this chapter. For instance, you can set up screen time monitors so you can determine if your children are using their mobile devices for several hours.

You can come up with an agreement that within the week, the child that gets the least amount of screen time will get the most number of treats come Saturday. Of course, you must live up to your promises and prepare a treat for them. The winner, of course, gets the biggest serving.

2. Mindfulness Space and Mindfulness Huddles

You can create some kind of safe space in your home where people can sit down, relax, and do some mindfulness meditation. Some people set up meditation rooms or meditation corners in their homes.

It doesn't have to take up a lot of space. The important thing is that it is a section of the house where you can go to be alone with your thoughts. Design it in a minimalist fashion. Keep the space clutter-free and digital technology-free.

You should put more than just one chair in the area since you're expecting the entire family to try the spot every once in a while. If you're not the chair setup kind of guy then you can layout mats of the floor, and maybe some cushions where people can sit.

Once you have your meditation corner/room set up, you can schedule certain times within the week when your entire family can gather around and practice mindfulness exercises.

These little huddles don't have to take a lot of time. You can do it once a week as an entire family and just let the meditation session last for around 10 to 20 minutes. Adjust the length of the session as needed.

Make it a rule to allow any family member to go to this designated mindfulness space. It can be your refuge from stress, problems, and confusion in your life. Allow people to join in when someone goes here to meditate. You can also use the said space for family meetings where you can discuss really important issues about your family.

3. Have Mindful Meals

Do you remember the raisin meditation exercise from earlier? You can use the same mindful practices when eating your meals. You have to skip the parts where you have to put food in your hands and stuff. Skip to the part where you chew your food well and savor the flavors in your mouth, and experience the sheer joy of good food.

But that is not all of it. Since you want to maintain your focus and mindfulness on the actual meal—meaning the food coupled with the discussion at the dinner table—you should also make it a rule that there should be no digital technology while at the table.

That means the TV should be out of sight or turned off while you have your meal. No mobile phones, tablets, or any kind of device. Everyone should focus on the meal and enjoy the few minutes when you can have an actual conversation with the people who truly matter in your life.

4. Mindfulness and Discipline

Let's face it—kids will be kids, and people will be people. Someone, sometime, somewhere will break a mindful habit. Your kid or your spouse may one day just spend too much time on their smartphone. Maybe someone in the family will binge-watch all through the night.

It happens.

Do you remember one of the phrases that we keep repeating whenever we practice mindfulness meditation? We forgive ourselves when we make mistakes. Extend the same level of forgiveness.

However, along with that mindfulness principle, as a parent, you should also impose some form of discipline on your kids just to help train them not to be too dependent on digital technology.

But how are you going to do that?

Here are a few tips:

- Listen first, ask why they binged, brought their phone to the dinner table, didn't want to join you in a mindful exercise. Don't lecture—it's the last thing they need. Learn to be understanding. In the words of Stephen Covey, "seek first to understand before you seek to be understood."
  After you have completely understood their reasons, then let them understand why you want them to participate both in your family's digital minimalism and mindfulness practices.

- Validate how they feel—acknowledge their feelings and thoughts. Empathize with them and try to see their point of view. Make sure to communicate that you understand how they feel and think.

- Redirect the dialogue to show how minimalism and mindfulness can benefit them. For example, if you discover that your child stays up late at night to play games with his or her phone, then here's what you can do.

  After listening to what they have to say, you can explain that if they don't rest early, they will have a hard time getting up in the morning, and they can be late for school the following day. Show compassion and reaffirm the fact that you care for them, and what you are doing is for their own good.

As you impose your house rules about minimalism and mindfulness, you should make it a point that you reassure your children that they can confide in you. If you have raised your voice, then apologize.

Ensure that every time you have pep talks with your kids that they feel that it is always safe to open up to you. Give them a sense of safety and reassurance that when you're leveling with them and being honest and open, they can do the same and that they can trust you.

5. Always Be Clear About the Rules

Your kids will need to know the boundaries that you have set for everyone in the house. Establishing boundaries translates to a clear definition of how far a child's autonomy goes, how much space in the house they are responsible for, and when and where they can use digital technology.

You can talk about these rules with your kids during a family meeting or a one-to-one pep talk. The important thing is that you can establish the said house rules clearly and understandably.

You can also put up reminders, like notes on the fridge and elsewhere. You can also remind your kids about these rules from time to time. You can have weekly family meetings and talk about your experiences and, of course, how everyone is doing when it comes to mindfulness and digital minimalism.

6. Make Mornings Mindful

Make it a rule in the house for everyone to stop using their phones and other technology for 15 minutes early in the morning. A lot of us have made it a habit to check our phones as soon as we wake up.

To help your kids practice digital minimalism and mindfulness a lot better, you can spend a mindful moment with them, as was explained earlier in this chapter. It doesn't have to take that long—just two minutes will be fine.

If they already have their phones or other devices in their hand, ask them to put them down for a minute and do a mindfulness exercise with you. All you need to do with them is this:

1. Close your eyes.
2. Breathe in and out to quiet your minds.
3. Take note and describe the emotions that you are experiencing right now.
4. Acknowledge and accept that emotion.
5. Breathe in and out, and allow these emotions to pass.

And now you can mindfully go on with your morning routine. You may need to do it with your kids from time to time until they can do it on their own.

Practicing digital mindfulness will be a big help to anyone who wants to practice digital minimalism. Minimalism allows you to separate yourself from your phones, tablets, computers, and other devices, identify the underlying emotions that influence your choices, and then purposefully and consciously use technology.

Key Takeaways

- Mindfulness as a practice has been around for hundreds of years
- Digital mindfulness is all about applying mindfulness principles and practices to our digital lives
- At any given time we can use mindfulness exercises to regain our focus and channel it into the present moment
- By using digital mindfulness, we reduce the impact and influence of digital technology in our lives

Chapter 6: More Tips and Life Hacks to Break Free of Technology Addiction

We covered technology addiction in chapter 2 of this book. A lot of the things that we talked about here, such as digital detoxes, decluttering, and minimalism, are helpful when it comes to breaking technology addiction.

In this chapter, we will go over several life hacks that you can do to break free of digital addiction.

Life Hack #1: Preventing Technology Addiction in Children

It was mentioned in an earlier chapter of this book that children are more prone to digital technology addiction. As guardians and parents, you have the responsibility to nurture and protect your children—that includes preventing digital threats.

It is easier to prevent digital technology addiction from occurring than to stop one that is already ongoing. I also understand that it is impossible to take technology out of the hands of our kids.

It is such a norm today, and they will also eventually use digital technology when they grow older. The smart way to do things is to train them early on in order to be more responsible users of digital technology.

Here are steps on how you can do that:

1. **Observe and monitor their tech usage**: You can use apps like Moment to monitor your children's use of their phones. It can give you warnings when your children have already spent too much time on their phones. We have already mentioned different screen time monitoring tools in a previous chapter as well.
2. **Watch out for the signs of tech addiction:** Review the signs and effects of tech addiction mentioned in chapter 2. If you see two or more of the side effects listed there, you should perform some direct interventions. Use the tips on digital declutter and mindfulness mentioned in this book.
3. **Do not completely ban their internet use:** As strange as it may seem, you should never ban their internet use. Kids these days need to learn how to responsibly use digital technology. The internet is a reality of our time, and it can be a useful tool. What we need to teach is how to be more responsible when using it.
4. **Test your child's social skills—and provide some coaching if necessary:** Does your child have difficulty interacting with other kids? Not all kids have the same social skills. You may have to model and coach your child how to talk to and react to other children.

The important thing is to ensure that your child gets a lot of real-world face-to-face direct human interaction. You will also have to enforce how many hours they can use the internet and digital technology. As a parent, you need to identify your child's gifts and talents and nurture them.

Life Hack #2: What If You Can't Get Rid of Technology Completely? Tips on Minimalist Tech Use

How can you be a digital minimalist when you need technology for work or life? I agree that in our modern world, it is impossible to get rid of technology completely. Digital minimalism is not about discontinuing technology use completely.

Here are a few tips and suggestions that you can use if you need digital technology in your life:

- Don't react to social media posts. This tip is from Cal Newport's book. Don't click like, don't click the reaction buttons, don't share the post, and don't post comments. This might be challenging at first. The like button and other reaction functions on social media are quick fixes.

  If you really like what your friend posted, why not give them a call instead and tell them how you felt about it? Doing this fosters real, meaningful interactions, and allows you to use digital technology more purposefully and more mindfully.

- Consolidate all your texting time. This can also be applied to chat boxes and other work notifications. How do you do that? Let the airplane mode on your phone be the default. Schedule 30 minutes of texting time several times during your day (say 30 minutes after lunch, breakfast, and dinner so that your meals won't be interrupted).
  This will also train your coworkers, staff, clients, and other associates that your time is important, and they can't just barge into your day, hoping to get an instant response.

- Minimize computer use to work-related matters only. Make sure that you only use a computer at work. There may be times when you will need to use your computer for personal purposes—maybe to check flights, confirm orders, etc., but they should be minimal uses (maybe around five to ten minutes). The goal is to reduce computer usage outside of work. Your personal time should be used for more person-to-person interactions.

- Use your good old alarm clock. Before you watch a video on YouTube, view Facebook feeds, check Twitter tweets, or view posts on Instagram, set an alarm. You get to decide how long you want to spend on social media; however, don't set your alarm for more than one hour. After setting your alarm, go through all the social media posts that you want. When the alarm goes off, then that's it. Turn off your phone and put it in your drawer. Get back to whatever it was that you were supposed to do.

- But what if you use social media for work? Let's say that you use Facebook for social media marketing, and you need to check your ad campaign metrics. What you should do is to bookmark Facebook for Business and log into that and not your personal Facebook account. You can find the same feature in Instagram and other social media channels.

  Go straight to the business section of social media and don't log on to your personal accounts. You can then check your metrics, launch new ad campaigns, and recalibrate your bot settings to better respond to product or service inquiries. Stay away from your personal Facebook account when using social media for business.

- Do a digital declutter. We already went through the details on how to do a digital declutter and inventory in chapter 3 of this book. In that chapter, we covered how to save time on your emails, how to decrease technology time, how to save time on your phone, and apps like Boomerang that will help you better manage your emails. You may want to review that chapter if you want to reduce tech time and practice digital minimalism while still using technology.

- Do a total disconnect one day each week. This is a concept that we can trace all the way to the Biblical Hebrews. It's called a Sabbath. The word is Hebrew for "day of rest." It's a day when these ancient people steer clear of all things work-related, which is something that we still do today. Stephen Covey, in his best-selling book, calls this principle *self-renewal*. You stay away from the hustle of work and digital life and spend time working on yourself.

  Designate one day each week when you will disconnect from the web and all things tech-related. Use that day to go out and get a massage, learn to cook a new recipe, sleep, clean your yard, do volunteer work for the needy, or simply just to meditate and be alone to ponder on things that are valuable to your life.

Life Hack #3: Use Art Therapy and Artistic Expression

Instead of using one of those coloring and art apps on your phone, switch to actual physical art. Let the guitar, piano, brush, clay, or mallet be your instrument and not just any art app on your phone.

One of your options when dealing with any level of digital addiction is to use art therapy . It is an experiential mode of treatment where a person addresses their needs through creative expression.

Human beings are creative beings, and we have different ways of self-expression. Kids love expressing their thoughts and emotions in different ways. But we adults can also find our own way of expressing ourselves too.

That is why there are different types of art therapy/art expression, such as:
- Poetry
- Music
- Acting

- Drawing
- Dancing
- Sculpting
- Painting

Sign up for an actual class on any of these arts. If you always wanted to learn how to dance, then sign up for dance lessons. You can even sign up online. Yes, you're using digital technology, but this time you're using it purposefully and mindfully.

Life Hack #4: Use Mandalas for Meditation

Mandalas are easy to find, and you can start with them right away. They are those circular pattern designs that tend to be quite mesmerizing. Drawing and coloring mandalas can also be used as a form of meditation, which is something you can do to help you be alone with your mind and get some time for self-renewal.

I tried those and found that coloring them can be quite relaxing and meditative. Studies also show that coloring mandalas can also lead you to practice mindfulness .

They're cheap too, and you can find lots of patterns on Amazon or other retailers.

Here's what you should do:

1. Order a mandala book online or download mandala patterns that you can print. You can start drawing on any piece of paper, that is, if you have some drawing skills already.

2. Set aside an hour on certain days. You can schedule your mandala time twice a week, three times a week; it's all up to you. If you're really busy, then schedule ten-minute mandala times every day.

3. Disconnect from the internet, turn off your phone, and turn off any digital tech (maybe just use your phone as a timer for this session). Set your alarm for ten minutes (or whatever time you have allotted for your mandala session).

4. Work on your mandala. Let your thoughts focus on the lines and colors that you put into your work. Take the time to appreciate the symmetry of the patterns. Pay attention to the details as much as possible.

5. When the alarm goes off, keep your mandala in a secure place. If you weren't able to complete the project today, you could always come back to it in your next session.

6. Take several deep breaths and go back to your work or the task that you had to finish that day.

Life Hack #5: Learn a New Life Skill

Choose a life skill like cooking, swimming, riding a bike, survival skills, self-defense, CPR, and first aid—anything that can be useful to you when the time comes. This is time well spent because it is your investment to become a better version of yourself.

You can sign up for a cooking class or have a friend come over to teach you a new recipe. This way, you are also enriching human experiences. You can buy a bicycle and if you don't know how to ride one then ask your neighbor or a close friend to teach you. This is something that you can't learn by just watching YouTube videos, by the way.

Life Hack #6: Pick Up a New Skill or Talent That Keeps You Away from Digital Media/Technology

This life hack is somewhat related to the previous one. Pick a skill or talent that you always wanted to learn. In my case, I always wanted to learn how to play the ukulele. So I ordered one on Amazon, and I searched for ukulele tutorials on YouTube.

I found that the chord patterns are much easier to remember since they're not that complicated compared to guitar chords. The only problem was that I bought a soprano, and it was a bit too small for my hand. But I got really good at it.

There were hundreds of tutorials on YouTube. The good part about it was that I picked a tutorial and watched YouTube for about 30 minutes until I learned the lesson very well. The great thing about it is that I was able to reduce my video streaming time.

I didn't need to watch YouTube over and over again. After I learned that lesson, I played that song or chord progression over and over for the entire day until I could do it with my eyes closed.

I really enjoyed learning new songs every day. I have also found out that you can use digital technology to help you find something that is equally enjoyable.

You can do the same. What is it that you have always wanted to try? Is it singing, drawing, boxing, dancing, pottery, jiu-jitsu, or painting? Pick something new and try your hand at it. Use tutorials that you can find on the internet.

Study one lesson per day and then disconnect from the internet so you can focus on practicing the new thing that you have learned. Keep at it until you have mastered that lesson. And then you can move on to the next one.

Life Hack #7: Use Digital Technology to Reach Out and Communicate

My team uses Zoom for meetings and presentations to clients who are overseas. However, that is not the only thing I use it for. I usually schedule virtual family reunions. Sure, we could have done that on Facebook Messenger a long time ago, but back then, my focus was just using social media and getting attention from the public.

Now, I use digital technology—Zoom, in particular—to meet up with long-lost friends and family. I don't just chat with them on Messenger, I get to see their faces and catch up. This is one of the positive ways to reinforce the proper use of digital media. I can also use it to share files and other media that might help rekindle old memories.

We're not just mindlessly using it to fill a void in our day. We use it intentionally and purposefully to reach out to our fellow human beings. Try this next time you need to use your phone. Download Zoom or Lark, Google Meet, or whatever online meeting app you would like to use.

Schedule a virtual get together with your friends—say, the following day or an hour from now—and then just go hang out with one another. Reach out and catch up to real people and not just some virtual character in a game you're playing.

Life Hack #8: Use the Power of Grey Tones

Do you know why the icons on your phone are so colorful? That is actually part of the positive psychological reinforcement to make you tap on them. That is one of the ways they were designed to attract your attention. Remember that certain colors tend to attract smartphone users.

Do you know what the least attractive colors are? It is grey scale. Studies show that when icons are in grey scale, the positive reinforcement in the design of those icons is taken away. You have removed one of the tools that steal your attention.

The good news is that grey scale color tones are already preinstalled in our devices. You can go to your phone's settings and then look for color filters. Choose grey scale as your color scheme.

Try it out and see if you feel a lot less likely to tap icons on your phone. It is the equivalent of turning off one of the pleasure switches on your device. Using your phone is no longer as fun as before because of the grey tones.

Life Hack #9: Take the Time to Read a Real Physical Book

A good friend of mine picked up a new hobby—reading actual books. It started when he saw reviews about a new TV series (yes, he's a binge-watcher) that is scheduled to premiere on Amazon called *The Wheel of Time*. It was said that this new TV series was based on a best-selling book series that spanned over two decades.

How could he have missed such a big story? He wasn't much of a book reader. But after learning about this upcoming show, he wanted to get ahead of the crowd. When *Game of Thrones* became such a big hit on TV, he loved it but never had a chance to read the actual books.

This time around, since it is rumored that *Wheel of Time* will be aired sometime in 2021, he wanted to see if he could change the experience a bit. He ordered the full 13-book set and started reading.

Some of those books were thick—and I do mean thick. Book 6 in the series had more than 600 pages in it—man, this Robert Jordan was prolific. He described his world in great detail, and the experience was so immersive.

My friend is now almost done with book 6, and I am just on the first book in the series. If you're reading a real page-turner, then you will be surprised that hours have passed since you cracked the pages open.

It's a great way to get off our screens and engage our minds. Try it. And here's a challenge that I would like you to do: read 30 pages a day. Note that with careful, focused reading, you can do that in one hour.

Life Hack #10: Go Out and See the World

You can beat technology addiction by disconnecting and going out to experience the real world.

Make a bucket list of places you want to see. Save money for weekend vacations to those places.

Going out to see the world doesn't mean your choices are only the exotic parts of the planet. Sometimes that means just getting out of the house. If you have the habit of staying stuck indoors, then spending time outdoors can already become a big improvement.

If you have a yard that desperately needs your attention, then schedule a weekend so you can work on it. Clean up your yard and get things organized.

You can even rearrange your furniture if you have no yard to fix and organize. At least you get to keep moving, and it's a great way to exercise. However, you should still dream about the places that you want to visit. Make your plans and save money for those trips.

QUICK TIP: Go out and jog for 15 to 30 minutes each day or just walk around the block. Do it every day—and I mean every day. If you meet someone, maybe a neighbor you haven't seen in awhile, spend two minutes for a short meet and greet. Savor the human interaction. It's a great way to reconnect with people and get some exercise. We also know that exercise reduces anxiety and depression, so you're also doing yourself a favor .

Lifehack #11: Use Minimalist Apps for Work

Going back to digital minimalism and work, there are apps that you can use at work that will help you to minimize your dependence on digital technology. We already mentioned several of these apps and plugins in the previous chapters of this book. Consider the following apps as additional resources that you can use to apply digital minimalism at work while still using tech for productivity.

Acuity

Acuity is a dynamic cloud-based appointment scheduler that integrates with many services. It even integrates with PayPal and other payment platforms, so you don't need to think about your subscription payments.

Bonsai

This is a freelancer app that you can use for managing your transactions. It integrates with a lot of other tools that you may already be using for work, from managing your invoices to timekeeping.

Gaia/Simple Habit

These apps aren't actually work apps, but you can use them during breaks. Use these apps for two to five minutes to do some guided meditation or mindfulness meditation during a busy day. It can help put some clarity on any tough, challenging day.

Squarespace

This is a tool that you can use for email campaigns, analytics, CRM, and content marketing management. It integrates into many tools, apps, and systems as well, so you don't have to jump from one system to the next. Everything you need at work will be all on one screen.

Offtime

This is an app that will block other distracting apps on your phone, like games and social media. It will even give you analytics on your phone usage so you can monitor how much time you spend on each of your installed apps.

Moment

This is a phone usage tracking app that your entire family can use. It can literally force you to stop using your phone via annoying screen alerts and other notifications.

Stay on Task

This is a productivity app on Android that is useful for someone who can get distracted easily. At certain times during the day, this app will ask you via notifications if you're still doing a task or you're doing something else. It basically reminds you to get back to work.

Lifehack #12: Life Hacks to Save Time on Office Spaces

Psychologists confirm that a cluttered environment reflects a cluttered mind. If you want to practice digital minimalism at work, then you should also practice minimalism in your office.

Here are a few tips:

- You should create as much white space as possible. That means space on your work desk that doesn't have anything on it. Maintain a white space as big as a piece of A4-sized paper on your dominant side.

  That means if you're right-handed, then this white space should be on your right-hand side of the keyboard. If you're left-handed, it should be on the left. You can use this space to sign papers, documents, reports, and organize documents. But as soon as you're doing stuff there, keep it clean and clutter-free.

- Limit the number of supplies you see on your desk. Paper clips, pens, erasers, envelopes, sticky notes, etc. shouldn't be lying around everywhere on your desk.

- Don't over-personalize your work desk. Sure, it's nice to have a picture of your cat or your family on your work desk. It serves as a motivator for you to work hard. But limit it to one or two personal items only.

- Put everything on a file. The file can be placed on the left or right of your computer screen. Use only one file, please. All papers, folders, envelopes, and work-related documents should be placed there.

- If you're using a phone in your cubicle, set it up on the dominant side of the desk. That way, you don't have to reach across to answer a call. You should also put it on the far side of the table away from your keyboard so you won't be tempted to reach out and dial now and then.

- The monitor should be at the center of your desk. It should be at eye level when you're seated on your chair and at arm's length from your body.

Chapter 7: Preventing a Relapse

It is easy for us to relapse into digital dependence, especially if we're just starting on our journey into digital minimalism. It's not going to be easy since it is very easy to open your phone and start tapping on an icon.

Here's an important mindfulness reminder: Even if you make mistakes and dip into your old habits, you can forgive yourself and bring your focus back to digital minimalism. Don't be too hard on yourself. Remember, you're not the first one to make mistakes. Pick yourself up and get back on track.

Here are a few tips that might help you prevent a relapse from happening.

1. Fill Any Empty Time Slots

As you go about trying to find new healthy habits that don't depend on digital technology, you should pay attention to your idle moments. Find something interesting that you can do to fill those idle times.

Remember that one of the lessons that have been emphasized in this book is that boredom is one of the powerful influences that make us reach for our phones and scroll through social media.

You can spend the time preparing a nice meal for you and your family, reading a book, exercising, engaging in a new hobby, or just trying to reconnect with friends. The goal is to try to stay grounded with reality and not jump back to your digital life.

2. Take Note of Your Triggers

Habits have behavioral triggers. For instance, you feel bored, and so your first instinct is to reach for your phone and to see the latest trend on Instagram. You should pay attention to these triggers and recognize them for what they are.

After that, you should try to avert the reaction to these triggers by doing something else. Here are some of the most common triggers that you should pay attention to:

- Financial insecurity
- Strained relationships
- Grief
- Depression
- Anxiety
- Feeling overwhelmed
- Fear
- Traumatic memories
- Isolation
- Loneliness

- Chronic pain
- Uncertainty

You can do mindfulness exercises to help reduce the effect of these triggers.

3. Reach Out to Someone

Whenever you can't help but use digital technology, then use it constructively. One way to do that is to reach out to someone. Check out who you can do a Skype call with. Find friends you can talk to on your messaging app. If you need professional help, then make sure there's a way for you to reach your therapist online.

4. Stay Accountable

In tip number three, the emphasis is on reaching out to get help from someone. This time, you reach out to someone to help *them*. By going out of your way—even when you're using digital tools—you still need to stay accountable for someone else.

You can use text messaging, phone calls, or video calls. The important thing is that you reach out to someone with the intent of helping them. Doing this is an acknowledgment that being alone is hard and that you are not alone in trying to overcome your dependence on digital technology.

Sometimes, when we go out of our way to help others, our own troubles seem less significant. We shift our focus away from ourselves, and in the process of reaching out to help others, we end up helping ourselves.

Key Takeaways

- As a parent or guardian, it is your responsibility to protect and nurture your children from negative influences—digital technology included.
- You can set up rules in the house when it comes to technology use.
- Learn something new, read a book, pick up a new hobby, get creative, use grey tones on your phone, and monitor your screen time.
- There are strategies that you can use to prevent a relapse, which may involve reaching out to someone for help, minding your triggers, and filling up your idle times.

Conclusion

Thank you again for purchasing this book. It is my hope that you enjoyed the content and that the information here has helped you in some way. I hope that you will practice digital minimalism and be free from technology addiction.

The next step is to use the different tips and strategies mentioned here. It takes time and practice to be a digital minimalist. I recommend that you start by doing some decluttering. That is something that you will do time and again—trust me on that one.

After that, you can try the mindfulness exercises until they become sort of a habit to you. It will take time to establish and follow digital minimalist rules in the house and at work, so be patient with yourself.

Give yourself time to reorganize and minimize things. Switching to a new minimalist approach to digital technology may be the best thing you will ever do for yourself at this time.

Book #3
Beginning Zen Buddhism

Timeless Teachings to Master Your Emotions, Reduce Stress and Anxiety, and Achieve Inner Peace

Introduction

Why do some people move on faster than others? Why are most people having a hard time coping with life's stresses and problems? Why are we still unhappy despite all the success we have? These are some of the most common questions we often ask ourselves when faced with struggles and difficulties.

Coping with life might not be as easy as we imagine. We set goals and plans on how we should live our lives, but when reality hits back and goes a different direction, we become confused and anxious. Each of us has personal issues, secrets, dreams, and desires. In most cases, one of them will eat us up, and we tend to lose focus on how to balance our lives.

I remember a good friend whose story fits well here. Charlie lost his father at a very young age. He fondly remembers going to music festivals together where he and his dad would dance and sing to the rhythm of the songs. They shared a really close relationship, and life was never the same.

Charlie was a smart kid; his mom never had problems with his grades and behavior at school. But growing up with a single parent practically meant raising himself. Everything seemed fine until he became an adult, met new people, saw new places, and tried new hobbies.

Going through life with very little guidance to shape his foundations took its toll. Charlie spent most of his time in bars, concerts, and parties, both with friends and strangers, smoking, drinking, and taking drugs. He enjoyed his newfound freedom and the new things he was experiencing. Nothing mattered. It was fun and terrible at the same time, but it also led to a turning point in his life.

When he was 21, he joined a marathon and fractured his ankle during the race. Charlie was then brought to a hospital to have it checked. As he sat quietly but annoyed by the situation, he saw an old man lying in bed, talking to a young lady. The elderly man looked weak and appeared to be crying. Minutes later, the man died. Seeing that brought him back to the day when his father passed. It was like a switch flipped, and just like that, Charlie felt human again. It was weird, but he found it to be one of the most remarkable moments in his life.

Looking back, Charlie realized that life wasn't really that complicated. As many years as a person can be blessed to live, it will feel short and simple towards the end. We are born, we grow up, we live, and then we die. However, in his case, it was ironic to watch a person dying in the same place where fresh souls are being born.

There are quite a few factors in our life that affects our disposition. Every seemingly bad thing has a good counterpart, and our perception will ultimately play a key role in how we go through life.

End and change

Death is inevitable, and so is change—whether it be a change in relationships, status, appearance, and whatnot, it will happen. The secret to conquering these things and achieving happiness and satisfaction comes from within, and we will talk about this more in the succeeding chapters of this book.

Life's challenges

When we were young, we were all told that things would always work out in the end, that everything would be just fine. But as we grew older and saw the world as it truly is, we realized that it doesn't always end well. Life will always throw curveballs and turn what was once mundane into a seemingly unending journey of struggles. These challenges are quite constant; they keep us on our toes. A perfect and conflict-free life is boring. The real challenge here is how we handle the situation. If you don't find your footing, you'll spiral away and find yourself in a losing battle all the time. Things can easily get overwhelming, and the line between rational and irrational decisions becomes blurry.

Distractions

Most of the time, we create problems for ourselves. Not intentionally, of course, but we do. Distractions are all around us, and sometimes, we allow these interferences to take over instead of taking control over the situation.

Typically, there are four types of problems people experience: simple, complicated, complex, and perplexing. We tend to spend all our energy worrying and complicating things. We must learn that problems are unique on their own, and each has a unique way of resolving.

This book could be the answer to all your doubts, questions, and dreams. It was written to serve as a testimony to life's realities, how to survive amidst all trials, and how to achieve real happiness despite suffering. The purpose of this book is not to create false hopes and promises to the readers; rather, it is meant to educate and open minds about how you can positively and beneficially change your life without the risks.

In the succeeding chapters, you will learn about the fundamentals of Buddhism and how its beliefs on life uncomplicate most situations. Understanding the principles behind Zen Buddhism will allow you to be fully in tune with the discipline to fully harness the benefits, practices, and how you can apply this to your daily life.

Chapter One
The Origin and Evolution of Zen Buddhism

"Your purpose in life
Is to find your purpose
And give your whole heart and soul to it."
-The Buddha

In the early centuries, Zen Buddhism was first brought to China by an Indian monk named Bodhidharma. It was during the 6th century that Taoism and Mahayana Buddhism were united, and Zen Buddhism was born.

Commonly called Chan Buddhism in China, it spread in different parts of the world. It was later brought to countries including Korea in the 7th century, Japan in the 12th century, and the West, where it became well-known during the mid-20th century.

Zen Buddhism was coined after "Zazen" and "Buddha," two significant aspects that contributed to the birth of Zen Buddhism.

If you look it up, *zazen* means "seated meditation," hence, it has another definition referred to as a deep intuitive understanding of the natural existence of things, including human life.

Buddha: The Enlightened One

Thousands of years ago, it was believed that there was once a simple yet noble man named Siddhartha Gautama, son of a king of the Shakya tribe, who was living a very abundant life with his family until he became conscious of the inevitable things all related to human beings and of the human life—sickness, aging, and death.

With an earnest desire to search for the truth, he then left his family and the palace, lived in forests, and went to different places where he met various people. He devoted all his time performing deep meditations, reflecting on his life's experiences, and deprived himself of any type of indulgence and earthly pleasure to show reverence to asceticism.

After a specific encounter with a monk, he decided to dedicate his life in search of peace and to resolve all issues on the suffering and death of the human being.

Motivated and hungered for solutions, Siddhartha Gautama studied and practiced all forms of philosophies previously existing. He went to prestigious philosophical and religious schools, which India had plenty of at that time, but none fulfilled him.

It was with desperation and strong willpower to answer his questions that he unquestionably sat down in *dhyana* posture, commonly called *zazen*, and contemplated. He decided to never move from his place until he untangled the mystery behind life and death. According to Buddhist writings, the Buddha did not move in his place under a Ficus religiosa tree for forty-nine days.

After mulling over everything—having to undergo oblivion and conquer his illusions—he found the most ultimate form of inner peace. He found it in his heart, breaking off the barrier between chaos and silence. It was during this time that he was called the Buddha or the Awakened One.

After being enlightened, the Buddha went to the Deer Park in Sarnath, where the holy city of Benares is. There, he had his first sermon, where he shared the subject of the Four Noble Truths.

Because of the genuineness of the *Dharma*, his teachings, he was able to capture the hearts of the people and convince them. He gathered five men who became his disciples later on. This marked the foundation of the Buddhist community.

The Buddha continued his meditations, illuminated his doubts, identified how suffering affected humans, and came up with a method on how one can free himself from it. At this point, he established the foundations of the philosophies that would be taught to generations throughout the years.

After the Buddha has passed away, his teachings began to spread and became the basis of today's Buddhism. More prominently in India, where it became the state religion, the followers of Buddhism established monasteries and advocated missionary works to areas in need.

As centuries passed, Buddhism eventually developed in other countries beyond India. Its philosophies and teachings were passed down in different interpretations contingent to the nation's diversity.

Today, the teachings of Zen Buddhism have reached many different parts of the world and greatly influenced many communities and believers. Three types of Buddhism were formed: Theravada Buddhism, Mahayana Buddhism, and Tibetan Buddhism, to represent particular geographical locations. Each type has its own interpretation and analysis of the Buddhist teachings. Thus, several topics have been linked to it, one of which is Zen Buddhism.

Many have lived by Zen Buddhism up to now, and countless people are still in pursuit of understanding it. With regards to this, we are all invited to start our journey towards a life of Zen by opening our minds and ourselves through the help of this book. In reading the full context, we are guided by the foundations of Zen Buddhism, how it affects our everyday life, and how we can walk the path towards enlightenment.

The followers of Buddhism do not recognize a god or a deity; instead, they virtuously focus on attaining enlightenment. Buddhism's founder and the Enlightened One is not a god. He is neither a son of a god nor a messenger from a god. The Buddha is a normal human being who exerted big efforts to acquire a deep interpretation and understanding of life. As a result, he was able to reach the highest form of state one can attain.

In this chapter, we have tackled the key points of Zen Buddhism, which are:
- Zen and Buddha are two important foundations of Zen Buddhism

- Zen Buddhism originated in China
- The term *Zen* was coined from the word *zazen*, meaning meditation
- Siddhartha Gautama is the Buddha, the Enlightened One
- Buddha is not a god; he is a real person
- The Buddha formed the concept of the Dharma, which will be discussed in the next chapters

Chapter Two

Buddhism: Karma, Suffering, Nirvana, and Reincarnation

"As she has planted,
So does she harvest;
Such is the field of karma."
-Sri Guru Granth Sahib

The principle of Zen Buddhism tells that all human beings are Buddhas and that each one must be enlightened to discover the truth within him.

In a simpler context, to be a human being means to be a Buddha. The mere existence of a human person is already an indication of being a Buddha. The term *Buddha nature* is a definition of *human nature*.

You and I are Buddhas, and each one of us is capable of being enlightened.

During my early years in writing, I realized there is nothing more comforting than enlightening people's minds. Sharing thoughts while earning is incredible but being able to educate is another thing. It is a fulfillment that completes my well-being as an author.

The key concern of Zen is to perceive things as they are, plain and simple. It centers on things as to how they are in a natural state rather than on how and what we see it is. The term *Zen*, as I have stated previously, could have several meanings. It could be a school, a meditating position, or a calm state of mind. However, Zen Buddhism's central efforts are all about the significance of life.

By any means, Zen technically stands as an action; it is something one must do. It could not be explained through words; however, it must be experienced to be fully understood. In other standpoints, Zen is neither recognized as a philosophy nor a religion. It is considered as a meditation practice or an art of discovering self-freedom. To control the mind through meditation is the first step towards enlightening the inner self. Thus, other similar techniques are helpful to escape the mind from logical thinking and allow the mind to wander.

Understanding Karma

Have you done something bad to someone, then afterward, something bad also happened to you? You feel like you are paying for your unjust actions regardless of when or where you did it. It just comes right after you did something. Same as when you did something good, for some reason, you begin to receive help, or some luck comes along.

The law of Karma is a concept that states the relation of one's actions, speech, and thinking towards the aspect of one's life. It is a theory mostly recognized differently in Eastern religions.

Karma came from a Sanskrit word, which means "action." From the word itself, the concept of karma considerably follows the law of cause and effect for every action that has been done. Thus, if one lives or acts in a way that is against the natural harmony of things, for example, involving greed or anger, one may experience conflict or pain. This works the same thing on the other hand. When one's actions are inspired by love and kindness, the person then could possibly be repaid with kindness, such as getting help from other people in the future.

- Two Levels of Karma

There are two levels of how Karma can be understood. The first level, as explained above, is based on a cause and effect situation. When one performs an action, it is expected that he will begin to experience its consequences later on.

One approach of Buddhism in describing karma is its usage of metaphorical examples to describe how planting bad or good deeds could result in bad or good fruits. If you planted a good seed and took care of it very well, you will reap a good fruit in time.

In the second level, karma is based on how one perceives things. It primarily focuses on the quality of one's thoughts or state of mind. Understanding karma on this level comes naturally. When one acts or thinks with a happy state of mind, the person then feels a blissful atmosphere around him; therefore, happiness becoming the fruit of his thoughts.

From a Buddhist point of view, we are capable of facing karma even beyond our present life. This implies that bad actions made during the past or present life can cause bad results in the next life.

Karma serves an important role in a person's life after death. It determines what kind of life or status one will have in his next existence. Good karma can be portrayed as being reborn in a heavenly state or living an abundant life, while bad karma can cause a person to be disabled or miserable in his next life. What's worse, rebirth as an animal or torment in hell could be attained because of bad karma.

According to the teachings and philosophies of the Buddha, there are six realms of existence: the higher realm of the heavens, the human realm, and the four lower realms of torment. The four lower realms are often described as Hell in layman's term. Hell, as we know it, consists of all types of rascals and horrifying elements—beasts, voracious ghosts, demons, and hell monsters. These realms indicate where a soul will go after his death.

The highest realm or state is intended for people who have lived their lives beyond what is in accordance with moral values. They are exceedingly noble and have spent their lives doing good deeds. The second one, or the human realm, is a state where the human soul is considered fortunate since it was reborn again in human form and was allowed to achieve Nirvana or end the rebirth cycle. As for those who chose to live in evilness and cruelty, the last realms of Hell await their souls.

Traditionally, Buddhists believe that even the Enlightened One was not excused from experiencing Karma. There is one renowned story about the Buddha, where one of his cousins attempted to kill him by dropping a large stone on him. The attempt was unsuccessful; however, it caused the Buddha's foot to be injured. The Buddha explained that this resulted from a karmic reprisal for an attempted murder he had planned on doing to his stepbrother back in his earlier life.

If we analyze it, karma is one of the most significant laws that greatly concern the happenings in our life. It is an essential ingredient in one's personal growth. When we live our lives based on what we know, we can reach an understanding of ourselves that others can't take away from us. This is when we are able to experience a great sense of fulfillment and peace.

From an artistic point of view, karma can serve as a law of human nature where one is capable of creating his own reality. We act as though we are artists painting on a canvas, but instead, our bodies, minds, and experiences in life are the mediums of our own life creation.

The objective of Zen Buddhism is for us to avoid the consequences of bad karma. We are cultured to follow Buddha's teachings and principles to help us avoid the occurrence of rebirth. Not necessarily to attain good karma but to be born in a more pleasant state.

Suffering and How to End It

In the Buddha's first sermon as the Enlightened One, he has talked about the *Four Noble Truths,* which expounds the idea of human suffering.

Ancient myths have told that he has come up with this idea upon witnessing four sad events of human existence and non-existence that greatly moved him.

- a.) The suffering of an old man
- b.) The suffering of a sick man
- c.) The death of man
- d.) The modest life of an ascetic (a monk)

It was in these moments that he was able to gather thoughts and deeply ponder on the reality of things in a man's life.

If you notice, the Dharma was overstating the idea of suffering many times, and you may think that Buddhism is just as miserable as it looks. Conversely, the Buddhist community does not view these either as depressing or comforting but fairly, a realistic perspective of natural life. It does not count on the positive side or the negative side but rather on what is actually real.

The idea of suffering does not only refer directly to grief and desolation, but it also acknowledges the existence of happiness and pleasure. However, as realistic as possible, the Dharma depicts happiness and pleasure as somewhat temporary. It only occurs in a short period of time or only during that particular moment.

To understand it better, let us talk about a detailed framework of the concept of suffering. The Four Noble Truths sum up the core of the Dharma. They are the product of the Buddha's awareness and realizations about life and death. Although seemingly vague and difficult to understand, they have endured centuries and were passed down in different interpretations by scholars worldwide.

The Four Noble Truths

First Noble Truth: Dukkha – The Truth of Suffering

The word *Dukkha* is a Pali/Sanskrit word, which means "suffering." According to Buddhist dharmas, the term is defined as "incapable of satisfying" or "not capable of resisting anything." More commonly, it refers to anything temporary or conditional.

The Buddha's first noble truth explains that nothing in the world will make a man contented. Man, in nature, is always hungry and never satisfied, making it the chief cause of all the suffering in this world.

Suffering exists. It is inescapable. The first three events that the Buddha witnessed (man's old age, sickness, and death) are all tantamount to suffering. There is no person on this planet that I have known who is incapable of experiencing distress. Even the richest individual or the luckiest person alive is subject to suffer. We may not know what kind of pain each one of us has to experience, but it is just a matter of time before it comes right before us.

Suffering comes in different ways and forms. It also depends on the gravity of the incident. It can be in the form of depression, emotional pain like anguish or jealousy, or worse, suicide attempts and physical agony.

The first noble truth attests to the underlying consequence of man's existence. We won't find the perfect happiness somewhere else because we are set to struggle in our lives. Life in all its forms is never ideal. In a reflective sense, life doesn't always go the way we expect it to. It is an endless battle to fight for.

Second Noble Truth: Samudaya – The Truth of the Cause of Suffering

In a day-to-day setting where we are involved in disputes and encounter personal problems and issues, it seems easy to recognize the cause of our pain and grief. However, in Buddhism, there is a deeper identified cause of all sufferings, a profound understanding of the root of our difficulties and fears.

The Buddha taught it in his second noble truth, which he described as the Three Roots of Evil, or the Three Fires of Hate. They are as follows:

- **Desire**

The desire to control and acquire things is part of human nature. Man has this unceasing thirst for satisfaction. The second teaching does not tell us that we must surrender everything we have to find real happiness. In that manner, there is a more subtle issue that lies behind it. It is the attachment to the things that we desire that puts us in trouble.

Desires can take several different forms. The most common examples are greed for money, desire for power, craving of carnal pleasure, aspiring to become famous, and even the desire to avoid unwanted happenings such as anxiety, sorrow, jealousy, and rage from happening.

The nature of humans is full of dreams and desires; however, it does not necessarily mean that much of the desires of mankind are destructive and bad. There are also good kinds of desires, such as the desire for peace and enlightenment, though at times someone's pursuit of happiness becomes a craving and, when overlooked later on, turns to greed. This seems to be true at some point in our lives. For instance, we are aware that most people need money to survive, however, others who already have enough want more. These types of people tend to think and do harm unto others for the sake of their wants.

Some people give love and want love in return, yet they could not receive it. Even if it looks like we are asking for the good, the second noble truth teaches us that excessive desire, regardless of the reason, may lead us to peril—or worse, to do evil things.

- **Ignorance or Delusion**

According to the Buddha, the desire initially grows from self-ignorance. We, as human beings, run into our lives chasing things at the same time. We do this for security—to have a sense of confidence about ourselves and the world around us. We tend to get attached not only to material things but also with thoughts, ideas, and opinions concerning ourselves. When this attachment continues, it usually turns to an obsession that makes us exasperated little by little when everything we want does not fall into place. This is where hatred comes in.

- **Hatred**

Consequent to ignorance are feelings of anxiousness built up inside of us. We are filled with a destructive urge, as described in *The Fire Sermon* that the Buddha taught; all is burning. When anger starts to build up in us, whatever we see becomes unpleasant and annoying. And so it goes, that whatever the eyes have seen (eye consciousness and eye contact), be it pleasant, painful, or not painful is burning with the fire of hate, lust, illusion, and anguish.

Third Noble Truth: Nirodha – The Truth of the End of Suffering

In Sanskrit, *Nirodha* means "cessation." To liberate oneself from the chains of attachment is to liberate oneself from suffering. The Buddha became a living example of the third noble truth. He has taught about our possibility of freedom and unveiled the secret to enlightenment.

Unlike the first and second noble truths, which tell us about the darkness of suffering, the third truth gives us hope to look forward to positive things that are yet to come. Moreover, it also tells us that the way out of *dukkha* is to end our attachment and cravings to excessive things.

Nirodha is like telling yourself to stop eating your favorite food. You cannot assure yourself to stop craving from now on just because you've said it. This doesn't work out easily because the conditions you've set for not craving will still exist.

Although it may seem difficult and impossible to cut back on our desires, the Buddha taught us that it is with diligent practice that we can succeed when we are able to see how impermanent everything is and when we can accept that grasping for ephemeral things will never satisfy us is the time that letting go is easier. It is when the craving seems to diminish on its own.

This is the point when we get to experience Nirvana.

Fourth Noble Truth: Magga – The Truth of the Path that Leads to the End of Suffering

Among the noble truths that the Buddha has taught in his forty-five years of sermons, the last one is the most spoken. The majority of the Dharma consists of life teachings about the *Eightfold Path*. In this section, I will talk about the Buddha's cure to suffering—a precept to the end of suffering and how it leads us to enlightenment.

The Eightfold Path, also called the Middle Way, eludes both indulgence and asceticism. Unlike in other religions and philosophies, Buddhism does not centralize the idea of believing in the doctrine alone but by living it and walking the path.

This path touches our day-to-day life in every way. It is a series of lessons and ethical conduct of our everyday activities to mindfulness. Every action, thought, and language is addressed by the Eightfold Path. It serves as a guide towards discipline and reconciliation. Without it, the first three noble truths will remain a theory.

The Eightfold Path

The first two steps of the Eightfold Path constitute a sense of wisdom that is believed to be present in each one of us if only we will open our inner self.

i. **Right Understanding (Sammā ditthi)**

The Buddha's teachings do not intend to be understood blindly by its followers. It is for them to experience and be able to realize if it were true. The first step is for us to understand that life in its ways is inevitable of human distractions, that we are prone to committing mistakes. Yet, we are called to open our minds and hearts of the truth that lies within. This is a momentous step of the Eightfold Path since it interconnects us to the reality of life. Thus, it stands as a preparation for the journey towards the path. In general, all of the Buddha's teachings are merely for practice. They are not created only as philosophies to be believed in or idolized.

ii. **Right Intention (Sammā saṅkappa)**

The second step is where we become faithful to the path. We begin to choose what is right and decide on what is best for us. Basically, Right Understanding demonstrates to us the naked reality of life, including the problems that revolve in it, while Right Intention guides us to where our heart desires.

The first step of the path marks an upfront discussion in understanding the perspective of suffering, its cause, and how we can end it. Now that we are interested in following the path towards freedom, we should begin to apply the perspective of Right Understanding to the intentions we live by so we can be able to identify and assess if our intentions either cause our suffering or not.

Our intentions are the principal basis of what we will think, say, or do. However, there is a deeper implication behind what we only want. It is more about the motive of why we want what we want. For instance, I am planning to buy a car. The basic intention might be for ease of transportation for myself or my family. It may also be for the intention of showing off to my friends or other people. Frequently, there are several intentions present in a desire; hence, if I solely think that my intention is just to impress, I may not consider other more important purposes of buying the car.

The intentions that we live by are significant in contributing to our mental health. They have a major influence on affecting our personality, psychological welfare, and our lives. When our intentions are motivated with happiness, we establish a habit of conditioning ourselves to greater happiness. To do so, the Buddha involved three Right Thoughts, which contradict the harmful intentions that lead to suffering. These are:

- Renunciation (Nekkhamma) - Nekkhamma, which means renunciation of relinquishment from lust, is a Buddhist practice that opposes the insatiable desires of the flesh. In Buddhism, renunciation is not referred to as something one must do, but it is something that one must understand with wisdom (considering the idea of cause and effect).
- Loving-kindness (Metta) – refers to acts of goodwill and compassion to other people, including oneself. It is the opposite of aversion, loathe, and malevolence.
- Harmlessness (Avyāpāda) – is the absence of the desire to injure. It refers to nonviolence and nonaggression.

Right intent requires a judgment emanated from the heart, a recognition of life's goodwill and fairness. It means having the determination and urge to continue the journey despite the hurdles that might come through.

iii. Right Speech (Sammā vācā)

What your mind thinks, your mouth speaks. When someone does something wrong to us, we tend to say foul words out of anger against that person. The quality of our thoughts automatically connects with our way of communicating because we become absorbed by our emotions at that moment.

The aim of the Right Speech is for us to refrain from speaking lies, insults that may cause a revolt, malicious language, and gossip. A rightful mind cannot speak harsh and hurtful speech. We, as Buddhas, must not only speak benevolently but also speak of what is only true. If, for instance, honesty comes with a lash, and it is not that necessary to tell, we just need to remain in "noble silence."

Communicating kindly helps us resolve disputes, unites us to others, and eludes us from living through regrets caused by dissent. By practicing thoughtful communication, we are more likely to come closer to living a compassionate life.

iv. Right Action (Sammā kammanta)

Right Action aims to promote only what is right, more particularly peace and harmony. In the sermon of the Buddha, he enumerated five immoral acts that we must abstain from: killing, stealing, telling lies, sexual transgression, and addiction to drugs and intoxicants. We are obliged to act in accordance with the moral teachings.

Aside from the aforementioned, we as human beings can distinguish what is right and what is wrong, and what can and what cannot harm others. Thus, it is our responsibility to spare any kind of action that is against the moral teachings.

v. Right Livelihood (Sammā ājīva)

Right Livelihood and Right Action work hand in hand. In order to progress towards the spiritual path, man must not only watch his actions but on his source of living as well.

Right Livelihood means that you should withdraw any type of livelihood which causes harm to human beings or animals. Such examples are: work that deals with weapons, liquors, intoxicants, poisons, gun shops, and the like. Slave trade is also discouraged since it deals with human abuse, astrology, and fortune-telling belief is also prohibited since it relies on a fixed future. The Buddha does not encourage certain types of work like these, which he detailed during his sermon.

The last three steps mentioned above (Right Speech, Right Action, and Right Livelihood) are related and constituted to establish moral ethics. Buddhism aims to promote peace and harmony both individually and as a community. This moral conduct serves as the basis of all divine accomplishments. Thus, without them, spiritual development would be impossible.

vi. Right Effort (Sammā vāyāma)

Right Effort, as described in the Eightfold Path, is a positive and balanced attitude towards our actions and decisions. It aims to prevent unwholesome behaviors that might cause evil to arise.

It is an energetic will that promotes optimism, promoting the mind to think of only positive, clear, and honest thoughts. Our minds are wholesome by nature, and the objective of this path is to trigger our thoughts to focus only on the positive things and drop down any form of negativity. Right Effort requires determination and thorough concentration to be fully achieved.

vii. Right Mindfulness (Sammā sati)

In line with exerting great effort towards our thinking, Right Mindfulness guides us to be fully aware and observant of our movements, thoughts, feelings, and ideas. Right Mindfulness asks us to be mindful of the moment; to focus on what is there at present.

When we go to a place, we see different elements—people, animals, buildings, trees. We hear noises—the sound of people chattering, the chirping of the birds, cars passing. We also feel the atmosphere of the place. This is the kind of moment that we have to focus on, not thinking of what will happen next and what we have left behind.

Right Mindfulness does not tell us to exclude our thoughts to the reality existing ahead of us. Thus, it helps us meditate and contemplate the goodness of the present moment. At this moment, we can control our habits and upcoming actions, including our fear.

Listening to a favorite song makes us forget all our worries. It makes us enjoy the moment while it is being played. At times, it puts us in a lighter mood not only when we listen to it, but even after we played it. Essentially, it helps shape our disposition and attitude towards the activities of our daily lives.

This is an example of what the Buddha is telling us. Be it in the form of art, music, a sport, or a hobby, we are all called to always live in the moment.

Have you lived your moment recently?

viii. Right Concentration (Sammā samādhi)

Right Concentration and Right Mindfulness may have a similar objective when it comes to focus. Both teach the mind to see and appreciate things in the moment as they are. Distinctively, the Right Concentration of the mind is a mental discipline where our minds are taught to select thoughts worthy of our well-being. Not everything that we see, hear, and feel must be welcomed; thus, we only need to concentrate on what may be valuable to us in our journey towards the path.

The last aspect of the Eightfold Path leads us to the four stages of *Dhyana*. The four *Dhyanas*, or most commonly called the Absorptions in the English language, allows us to experience the essence of the Buddha's teachings directly. They serve as our entrance to enter the state of Nirvana.

The Stages of Dhyana

1. Before experiencing the *Dhyanas*, one must be able to conquer the five hindrances in Buddhism—sensory desire, ill will, sloth and torpor, restlessness and worry, and doubt. Each of these must be replaced with happy and healthy thoughts for the mind. This is the first stage of the Dhyana.
2. In the second stage, the mind is slowly becoming inactive. There is a feeling of calmness and one-pointedness (Ekaggatā) in the mind. The sense of euphoria in the first stage is still present.
3. In the third stage, equanimity (Upeksā) resides. The feeling of euphoria leaves the body. There is real mental calmness and clarity.

4. In the fourth and last stage, the sensory abilities stop. The state of mind and soul seem to separate from the physical body. Equanimity is the only thing that remains.

Achieving Nirvana

Yes, you've probably heard of Nirvana in other places. The word is so pervasive that its real implication is a lot of times mislaid. Legendarily, the term Nirvana was used by a famous grunge band in America in reference to their actual band name. The meaning of Nirvana is so impeccable that it was personally picked by the band's frontman, Kurt Cobain, in honor of the Buddhist philosophy.

But what does Nirvana really mean?

Nirvana, in Sanskrit, means "to extinguish" or "to blow out." In the spiritual definition of Buddhism, the ones being extinguished are the fires of evil where hate, greed, and lust instigate. As discussed in the previous context, the Buddha enumerated and expounded in detail the Eightfold Path that guides us towards experiencing Nirvana. The eradicated fires must be transformed with deep reconciliation and peace. In a simpler sense, Nirvana is achieved when suffering (hate, greed, and lust) and rebirth are ended.

Other non-Buddhist traditions and philosophies, like in Hinduism, where it is defined as a rebirth of karmic predispositions, have a different interpretation of the term Nirvana. However, the most widely known Buddhist perspective is where the Buddha has exhibited living proof of enlightenment.

According to Buddha, Nirvana is the highest state one can reach. As he defined, one can achieve it at the end of life or in the course of existence.

We must understand that Nirvana is not a place but rather a state of existence. Although labeled as such, the Buddha warns us that whatever we say or conceive of Nirvana would be wrong. A state of perfection could never be described into words alone, especially in an ordinary survival setting. Therefore, it is beyond reason. There is no scientific explanation that can better define the state of Nirvana. It is beyond space and time, and it is a state that can only be experienced.

Through the years, there have been different analyses as to how the Buddha's teachings were addressed. In other scriptures, some people believe that we can enter a place called Nirvana, just like we enter a room in a house. Other beliefs came from the Mahayana sutras, where it was believed that only individuals who are reborn as men are allowed to enter Nirvana. Yet, it was refuted by the Vimalakirti Sutra, defending that all genders, male and female, all social status, and the laypeople are entitled to become enlightened.

Reincarnation

Do you ever wonder why some things seem to have already happened to you? A place or a person looks familiar, or you felt that you used to be someone else?

In several native regions, the belief of having to live more than one life is normal. It is a belief that when a person dies, his or her soul goes out through the nostrils and the mouth, leaving the physical body. The soul then transfers to another body either in the form of a human, animal, or an insect. The belief goes that the rebirth of the person depends on how he or she has lived his or her life in the past.

In Southern Africa, there is this idea that after death, the soul of the person stays near the grave where its dead body was buried for a short period of time. Once it has reached a certain number of days, it will then find another dwelling place or another human body where it will reside.

In other parts of the world, reincarnation is mostly considered in Asian religions. Most especially in India, where Buddhism, Jainism, Hinduism, and Sikhism are all practiced. One thing they have in common is the role of karma in reincarnation.

There are many stories and testimonies from people worldwide as to how they believed to have experienced reincarnation. In many different cases, it was found that such experiences occur most likely in children ages two to six years old.

I remember reading a story from one of my father's books about a young girl who was believed to have reincarnated. It happened the night when she was asleep; she began to mumble unfamiliar words loudly and quickly awakened her parents.

They recognized that she was speaking in the French language, which was strange, knowing that neither spoke French nor had gone outside of the country. The parents of the young girl only knew a little of the language, which gave them a hard time understanding what she was saying. This left them with no choice but to record it.

The young girl was six years of age and had never been exposed to someone who spoke French. Confused, the parents went to a French teacher of a resident high school who could translate the recording. They found out that the girl on the tape was looking for her mother, who seemed to have been missing after the Germans attacked their community. The parents never believed in reincarnation, but the facts given were really unexplainable.

Based on science, the occurrence of speaking a foreign language, which was not purposely learned, among children and adults is uncommon but possible. According to Dr. Charles Richet, a well-known French physiologist and parapsychologist and a recipient of the Nobel prize, there is still a likelihood for such events. This finding was called "Xenoglossy," a term he had coined.

However, for a person of a categorically young age who has limited knowledge and experience, it is quite convincing to consider paranormal explanations with which is reincarnation.

Key Points
- All human beings are Buddhas
- Each person is invited to live a life of Enlightenment
- Suffering exists, and it is an inexorable aspect of life
- The Four Noble Truths explains how suffering is relevant in our life:
    - The Truth of Suffering
    - The Truth of the Cause of Suffering

    - The Truth of the End of Suffering
    - The Truth the Path that leads to the End of Suffering
- The Eightfold Path is eight practices created by Buddha that, when followed, guides us to the path towards enlightenment
- Karma is the result of one's actions in his previous life; it primarily dictates the fate of a person's life in his future existence
- Nirvana is the supreme form of state that one can attain
- Reincarnation is the rebirth of one's soul to a new life after death

Chapter Three
Zen Buddhism: Benefits and Techniques

"Do not let the behavior of others destroy your inner peace."

- *Dalai Lama*

I remember it was a Sunday night in September. I went to a fancy party, where a former colleague from work invited me. I was sitting at a table with other individuals when I met this middle-aged lady I thought was sort of familiar to me. Turns out, I've met her once on a writers' conference way back when I was starting my writing career. I recognized her because she did a talk about Zen Buddhism and how it helped her survive depression.

Ever since, I was always curious about spiritual techniques and philosophical practices. I wondered how they worked and how they affected people's lives. Being passionate about fitness was my way out of the constant hassle and stress of everyday life. I'd tried various activities, including yoga, but I hadn't tried Zen meditation yet. And so I've decided to learn and hopefully master it.

One of the best techniques to practice Buddhism is through meditation. Basically, when we talk about meditations, they often provide us with relaxation and stress relief. It is a given advantage that most forms of meditation provide. But unlike others, Zen Buddhism offers a more profound intention that sets both the human body and soul in harmony. As discussed in the other chapters of this book, the practice of Zen meditation instills in us the values of mindfulness and inner peace. But what is more, is how it can benefit us on a long-term basis.

The main benefit Zen meditation gives in the Buddhist tradition is its ability to provide awareness on how the mind works. Honestly, my first Zen journey was challenging due to numerous factors. When I first tried it, I found it hard to focus, maybe because I was used to the hustle and bustle of the city life.

First Stage

As expected, just like any other day, my schedule was jam-packed with projects, assignments, and commitments that I had yet to accomplish. I had no time or good reason at all to start it, but opportunity knocked. I was given a task where I was assigned to do a short journal article about meditations, so I did it anyway.

I performed my first Zen meditation in my old apartment. I did not have a meditating space, so I just used an exercise mat where I could sit comfortably and placed it beside my bed next to the window, hoping to get a peaceful vibe out of my makeshift meditation space.

It was nearly five in the morning; I chose to listen to an online meditation podcast just like any beginner would. I followed every step earnestly with the best of my abilities, but whenever I close my eyes, my mind becomes active and restless. I couldn't seem to calm my thoughts.

I sat down for a few minutes and tried hard to shut off my mind, but I couldn't. I was totally annoyed with myself for being so cranky. What I was expecting to bring peace to my mind was an absolute opposite. The more I forced my mind to relax, the more thoughts that popped into it.

I also found it hard to turn off e-mail notifications and calls because I was worried that my boss might need me while I was on the verge of my meditating session, and at the same time, I was used to checking my social media accounts. This was the first obstacle I encountered in my first effort to try Zen meditation.

I started doubting if I had what it took to be a Zen person. Hence, after evaluating my experience, I opted to do research and found an inspiring piece from a book where the author emphasized the wrong ideas of Zen meditations. The reality is that we cannot stop our thoughts; we can let them pass by. Zen meditation helps us to be aware of our thoughts without using judgment.

After an enlightening discernment, I have come to realize that it was right and possible. In my attempts to try Zen meditation, I have come up with a few realizations about how it would be best to perform it, especially for beginners.

- Make sure that you are prepared both physically and mentally
- Do not rush; take the time to condition yourself
- Not required, but you may want to allocate space for your meditation
- Try to research and have a background about Zen and its techniques
- Turn off devices and gadgets that could distract you

Second Stage

Through consistent practice, I was able to perform it successfully. I didn't notice it until I finished the session, and I saw that thirty minutes had already passed without interruptions. During the experience, I felt lightness and peace. I felt like I was very light, like that of a feather. There were complete serenity and calmness. The effect to me was somehow hypnotic, and I became sleepier than before. As guaranteed, the effect of Zen meditation was really promising. Evidently, one of its main benefits is relaxation. In science, good breathing relaxation increases the body's oxygen level, which conditions both the mind and the body to function less. In effect, sleeping is much easier and better.

In my attempts to continue with what I started, I switched up my morning sessions to an evening schedule before going to bed. It made my sleeping pattern easier because I was able to sleep immediately after each sitting. It was also surprising because my gadget dependency lessened. I can say that the experience was extraordinary and worthwhile. It improved my day-to-day life and reduced my levels of stress and anxiety.

Third Stage

At this point, I was able to practice it consistently. I made it a point to perform it every week before I go to bed for thirty minutes to an hour or depending on how flexible my schedule was. Practicing Zen was a commitment and, at the same time, an investment. It significantly changed my life for the better, and I become more appreciative of its essence.

On a personal note, Zen taught me a lot of things and helped improve my well-being. It worked wonders in my sleeping pattern and with my way of thinking.

1. **It improved my focus and memory**

   Of all Zen's benefits, the most recognizable is its ability to improve focus and concentration. As stated in various studies, stress causes a lot of issues and problems, including mental function. It directly impacts memory and even intensifies mental illness. When a person is stressed, his memory tends to slow down, and the ability of the mind to focus and retain information is impeded.

   In my case, I was able to accomplish my assignments and projects ahead of time. My usual distractions no longer distracted me because my attention span had improved, and I even had extra time for my sports and other hobbies. Having a retentive memory and a healthy mindset helped me to easily finish my tasks. Also, it kept me away from unwanted diversions that might distract me.

2. **It boosted my mood and confidence**

   Ever since I performed my Zen sessions, I started going to bed earlier and more comfortably. As we all know, getting the right amount of sleep helps improve our moods. Thus, a positive mood leads to a positive way of thinking.

   In my fifth week of Zen meditation, one of my bosses suddenly commended me at work for successfully accomplishing a project at that time. I didn't realize that I was becoming highly energetic and more motivated at work, not until that moment. Since then, I started becoming more confident in myself, and that continued throughout my Zen journey.

3. **It enhanced my creativity**

   Before, I was only into sports and writing. I didn't have much of a hobby until I became interested in music. I think it started when I listened to mellow tracks during meditation. Of all the different genres of music that I have explored, the most remarkable one that fascinated me was classical music. The relaxing and peaceful feeling it gives is what I loved the most about it.

   With great fondness for music, I watched online tutorials on how to play the piano whenever I have the time. Truly, Zen meditation opened me to more opportunities to enhance my creativity.

4. **It boosted my energy levels**

   According to a study at the University of Waterloo, practicing quick sessions of mindful meditation with Hatha yoga involved at least twenty minutes a day can remarkably increase brain function and energy levels. Meditation is a form of relaxation that allows our bodies and minds to relax, providing us with better sleep and a good energy level.

Hatha yoga and mindfulness meditation are two effective practices that allow our minds to limit the processing of unnecessary information so that our energy can be reserved for other activities.

As time has gone by, I have found more ways of practicing Zen meditation. Actually, there are a number of casual techniques on how to apply Zen in our everyday lives. Beyond sitting in meditation, we can also achieve stillness while walking, drinking our coffee, or even while doing our routines.

Zen meditation has a lot of methods that we often doubt and overlook. The most common misconceptions involve its contemplation style and setting. A lot of times, we think we must climb mountains, shave our heads, and be like a monk in order to succeed in it, but in fact, it doesn't really matter.

Regardless of who we are and where we came from, anyone can follow the path of Zen and do well. There are no right or wrong ways of doing Zen. Whether formal or informal, its effectiveness depends on how we perceive and believe it.

The essence of Zen Buddhism inspires us to seek peace and satisfaction from within ourselves. It does not conform to what is common, just like other meditational practices that only provide fleeting benefits. Zen Buddhism's principle emphasizes that we can only attain true harmony through continuous experience and not rely on its idea per se.

As ironic as it might seem, the Zen meditation technique works best when we are busy. This is because it is the time when we need peace and quiet the most. There is an old Zen saying that goes like this: "You should sit in meditation for 20 minutes a day. Unless you're too busy, then you should sit for an hour."

For beginners, you can start meditating for at least five minutes each day. You may start by taking slow deep breaths, listening to soft background music or your surroundings, or just barely looking up to the sky. Take time to enjoy the moment without doing or thinking of anything. You will be surprised that after doing this, your mood has significantly improved. Undeniably, a few minutes of silence is essential to clear our minds from constant noise and stress.

Day by day, increase your time to ten minutes or more until you reach the standard thirty-minute meditation. It is recommended that you find time to do this no matter how busy you are because the effects are worthy in the long run.

Zen meditation techniques can regulate our emotions and mental inclination. When our minds are clear and stable at all times, our thoughts and attitude towards the things around us become more positive. It becomes noticeable in us that we are slowly recreating a better version of ourselves. Hence, the core of Buddhism progressively affects us.

Buddhism is known to be concerned about open-handedness, as it teaches "the more that you give to others, the more you will receive." The concept implies a stylistic expression of how generosity offers us a larger threshold of opportunities. When we are selfless, we do not expect anything in return, which makes us free from imminent distress caused by too many expectations. Thus, people are more than willing to help us if we need help in the future. This goes back to the concept of Karma. Relative to the cause and effect of things, we attract positivity when we live our lives positively; what we do unto others comes back to us in a different form but with the same gravity.

In a common context, Zen practice often encourages us to live a life of compassion and simplicity to avoid unwanted things from happening. According to a Zen master, when we seek inner peace, the more it would be difficult to find it. Hence, when we do not ask for any reward despite extending help, and when we choose other's happiness instead of ourselves, there is a greater possibility of attaining peace.

We learn from this idea that unlike other meditations that provide short-term solutions to life problems, Zen is focused on addressing the main issue, the core of the problem. It delves into a more serious issue that helps improve not only our physical well-being but also our spiritual identity.

The way to achieve peace and openness is not complicated as it seems to be. It is simple, yet requires a thorough effort to understand. Beneficially, when one attains the Zen technique, there will be remarkable changes in a person's life. You do not necessarily need to be a Zen master to prove that it is effective for you. Whether you enrolled in a meditation class or you just learned it by yourself, the effects will reflect in time.

Truly, the Zen technique of Buddhism serves as a medium of self-discovery and self-improvement that is morally upright. In addition, it encourages its followers to become appreciative of everything we have, even in the slightest form. When we look at everything with gratitude, we are able to obtain a sense of happiness within ourselves for the reason that we do not allow pessimism to lead our lives.

Takeaway Points

- Zen Buddhism can help you become a more positive and appreciative person.
- The essence of Zen Buddhism is to seek peace and satisfaction within oneself.
- One can only attain true harmony by continuously practicing the principles of Zen Buddhism and not merely fixating on its ideologies.
- Zen Buddhism can lean you towards the path of self-discovery and self-improvement.

Chapter Four
Buddhism and Mindfulness

"Mindfulness is a way
Of befriending ourselves
And our experience."
-Jon Kabat – Zinn

In our modern world, the mindfulness technique has inevitably gained a reputation in terms of the psychological help it has given to people. There are previous findings that mental rehabilitation based on mindfulness has been effective in preventing the recurrence of depression and anxiety.

In certain mental and psychological institutions, there are proven cases where individuals who suffer from mental illnesses and anxiety disorders have claimed that their perspective of life has improved. Nevertheless, it would be more preferable to say that the technique did not solve their conditions, but it helped alleviate their symptoms.

In other areas, mindfulness is a state of mind; for others, it is a practice. But according to the Buddhist teacher Joseph Goldstein, mindfulness is "the quality and power of mind that is aware of what is happening, without judgment and without interference."

Mindfulness is about cultivating. It aims to create awareness of thoughts and emotions in our surroundings without using judgment. It is a technique adapted from Buddhism to aid us in our typical day to day problems. Palpably, the mindfulness technique instituted an effective system of addressing mental health issues.

Even though there are studies that show how effective it is in providing psycho-biological effects in reducing anxiety, there is no clear explanation as to how it works. Mindfulness and meditation are two important aspects of the success of mindfulness-based mental therapy. Some people have claimed success from the therapies, but for others, it did not work.

Considering that the practice of mindful meditation has brought positive effects to certain individuals because it is indeed harmless and easy to follow, there are also quite a number of downsides. While meditation often leads its practitioners to enlightenment, others are able to resurface negative thoughts and emotions during the sessions. Often, this happens to people who have experienced a traumatic past. Thus, we must remember that the Buddhist mindfulness was not created to serve as a medication to heal us or to give happiness in our life. It is a practice that seeks beyond what is common to our needs. It is a more profound understanding of how we live our lives in a better way.

In different ideologies, the efficacy of mindfulness only depends on how the person handles the circumstances. When practiced carefully and morally, it reduces suffering. Also, when we apply it in our everyday life, we can follow the Dharma teachings. According to the Buddha, the goal of mindfulness is to end suffering. That is why he established the Eightfold Path for us to be guided on how to practice mindfulness effectively.

As the Buddha continued on his sermons, he gave responsibility to his senior monk Bhikkhus, to educate their students about the Four Foundations of Mindfulness.

The Four Foundations of Mindfulness

- *Mindfulness of the Body*

    Practicing the mindfulness of the body means that you should look at "the body inside the body," meaning to say, the Buddha wants us to recognize that our bodies are not unified or barely compact. The body consists of different small parts that are individually formed. It comprises the brain, heart, lungs, teeth, bones, eyes, etc. Each "body" portion is positioned in a much wider body.

    Through this, the Buddha teaches us that the composition of body parts represents a physical form that comes into existence, which only endures in a specific amount of time. The human body is inclined to experience injury, disease, and, eventually, death. Our lives are temporary—so is our happiness. Since our bodies are not permanent, then we can say that our bodies are not ours to keep. Thus, we must distinguish "the body as it really is," as stated by the Buddha.

- *Mindfulness of Feelings*
    Similar to how the Buddha wants us to realize the mindfulness of the body, the practice of mindfulness of feelings is to realize that there is a "feeling in the feeling." Our feelings or emotions comprise of subdivided feelings which are activated at a particular moment when are sensation is stimulated. These are pleasant feelings, unpleasant feelings, and neutral feelings.
    When we are feeling happy, the pleasant feeling is activated. Therefore, neither the unpleasant nor the neutral feeling is present then. This happens the same thing when we are sad or in a neutral state. There is only one feeling currently triggered, and the other two are inactive.
    We are taught to view our feeling this way for us to recognize our feelings as only a part of a bigger emotion. As that particular feeling arises, we notice that feelings are somehow temporary. When we are delighted, it looks like it only lasts for quite a while, but when we are angry, it seems like we have been angry forever. This is the reason why we know feelings could be disappointing sometimes. Due to this, the Buddha calls us to recognize "feelings as they are" and that we are not subject to it.

- *Mindfulness of the Mind*
    Looking through our minds, we might think that the mind is a distinct state. Hence, the mind is just a progression of another mind, which is vaster. The information is sent to our brains once

our senses are prompted at the moment. Our consciousness covers a wide range of senses, which are, as we all know, the sense of sight, hearing, smell, taste, and touch. These five main senses are significant in the processing of our internal intellectual state. The mind is such a powerful space that we can stock up on millions of dreams, thoughts, ideas, and memories in it.

Though, if you will observe, the mind only depends on internal and external factors. It isn't permanent, and it could change from one minute to another. Every feeling passes by in a glimpse. It comes, stays for a while, and goes away eventually. For this reason, we are taught to understand that we are not our thoughts, and we could not be defined based on our thoughts alone. The mind is a channel of constant impermanence. As the Buddha teaches, we should look at the "mind as it really is."

- ***Mindfulness of the Phenomena or the Dhammas***

    The Buddha always teaches us about the context of the dhammas, that we must not only learn it as it is but to understand it more deeply. Naturally, the human being was born with an endless curiosity, and the Buddha supports this, but only what is true and moral. He, too, was ambitious to seek the truth about life, so he did everything to succeed.

    Out of inquisitiveness, he continued his pursuit of the truth in almost everything and even sought the maker, our source of existence. This is where he discovered that no one else and nothing in this world could gratify him. Hence, he was able to discover a more significant point. He found out that man is subject to experience such phenomena in life. Man must undergo birth, growth, aging, pain, illness, and death, all of which are inevitable to mankind, to understand the essence of one's life. The Buddha learned that it is not only a problem that he must battle alone but of each human being. Accordingly, he searched for answers within himself and found enlightenment.

The Four Foundations of Mindfulness are the key things that we should be mindful of. They are intended for us to see things as how they really are, far from our conjectural ideas of them. As a result, we are able to see reality and truth more transparently.

According to Buddhism, there is nothing wrong with human beings. The problem exists because we are not able to understand the nature of reality. Thus, the Buddha aims to help us develop our responsiveness towards reality by providing ways to practice mindfulness.

To help you get started, here is a step by step guide of Applying Mindfulness through Meditation that you can easily follow anytime anywhere:

1. Allocate a quiet space or a room where you can freely perform your meditation. You may want to make sure that the place is peaceful and comfortable. Sit on the floor with your legs crossed, similar to a "full lotus" meditating position. If you find yourself uncomfortable in this position, sit straight on a chair without leaning at your back and stretch your legs with your feet flat on the floor.

2. Place your hands on your lap, as if touching each of your thighs. Maintain a good posture while sitting and ensure that you are not slouching. Look forward and keep your chin up.

3. Relax your posture and keep your shoulder blades engaged to avoid tension. Your lower body must feel the weight, and the upper part must feel lighter.

4. Do not close your eyes entirely. Allow your eyes to gaze comfortably on what's in front of you. Do this for a minute, then slowly look downwards about five feet in front of you.

5. Focus on your breathing pattern. In this state, you are still aware of what's going on around you. Take time to absorb the moment then slowly, listen to yourself as you inhale the air and exhale it through your mouth and nostrils. After each breath, envision yourself being released together with the air.

6. Whenever you feel that you are getting distracted, say the word "Zen" and focus again on your breathing. At this instance, any form of thought, idea, or emotion that could cause interruption of the meditation must be disregarded immediately by means of referring to the term "Zen."

7. Do this until you feel relaxed and refreshed. At the end of the session, you must be able to set simplicity, calmness, and mindfulness in yourself throughout the day.

These techniques seem very easy if you would just barely theorize them, but in point of fact, it takes a lot of practice to prove its efficacy. The application itself requires seriousness and takes time and effort to perform it successfully.

As mentioned earlier in this chapter, the effect of mindfulness on various individuals is visibly manifested in the modern psychological foundations today. According to Professor Jon Kabat-Zinn, mindfulness practice can be brought and integrated into conventional medicine to improve physical and emotional symptoms among patients. He also believed that the practice could show progress in the behavior, attitude, and mental health of certain people suffering from cognitive and emotional illnesses.

Stress happens to anyone, regardless of age, gender, time, and status. It is a normal part of life; however, it may not be the same for everyone. Dealing with stress depends on a person's way of responding to it. What is stressful for me may not be stressful for you, and vice versa. Thus, the skill of mindfulness is intended for those who experience high levels of stress for them to handle it with ease.

Several studies today have been carrying out research involving children and students since they are more willing to participate than adults. Results show that stress has become common not only to adults and to the workforce but also children and teens. The good news is how mindfulness can benefit persons of all ages without causing harm or risks. Mindfulness techniques are safe and enjoyable. They are proven to provide comfort and ease to beginners and long-time Zen practitioners.

Students, especially teens and young adults, are prone to stress due to sleepless nights, pressure, influence, etc., which lead them to alcoholism and drug abuse. Thus, mindfulness meditation can be taught as early as now for them to be prepared at a young age. In one of the studies from the *Journal of American College Health,* four hundred college women who practiced mindfulness were found to have better physical health, healthier eating habits, and improved sleeping patterns than students who did not undergo the practice.

If you will recall in the previous chapters, one of the benefits of Zen meditations is its ability to control our emotions and way of thinking. Thus, numerous findings support how mindfulness is effective in fighting stress.

Stress reduction programs and exercises are mindfulness platforms that involve thousands of practitioners and experts to administer the programs to identified sufferers. Through these specific courses, symptoms of stress, such as a constant feeling of irritability, restlessness, headaches, lack of energy, etc., are alleviated.

The mindfulness technique teaches a breathing pattern that stimulates our senses to relax. With this, we are able to reap the benefits of lowered anxiety levels, blood pressure, heart rate, and even enhanced our ability to deal with certain illnesses.

The Benefits of Mindfulness to the Young and Old

1. Reduces stress and anxiety
2. Improves physical and mental health
3. Reduces risk of depression
4. Improves academic performance
5. Reduces psychological distress
6. Promotes confidence and boosts self-esteem
7. Boosts creativity and tolerance to stress
8. Improves sleep
9. Increases attention span and focus
10. Develops patience and calmness amidst difficulties

Key Points

- Mindfulness can both be a practice and a state of mind.
- Mindfulness can help you get a grasp of reality.
- Stress, worries, and anxieties can affect anyone, regardless of age, gender, and status. They can have severe implications for life. Nevertheless, they can be managed by practicing mindfulness.
- There are a variety of benefits you can get from practicing mindfulness. Likewise, there are numerous programs and exercises that you can try to practice it.

- The foundations of mindfulness are meant for you to understand what things really are rather than believing in your own concepts of them.

Chapter Five
Experiencing Zen in our Everyday Life

"Knowledge is learning something every day.
Wisdom is letting go of something every day."
-Zen Proverb

The practice of Zen Buddhism or Zen does not merely revolve around meditation. It can also be applied to various aspects of our everyday life. Surely, we are all set to experience day to day problems, and the teachings of the Buddha are created to guide us towards a more tranquil and stress-free life.

In our modern world today, numerous distractions tend to disengage us from ourselves and to others. The world is evolving too fast that sometimes we aren't able to get along with it. Hence, the teachings of Buddhism serve as a guide for us to remember how to cope with life.

Buddhism teaches us to learn the art of focus and concentration when we are experiencing confusion. Every day, we are using gadgets and computers to aid us in our work and personal business, and we tend to unconsciously lose our attention to the more important things in our life.

We are so out of focus that we forget to live in the moment. Zen Buddhism not only entails us to practice meditation alone but to bring those learnings in our day to day existence even if our life seems to be full of the hustle and bustle.

One thing about the beauty of Zen is its view of the plainness and tranquillity of everything around us. Seeing a flower, breathing fresh air, or even taking a sip of our favorite coffee, these are the simple things which are common in our everyday lives that we often overlook and forget to enjoy.

Living a life full of earthly possessions, we, at times, get too attached to material objects. This is where the Buddha's teachings come along. Being awakened to the ephemerality of things leads us to acceptance and non-attachment to temporary things, evading us from experiencing suffering. When we do that, we can value more the simplest acts of life, realizing that they are worth living for. Life then is lived in harmony with the body and soul.

What do we do when we are hungry? We feed ourselves to nourish and satisfy our hunger to keep going. Apart from this, it is indeed essential to feed one's soul to see how beautiful life can be. It is not only physically that we live, but by being spiritually full, that makes us truly alive.

When we learn to value simply what is there, we began to see the beauty in everything. Look around and see that all of what exists is made beautifully and uniquely. Unity and harmony invite us to get closer not only to others in the community but also with nature, thus, developing a sense of connection to everything that surrounds us. With this, we are able to manifest in us the values obtained from the Buddha.

One of my favorite sayings that I have followed and lived by personally is an aphorism stated by a monk, Shunryu Suzuki. It goes like this, "Zen is not some kind of excitement, but concentration on our usual everyday routine." Truly, to experience Zen requires more than a feeling. It involves thorough concentration to be fully achieved.

In my everyday life, I always find time to pause for a while from the chaos of the modern world. Taking a short break for oneself is not a sign of unproductivity and selfishness but a useful means to keep going through life. When we begin to discover how to find peace out of conflict and order out of chaos, it is easier to battle our day to day problems.

To help you have a more meaningful life, here are some tips and tricks that might help you find more Zen amidst the confusion.

Zen at Home

1. **Take one step at a time**
   This is a rule that is common to many but rarely followed. Often, we are always in a rush to finish things that we think of doing them at the same time is the best way. Well, multi-tasking could work for others, but to Zen seekers, it may not always be the best way. Multi-tasking tends to cause confusion. Instead, do things one at a time.
   List down all that needs to be done and take note of what should be accomplished first. In this way, you are able to do things in order and with accuracy. Watching while eating, playing games while doing an assignment, talking while working; these are some examples of day to day activities that could be improved if you are seeking Zen. When you eat, finish it first. When you work, focus on it alone.

2. **Allot a quiet hour**
   Sometimes allowing yourself to be alone is a sign of a healthy desire—a desire for peace. It does not technically mean being selfish but more of listening to yourself to discover your inner peace. Finding some quiet hour for yourself can be healthy both physically and mentally. After all the tiring and loud noises that we hear every day, our ears deserve to relax. It is also with silence that we can hear what might be going wrong or what the situation calls for. When we acquire these, we become rationally stronger.
   Before going to bed, you may want to set your alarm one hour earlier than your actual waking time. In this way, you can meditate, gather your thoughts on what plans you have for the day, write down on your journal, or even perform some exercise. The quiet hour is all yours to take, and you can do whatever you want at that time with peace.

3. **Close your eyes and breathe**
   Sometimes when we are full of things to do and do not know where to start, it is much better to just close our eyes, breathe, and relax our minds. This may not look effective but believe me, it is

a good starter for relaxation. Closing your eyes is like shutting off the world for a while to relieve your stress. Thus, it also lets us recognize the beauty of the stillness inside us.

Close your eyes. Calm your thoughts and allow your mind to wander. Listen to your surroundings, and try not to think of anything that may disrupt your meditation. Slowly, take deep breaths at a time. Feel the air going through your nostrils and going inside of your body. Exhale all the negative aura and inhale as if you are breathing the freshest air in the world. Focusing on each breath, you will find yourself slowly getting back to your senses.

4. **Consider productive habits as meditation**

   Meditation is a practice in which you are putting your complete focus on something. It is a means to achieve serenity and composure amidst all complications and confusions. One misconception about meditation is that it is only effective when one sits still and closes his or her eyes. This is the most identified form of meditation; however, there are also a lot of ways to practice it. Cooking, washing the laundry, and cleaning are examples of productive habits that you can consider as a form of meditation.

   How?

   Focus on each chore. If you are cooking, put your entire attention to it. Do not multi-task, or you may end up burning it or ruining it. Concentrate on making a delicious meal and do it slowly and passionately. You will see, food tastes better when prepared with full attention. Same as through with other chores, finish them one step at a time to achieve better outcomes.

   The concept of Zen is not only about immovability but also about focus. When you practice meditation in your everyday activities, you would eventually make it a routine and get used to it; hence, even the most hated chore won't be a burden to you the next time you do it.

5. **Learn to disconnect when necessary**

   Take a period where you don't need to answer phone calls, respond to e-mails, or check social media accounts. It is essential to build healthy boundaries from time to time. Being connected at all times will only cause constant stress due to the continuous flow of information coming in. In instances like this, you are more prone to irritability and a bad temper. Give yourself a break from the busy world. Turn your cellphones and computers off for a while so you can allow your mind to rest.

   Technological advances like the internet and the evolution of social media both have advantages and disadvantages. They serve as a means of communication and news update. However, some studies have shown how frequent checking of social media accounts like Facebook, Twitter, and Instagram may affect a person psychologically and emotionally. Looking at other people's lives and status may trigger envy and a desire to acquire what your neighbor has. So, to avoid these occurrences, concentrate on improving yourself instead of comparing yourself to others.

Aside from disconnecting from these technological devices, it is also fine to disconnect from the people around you. It does not mean that you will cut people off from your life. What you would do is to just focus on yourself and stop checking on other people.

6. **Live a simple life**

    If you observe the life of monks and other followers of Buddhism, they are all living a humble life. They use what is only essential for them. The definition of essential to each human person is different; what may be essential for me may not be essential to you and vice versa.

    The essence of living simply is for us to appreciate even the smallest type of things. Being appreciative of things spares us from the shadows of greed and discontentment.

    Try to get rid of anything unnecessary, especially material things. Separate your needs from your wants to help you identify what you will keep and neglect. What is essential for me is my writing equipment, reading materials, and exercise apparatus. I can live without other things except for these that I have mentioned. As for others, they might not need reading materials; instead, they might need art materials or cooking supplies. There is no specific rule that states what you must and must not have. It depends upon the person's needs. However, you must always consider what is really important in your life and focus on it by removing the less important things.

7. **Find time to be silly**

    Zen is all about finding peace and happiness. It is not bad to be silly sometimes. After all, we live in order to be happy. Life is not all about study and work. Do not forget to laugh and smile once in a while. As we grow older each day, we tend to lessen telling jokes and silly things. Try to make the most out of your day, for tomorrow it may not be the same.

    Laugh while you can and smile often. Sing in the shower while taking a bath, dance while preparing your breakfast, talk to your plants and pets. These are just some of the small things that you can do to make yourself smile for a while. Find time to do what you love, even just for a minute. You will see a big difference in the way you perceive and do things.

8. **Practice a healthy lifestyle**

    When was the last time you had a good run or an exercise that made you sweat? Have you been sleeping enough for the past weeks?

    At times, when our schedules are full and hectic, we don't notice anymore how unhealthy we have become. Due to lack of energy and time, we always resort to "shortcuts" in our everyday living but are they worth it? Instead of preparing home-cooked meals and making salads, we opt to grab on some burgers and instant foods full of artificial enhancers and preservatives. The meals are tasty and hassle-free but remember that it is your health that is at stake.

    Maybe you are also too busy preparing a sales report and presentation for tomorrow that made you stay up late, or were you just being too obsessed with checking your social media accounts, and that's why you were sleepless? During weekends, do you allow at least a thirty-minute walk, or do you choose to collapse on your bed and gobble up some chips and ice cream?

A stressful way of living requires at least some healthy habits too. If you are guilty of these things, you should consider changing your unhealthy routines. To live a life of Zen involves healthy practices to attain a healthy state of mind. Being unhealthy has many side effects and risks; it makes you physically weak, emotionally unstable, and even affects your way of thinking.

9. **Appreciate Mother Nature**

   In our life, we spend most of our time inside the office, our cars and vehicles, and inside our homes. We are so busy accomplishing our duties and responsibilities that we hardly get a chance to visit and spend time outside. During the weekends and holidays, when there is a chance to go on a vacation, most people choose to go to shopping malls instead of parks or gardens. There is no wrong in choosing where you want to spend your time, but you may want to consider spending time alone with Mother Nature.

   There are numerous benefits of interacting with nature (psychologically, cognitively, socially, physiologically, and spiritually). Viewing the sceneries itself relaxes not only our eyes but also improves our moods. Scientifically, it is found that engaging in nature has a reflective impact on our intellects and behaviors. Nature is believed to help us reduce experiences of anxiety and stress. Thus, it helps develop creativity and improves our ability to connect with other people.

   Try to go to a garden or a park. Sit down and observe how wonderful our nature is. Appreciate it and enjoy the moment. Breathe the fresh air coming from the trees, gaze on the greens, and relax your sight. Listen to the rustling of the leaves and the gentle breeze.

   Nature can never be replaced by any type of hotel, mall, or other recreational area created artificially. Our nature is the only one that can provide us with breath-taking scenery, supply us fresh air, and improve our health issues.

Zen at Work

Regardless of what type of job we do, we must practice Zen every so often. Work, typically, is stressful. Whether it is related to your boss, your workmates, or the environment itself, everything related to work seems suffocating sometimes. Due to busy schedules and heavy workloads, we can't take vacations even if we need to. We make the most out of the time given to us in order to meet our deadlines and responsibilities. But how can we be committed to our jobs if we are constantly stressed and unmotivated?

1. **Slow things down**

   In a fast-paced world we are living in nowadays, it is ironic to think that even though technology helps us finish our jobs quicker and easier, we do not use that advantage efficiently. Instead of finding time to relax and enjoy after we have finished our work, we tend to waste our remaining energy abusing the internet, our gadgets, machines, etc.

   As the Buddha taught, to live a life of Zen is to acknowledge what is presently there. Technology, as we all know it, is manmade. Hence, we are all so caught up with it that we forget to enjoy the real things presently happening. Instead of clinging on to your phone, why not engage a conversation with a friend or a colleague? A cheerful greeting will cost you nothing; hence, it may even get you great connections. Learn to appreciate the stillness of the morning rather than rushing off to work just to be absorbed by technology again. These simple things teach us only one lesson—to slow down and delight in life even more.

When we are always in a hurry, we tend to oversight things. Hence, do tasks one at a time to improve your accuracy in doing your duties. Take time to finish one thing slowly but surely. Do not rush. The more you rush, the more you are prone to committing mistakes and missing details.

2. **Set aside work from your "me time"**

Learn to manage your time wisely. Do not let your time for work and time for other things mix up. When you work, focus on your work alone to finish it on time, and you won't have to sacrifice your "me time" for other responsibilities. Try to balance your time for work and play. You may want to create a schedule so you can track your time.

Most of the workforce encounters problems like this because they are not able to manage their time well.

3. **Set daily reminders**

Make a daily reminder of your meetings, appointments, and other errands so you can track your activities for the day. Include photos of your family or loved ones, your pet, your favorite quote, a beautiful destination, or even a background song that motivates you. In doing so, you can be more inspired to work, making you more productive. It also lessens the pressure and stress brought by work.

Daily reminders do not necessarily comprise activities and responsibilities. You can also use daily quotes and Bible verses that help you boost yourself and uplift you as a person. Sometimes, what others think about us is not what matters. It is how we feel about ourselves that is more important at the end of the day.

4. **Do not work while eating**

Eating a nutritious lunch is a proven way to be healthy. It also boosts the immune system. Thus, when we are healthy, we tend to be more productive throughout the day. However, we must take note of where and with whom we eat our lunches. Certain researchers have said that improper lunch breaks have caused fatigue and unproductivity among employees and the workforce.

Hence, the best way to avoid this is to eat inside a cafeteria or a canteen instead of eating in front of your desk. Taking a proper break allows your brain to recharge and detach from the energy-draining issues at work.

Try not to answer calls and e-mails while you are eating. Stay away from things about work that could interfere with your lunchtime. Savor each bite of your food and resist the urge to talk about issues from work during lunch. Enjoy eating your meal, and use your time to rest or take a nap afterward. You may also take a walk or use that time for personal hygiene practices.

5. **Allocate a space or breathing area where you can calm down in times of stress and anxiety**

   Take regular breaks and perform breathing exercises. This is a helpful Zen technique that you can apply during work. It can help you calm your senses and get you motivated again to go back to work.

   You can also practice these techniques while you drink your tea or coffee. A minute of calmness is indeed helpful in stimulating one's mind.

6. **Create a healthy working environment**

   Companies, offices, and workplaces are known to attract a lot of stress and pressure. A lot of times, we even get irritated or angered because of several factors. It may be due to an unfinished or wrong report that got you reprimanded by the boss, an annoying office mate, or you were just late due to traffic. Due to these reasons, we tend to exhibit bad behavior towards our peers.

   By establishing a good relationship with your co-workers, you can create a happy and healthy working environment. Don't look at your superiors, colleagues, and subordinates as enemies or competitors. Instead, treat them as buddies. Appreciate your co-workers once in a while, not only when they have achievements and accomplishments but also with their good qualities.

Zen in Relationships

In Building relationships

Have you met someone, and for some reason, you've already judged him or her by the way he or she gives the impression to you? Most of the time, when we meet people and get interested in them, we are in a rush to know them. We think we've known them already, but really, we might be wrong.

The human mind is primarily empty in nature, meaning it is a state that requires judgment and knowledge in order to be full. An empty mind is always craving for something; hence, it is open for everything. But if we always rely on our judgment of people, we might miss prospect relationships. Deep connections are hard to find. The reason why this happens is because of our rash conclusions that lead to wrong impressions.

The role of Zen in relationships is to empty our minds so that we can be able to receive more wisdom and possibilities. Being able to do so, we understand how significant it is to learn more about a person by being more open and more curious about them.

- **Open yourself**

    The quality of open-mindedness to things is one of the key foundations of Zen Buddhism's beliefs and practices. It is an attribute that allows us to gain more knowledge of a certain person or event apart from the existing familiarity that we know from them. Thus, opening ourselves not only exposes us from a lot of opportunities but also makes us mentally stronger. When we are open to new experiences and ideas, we are honed to become more equipped and excited about the endless challenges that come along in our lives. We become resilient and optimistic in everything, including our relationship issues.

Keeping an open mind is encouraging, but it can be a little bit challenging. The human mind is designed for viewing models of information as a whole. Thus, when our minds receive new information, we tend to undergo a mental process wherein our minds adjust to what we already know.

Misunderstandings and disagreements are a few of the main reasons why some relationships fail. Hence, in this chapter, I will share some proven ways that could guide us towards becoming an ideal open-minded person.

- **Intellectual Humility**

    Being intellectually humble is a method of thinking in which a person does not resist any type of knowledge or information he or she is given, even though it is unfavorable in his or her part. Instead, he or she is more attentive to learn from others.

    Researches have shown that sometimes, being well-informed about something can lead to closed-mindedness. This is for a fact that when we believe that we are knowledgeable of something, we tend to stop learning about it because we think that what we know is already enough.

    Because of that, real experts tend to be essentially humble about their knowledge. They believe that learning never stops and that there is always something to learn from others. So, if you think that you already know everything, odds are you don't.

    With this, we know that being closed-minded often leads to cognitive ignorance. It limits our wisdom of what others know and the opportunity to establish a relationship with them.

- **Take some time**

    Before judging what you see or hear, take a little bit of time to listen and consider what others have to say. Commonly among us humans, we tend to instantly disagree when someone talks about something. Instead of trying to listen, we easily heat up and prove how wrong the idea or the person is.

    The problem with this kind of thinking is kin to our fast emotional response. Often, it is easier for us to criticize than to accept the diversity of things. As an alternative, giving ourselves an ample amount of time to mull over and evaluate thoughts before judgment can avoid arguments.

    Being open-minded technically requires cognitive effort. If you aren't willing to consider other ideas and opinions, it may be really difficult to be open-minded. Dogmatism, in all its forms, contradicts the concept of what Zen Buddhism tries to demonstrate. Thus, to avoid this, taking a short time to evaluate your response first is recommended to avoid careless judgments and decisions.

Characteristics of an Open-minded person that can help build or save relationships
1. Believes that others have the right to share their beliefs and feelings
2. Welcomes other people's opinions and respects them
3. Does not get angry when wronged
4. Appreciates other people's suggestions and ideas
5. Loves new learnings and growth
6. Thinks positively even when things don't go as expected

In Saving Relationships

- Listen more, talk less

    When your partner or one person talks to you, do you listen to a reply or to understand? This is a good question to consider, especially when saving relationships. Most of the time, we are in a rush to solve problems, which is why there is this natural tendency in us to only just communicate and not comprehend. When we merely communicate, we are only talking without addressing the topic or the problem. But when we comprehend, we are giving our full attention to the person and the topic.

    The good thing about this concept is its applicability to every type of relationship—from a beginning friendship or a long-term relationship. Misunderstandings happen at times. Whether we are creating friendships or saving relationships, the best thing that we can give to a person is respect and understanding. When we are able to make someone feel understood, we are giving them an extraordinary gift that not everyone can give. With this, a sense of trust is being established in both parties.

Becoming Stronger in Relationships

- Let go

    Break up, death of a loved one, feud with a colleague, misunderstandings, traumatic experiences—these are some of the many reasons why a person can feel frustrated and lost in life. Such events are expected to be experienced in this world. It is part of human nature to get caught up with such episodes at a certain point in our lives. Consequently, the Buddha's teachings encourage us to persevere amid difficulties.

    The path to enlightenment aims to free us from any form of hatred and resentment towards a person or an experience in the past. By letting go, we can understand ourselves more deeply, become stronger, and be exposed to all kinds of predicaments that we may encounter in the future.

    Letting go means you are willing to let go of anything, big or small, that holds you back into living your life peacefully and freely. If you have any emotional baggage from past experiences, you may start by listing them in a journal. Each day, write about what you feel. Have you been okay lately? What are the things you are currently up to? Are there things bothering you? Ask yourself these questions and evaluate your present situation.

Take time to heal yourself from past trauma and help yourself recover. Sometimes, all it takes to move on is to just accept what has gone, let it go, and find something to look forward to.

Key Points

- Zen Buddhism is more than just practicing Zen meditation. It can be applied to various aspects of life.
- Zen Buddhism can help you learn how to let go and achieve freedom. It can help you heal and move on.
- You must learn to let go, no matter how big or small it is.
- Zen Buddhism teaches you to adopt the right traits and/or characteristics that are necessary for achieving true happiness and peace.
- A life of Zen is a life that revolves around the present moment. It does not hold on to the past or get anxious about the future.

Chapter Six

Transforming Your State of Mind through Kindness and Compassion

"When there are thoughts,
It is distraction:
When there are no thoughts,
It is meditation."
-Ramana Maharshi

Life, as you know it, is difficult. This is why compassion is necessary. Everyone is prone to injuries and diseases. Everyone has a life that inevitably starts and ends. Everyone encounters unexpected events and experiences. No one can ever escape the uncertainties of life.

It would be much easier to go through life with compassion. When people work together, journeys become more bearable. There is a Buddhist tradition that describes this. It says that just like others, you wish to be happy. Likewise, just like everyone else, you wish to be free of suffering.

Such recognition of common yearning and fear is where compassion stems from. Although compassion may not be very easy, its general view is simple. Compassionate individuals are sensitive to suffering as well as committed to trying to prevent and alleviate it.

Take note that suffering must not be confused with any positive emotions, such as love, because the most difficult form of compassion is for those who you love. Likewise, it is much more difficult to have compassion towards people who are not like you. You have probably felt more compassionate towards those who share similar interests or points of view with you.

In addition, your experiences in life may also diminish your ability to receive and give compassion. More often than not, those who attend therapy get entangled in psychological loops that hinder their ability to receive compassion from themselves or other people.

Nevertheless, it is possible to break such loops when you become aware of the way your brain works. In other words, you can break from your psychological loop if you can be aware of your own awareness.

Once you are able to do that, you can start to cultivate compassion. You can learn how to cultivate compassionate thinking, compassionate attention, compassionate behavior, and compassionate feeling. You can also learn how to be open towards the suffering of other people, aside from the suffering in yourself. This would help you act towards alleviating such suffering.

The Relation between Suffering and Your Brain

According to biology, your brain is created by your genes. Hence, you did not have any control over its development. It was controlled by evolution. While it is true that your brain can do so many great things, such as finding ways to treat and cure diseases, it can also do a lot of awful things, such as starting a war.

The way your brain has evolved means that it can give you trouble. In fact, you have two brains—an old one and a new one.

Your old brain has desires and motives that have already evolved years ago. You share this experience with other animals. Just take a look around you and observe your surroundings. For instance, you may notice that your pet dog avoids things that may harm it. It may bark at anything that looks unusual. It may also be territorial and possessive. Moreover, dogs are naturally concerned with hierarchy. This is why there is such a thing as an alpha dog.

Humans are just the same. They are also concerned about their status, particularly in society. They like to be part of groups as well as are inclined to develop friendships and personal connections. They are also naturally inclined to reproduce and take care of their offspring. Furthermore, humans do their best to avoid anything that might bring them harm. They also feel happiness, sadness, anger, and a wide variety of emotions.

Then again, humans are a lot different from other animals. Millions of years ago, ancient humans began to evolve and developed intelligence. This explains why you are capable of reasoning, visualizing, using symbols, and using language.

This new brain of yours is amazing when you use it wisely. Then again, you have to keep in mind that this also depends on the way you use it with your old brain.

Say, you spot a lion and a zebra in the same area. Once the zebra sees the lion, it would surely run away. This is its natural instinct. It knows that its life would be in danger if it does not stay away from the lion.

Your old brain works the same way. It has a primal instinct to detect and respond to threats. So, when the zebra successfully escapes, it would head back to its herd to eat and live. It would not recall the recent event.

Then again, there is a new brain. It is what makes humans different from wild animals. Since you are a human being, you would think about the possible consequences of your actions. You would ponder on what just happened. You would also probably wonder what you could have done differently if you were in the position of the zebra.

This is also the reason why you think about the future. Your new brain allows you to plan ahead of time so that you can increase your odds of getting what you want. You can also think of the steps that you may have to take in order to stay safe and secure.

Even though this is helpful and beneficial, it is also quite disadvantageous. Anxiety, for instance, is a usual result of thinking using your new brain. The threat may have long been gone, but your new brain still holds onto it. It simply cannot let go that easily.

Human beings tend to run simulations in their heads. They tend to ruminate and visualize "what if" scenarios. If they are not able to control their thinking, they can become anxious and depressed. They can also be in constant fear of the future.

The Emotional Memory

Humans also have an emotional memory. For example, you love holidays. Whenever there is a holiday coming up, you become excited. You look forward to the festivities and seeing your family or friends. You start to pick out clothes or even shop for new ones. You are always in a good mood when there is an upcoming holiday.

But what happens if you experience something bad during your favorite time of the year? Say, you get beaten up by a random group of men. They robbed you, and you eventually end up in a hospital. Your holiday is ruined. You no longer associate your favorite time of the year with fun and festivities. Because of this unfortunate event, you no longer become excited. Even worse, the incident has left you traumatized. You become anxious every time you remember it, especially around the holidays.

This very same mechanism works with children who experience trauma in the hands of their parents or caregivers. Humans have an attachment system in which part of their brain facilitates the loving connection with their parents. Then again, this part also gets connected to the fear system. Hence, if a child grows up in a toxic environment, he tends to form unhealthy attachments with other people in adulthood. His emotional memory becomes unpleasant, and he becomes prone to mental health disorders.

A lot of people have mental health issues. They become stuck in a loop, ruminating about the things that make them fearful and anxious. They solely focus on the negative; they reject the positive.

It is important to take note that this is not their fault. They simply have an old brain threat bias. According to Dr. Rick Hanson, a psychologist and author, the brain works like a Velcro for threat-biased and negative things. Conversely, it works like a Teflon for positive things.

Mindfulness as the Solution

Humans indeed have an old brain and new brain that makes them happy and sad and courageous and fearful at the same time. If you ever feel anxious at times, you should not worry too much about it. Know that you are also capable of reconciling your new brain with your old brain.

You can use the mindfulness technique. It involves moment-to-moment awareness of feelings and thoughts. Every human being is capable of being aware of awareness. Thus, you are capable of observing and learning about the tricks that your mind plays on you.

Mindfulness is such a vital and wondrous evolutionary quality. In fact, it is akin to the development of a visual system. Take light, for instance. It exists. However, it cannot be perceived by anyone or anything that is not capable of being aware of it.

Since you are a human being, you are capable of being aware of light as well as life. Unlike wild animals, you do not simply go throughout your day eating and sleeping. You also spend time thinking of what you want to do, such as losing weight and becoming fitter.

With mindfulness, you can understand that attention is similar to the spotlight in the sense that whatever it focuses upon becomes brighter and emphasized. So, in your mind, whatever thought you focus upon would become more profound and affect you more significantly.

To help you understand this further, you can try visualizing yourself going on a vacation. Imagine that you have finally gone on the trip of your dreams. You are feeling very excited. You have finally experienced going to your dream destination and doing what you have always wanted to do all your life.

Focus on this thought for one minute. Observe your body. What happens when you dedicate an entire minute to this thought alone? Do you feel any sensations? What are these sensations?

When the minute has passed, you can purposely think of something else. Switch your focus and attention to another thought, particularly one that worries or concerns you. Focus on this thought for one minute, and just like what you did before, observe its effects on your body. Does the concerning or disturbing thought make you feel differently? How does it make you feel?

While attention or focus can bring things into the spotlight, it can also take it out of it. It can bring things into the dark. For example, you are doing your Christmas shopping. You go inside ten shops with nine of them having very helpful sales personnel. In one of the shops, you encounter a rude salesperson. This person makes you wait and does not answer your questions about the products being sold in the store.

Because of this experience, you are able to remember this one rude person out of all the others. This particular salesperson stands out from the rest of the sales personnel you have encountered throughout the day. Even if you go to more shops, you will still remember this person if the sales personnel in the other shops are also friendly and helpful.

When you reach home, you may still think about your recent experience. You may ruminate and think about possible consequences. You may have "what ifs" as well as wonder why some people act that way. You may wonder whether you should report the incident to the store manager or just let it go. You may also wish for the rude salesperson to lose his job.

This puts you in a loop. You stay in an anger system for a significant period of time. You do not think of the other sales personnel who were friendly and helpful. You merely focus on the one who was rude and unhelpful to you. The helpful ones stay in the dark while the unhelpful one stays in the spotlight. This example shows how people forget a huge part of their experience by focusing on just one thing, particularly a negative one.

Then again, the moment you notice what your mind is up to as well as determine why it is up to it, you can take control over your attention. You are also able to use it practically and mindfully.

So, going back to the previous example, you can purposely bring your thought back to the other nine helpful sales personnel. You can exert effort to remember how friendly and nice they were to you. You can recall how you were able to find what you want and felt happy about it. Such thought can put you in a good mood and allow you to forget about your unpleasant experience with the rude salesperson.

When you take this step, you can break out of your anger loop. Nonetheless, this step requires your attention, which is the key to developing compassion.

Keep in mind that compassion stems from your brain system. It has a lot to do with motivation and intentionality. When you orient yourself towards compassion, you can change the entire orientation of your mind.

The key is to understand and know that you have the capacity to purposely select your basic motivational system. For instance, you can consciously choose a motivational system for caring and then cultivate it. You can also make it grow through consistent practice.

In addition, you have to know exactly why it is important to do this. Well, you need to do this because it changes your brain and gives you more control of your life.

Courage and Compassion

With therapy, you can develop compassion. You can be trained to recall and observe kindness as well as build upon your memories. Matthieu Ricard, author and Buddhist monk, says that the mind is like a garden that grows naturally. If it is left uncultivated, it can be influenced by external elements such as the wind. It can also be affected by the changing weather. Some things tend to grow large, while others tend to shrivel. In the end, some of the results may not be favorable to you.

As a human being, you have the capability to understand how and why you need to cultivate compassion within yourself. This, in turn, would let you heal and reorganize your mind so that you can become the person that you want to be.

However, you also need to be courageous. For instance, if you are agoraphobic, you have to do some modifications to your behavior. You will not achieve compassion by always staying at home, wallowing, and doing easy things. You need to have the courage to face your fears as well as overcome your anxieties.

In essence, there are two kinds of courage: physical and emotional. Many men possess physical courage, but only a few possess emotional courage, which involves the ability to navigate into areas of deep pain and suffering.

When you have compassion, you would be able to move in these areas. However, you also need to be prepared to confront and alleviating the pain within yourself.

Your old brain and new brain can both be a blessing and a curse. It all depends on how you use them. Your old brain, in particular, should be used wisely. You must not allow yourself to get lost in your basic motives and emotions. You must also refrain from being distressed and too affected by the issues of other people.

Thanks to evolution, you have been given an extraordinary competency that allows you to sense and experience the consciousness of consciousness. The nature of your mind is so wonderful that you can cultivate the necessary emotions in your life. You can be awakened and enlightened.

Key Takeaways

- Humans are evolved creatures that possess both an old brain and a new brain. Your old brain makes you akin to wild animals while your new brain differentiates you from them.
- The old brain and the new brain can both be a blessing and a curse depending on how they are used.
- It is necessary to learn how to use your new brain properly in order for you to reap its benefits and/or rewards. If you are not able to use it wisely, then it will not work in your favor.
- Kindness and compassion can transform your state of mind and allow you to be free from worries and stress.
- Humans are wonderful creatures with lots of possibilities. They can cultivate compassion as well as understand why it has to be cultivated within oneself.
- Compassion may not be very easy to develop. Nevertheless, it can be done with the help of therapy.
- Mindfulness can solve problems that relate to stress and anxiety brought about by human feelings and thoughts.

Chapter Seven
Center Your Life and Awaken Inner Peace with Zen Buddhism

"Meditation makes the entire nervous system
Go into a field of coherence."
-Deepak Chopra

The Zen practice is the way to true happiness and peace. Zen Buddhism shows you the way. The Buddha taught people how to achieve enlightenment. However, he did not elaborate on what it was.

It is important to note that concepts may have a certain importance. Then again, it is the actual path that is much more important. Simply thinking of what something may be like without actually knowing it or walking the path on your own does not really matter.

Zen Buddhism is about direct experience. When you study the schools of Buddhism, make sure that you study the "sutras" or the texts as well as practice using your direct experience.

Remember that the Buddha told his disciples to never follow or believe in anything that they merely heard. They should not readily follow anyone, including himself, without proper judgment.

This part of Buddhism is appreciated by many, including myself. Doing something based on blind faith alone is indeed ridiculous. One must always study the text and use wisdom to verify its authenticity. Each and every one of us is gifted with a wonderful mind. Therefore, we should use it.

The practice of Buddhism can be ultimately described as the process of working to gain moments of insight, including the ones gained from direct experience.

What Zen Is All About

True change can only happen when we experience things for ourselves. This might seem a little overwhelming, but it is necessary. Hence, you must not hesitate to ask yourself questions that would eventually lead you to the right answers.

Keep in mind that Zen is about slowing down. More often than not, people live in such a hurry that they no longer become mindful of what they are doing. They tend to go on autopilot and do everything on a routine.

While it can be practical to go on your daily routine, it can also hinder your spiritual growth. Speeding things up to save you time robs you of the opportunity to reflect, meditate, and practice mindfulness. You need to learn how to slow down when necessary. Do not worry because you will still be productive.

Other things that people want are fame, power, and money. Sadly, many of them believe that these things will bring them genuine happiness. With Zen, you will learn that this kind of thinking is wrong and dangerous. If all you do is chase after success and material wealth, you will not be content. You will not feel any satisfaction, no matter how rich and powerful you become. You will not be happy.

Zen is about being peaceful, content, and happy. Zen is also about having understanding and compassion. You must not harbor ill feelings towards others. You must learn to forgive and let go. It is only when you can do this that you would truly heal and be at peace. Furthermore, you must remember that everyone is connected intrinsically. So, whatever you do onto other people, you also do to yourself.

Through Zen, you can achieve genuine happiness and peace. It can teach you how to work from within yourself, see through illusions, discover your real nature, and break free from attachments.

Let's say you have your own business. Your business should treat everyone with compassion. Teach your employees to nurture and support the well-being of one another. Likewise, they should learn how to treat customers and/or clients fairly.

When you do not solely focus on making money, you can treat other people and yourself with compassion. This would allow you to achieve genuine happiness and peace.

How Practicing Zen Changes Lives

The practice of Zen is recommended to everyone, regardless of age, gender, or social status.

Zazen or Sitting Meditation

Zazen, also referred to as sitting meditation, creates a significant impact on the lives of people. I, myself, for example, have never been prone to anxiety and stress. However, when my first child was born, I have begun to feel as if time constantly runs out. I recalled my past actions and thought that I had not had any major life achievements. As a result, I forced myself to do something great; but this only made me more prone to anxiety and stress.

One day, I learned about Zen Buddhism, and I was fascinated. So, I started meditating right away. Several weeks later, I noticed that my anxiety and stress had been significantly reduced. It was as if I was a completely new person! I realized that practicing meditation has made me more productive and less stressed. My chaotic mind has finally attained peace.

Through Zen Buddhism, I became a much happier person. I now find contentment in everything. I feel happiness in everything I do. I also feel more resilient. Each time a challenge comes my way, I can face it without worries or doubts. I know that I can do it. I know in my heart that whatever outcome I get, I can surely accept it.

For this, I highly recommend zazen or sitting meditation. If you are a beginner, you can find tips and information online. There are plenty of websites and articles that you can check out. You can also watch tutorial videos or read books about this topic. Once you have been introduced to this practice, you can start living a new life using Zen Buddhism.

Mindfulness Meditation

Frequently, people become so immersed in their jobs and daily chores. Rather than become mindful of what they are doing, they move on autopilot. This causes them to miss out on the beauty and wonders of life. They become so focused on their work that they no longer have time to relax and refresh their minds.

Through mindfulness meditation, you can reprogram your life. Mindfulness is actually meditation in action. According to Thich Nhat Hanh, Zen master, mindfulness is about keeping your consciousness alive to the current reality. In essence, it means following your breath.

Every living creature breathes. So, no matter what you do, you breathe. This is why breathing is such a good anchor. When you keep your focus on your breathing, you remain grounded in your present moment. Whether you walk, talk, or do something else, you can focus on your breath. When you do this, you practice mindfulness.

You see, there are lots of advantages to mindfulness. So, you should always take a moment to notice and follow your breath. You can also practice mindfulness as you walk, sit, or lay down. This can help you regain a sense of happiness and peace and allow you to regain control of your emotions.

Like I mentioned previously, I used to have a chaotic mind. It was only when I learned about practicing meditation that I was able to gain peace. I used to be anxious and worried about not having enough time for my tasks. I was always in a hurry.

Now that I have learned to practice meditation, I no longer feel the anxiousness or the need to rush everything. I feel that I have ample time to do everything I have to do. No matter what I do, I feel that the moment is mine. This allows me to be more peaceful yet productive.

You, too, can be peaceful and productive at the same time. Mindfulness would nourish your mind and body. It would enable you to find genuine happiness and peace instead of the shallow and temporary fixes of material things and nonsensical activities.

Compassion Cultivation

Through Buddhism, you can learn about developing compassion. Compassion is a major aspect of every Buddhism teaching, including Zen. According to the Dalai Lama, compassion is not merely a passion emotion but rather an aspiration. Thus, one must work on expressing it towards other people. When you can do this, you can realize the real nature of your existence as well as discover a deeper sense of happiness and peace.

The teachings of the Buddha also emphasize enlightenment. For you to achieve enlightenment, you need to have compassion and wisdom. Some people find this difficult, but it can be done in simple ways.

For example, you can start by being kinder to other people. As you continue to do this, you would eventually realize that it is fulfilling to do something good for other people without expecting anything in return. If you still harbor the thinking of needing to get something in return, then you are not yet truly wise and enlightened.

The illusion of self is, in fact, the greatest illusion. Through compassion, you would see this truth. Once you become enlightened, you would awaken from such illusion. You would learn how to eradicate attachments and illusions as well as look deeper within yourself.

Discovery of the Real Path to Happiness

A lot of people think that the real path to happiness involves money, success, and power. However, this is not true. Material wealth, for instance, only brings shallow and temporary happiness. Even those who believe that chasing their dreams would make them happy are wrong. The truth is that genuine happiness exists within yourself, not outside.

When you can use mindfulness and live fully in the present moment, you can achieve happiness and peace. Use sitting meditation to look deeply within yourself and treat everybody with compassion. Do not worry because this kind of happiness is unlimited. You can renew it as much as possible, as long as you take control of your happiness.

Learning About Mindful Consumption

Everything you use and consume creates a significant impact on your life. So, everything that you eat, watch, listen to, and take makes you the person that you are.

If you are like most people, you probably complain a lot about your job, your boss, your co-workers, your relationship, etc. You also probably talk about others behind their backs or engage in gossip and drama. All of these actions have a negative impact on yourself.

Fortunately, you can still bounce back and have a mindful consumption. Take one step at a time. For example, you can begin with quitting television and reading a book instead. Whenever you have free time, you can pick up a self-help book to improve your wellbeing. Ditch the habit of watching television, for it does nothing helpful to you.

You can also learn a new skill by watching tutorials. Likewise, you can expand your knowledge by reading articles or listening to podcasts. Do your best to more productive during your free time.

Next, you should work on your communication skills. Improve your conversations with people at home, at work, and in the community. You can enroll in language courses and take classes, whether offline or online. You can practice what you have learned by being more outspoken, engaging in small talk, and joining clubs. Make your social circle bigger so that you can communicate with more people.

These simple activities are effective in helping individuals make changes that have profound results. Keep in mind that it is easy to change the things that you consume as well as change the ways you act and feel. What's more, it is all right to be imperfect. You may devise plans and end up not following them exactly. That is all right, as long as you stay focused and continue to create progress.

Discovery of Your True Nature

If you aim to find the purpose of your life, you cannot use Zen to do that. However, you can use Zen to discover your true nature.

A lot of people are searching for their life purpose, and many of them are searching in the wrong places. Through Zen Buddhism, you can fulfill your desire to feel found and connected. This is even though you do not find your purpose.

You will learn that the part of your nature that you see is not really you. The "small you," which you see is not your true nature, but rather the "big you" that you have to discover.

Thich Nhat Hanh explains that the "small you" is merely the phenomenal world or the world you see and know. It is merely a wave. The "big you," on the other hand, is the noumenal world or the ultimate dimension wherein there is no separation between you and others.

Take note that Zen Buddhism is not about understanding, but rather about gaining insight and direct experience. In order for you to start heading to the path of gaining insights and learning about your true nature, you need to practice. This means that you have to practice Zen meditation.

The takeaway is for you to know that what you want is not a sense of purpose but rather a sense of connection. You want to connect to the whole world around you.

In general, this sense of connection with others can cause you to want to contribute to the greater good. When you contribute, you will be able to find a deep sense of connection with others.

There are so many things you can do throughout your lifetime. Nonetheless, whatever you opt to focus on, see to it that it lets you help other people. This would make you feel the sense of fulfillment and sense of connection you have been searching for.

Simplification of Life

Through Zen Buddhism, you can learn how to make your life simpler yet more fulfilling. If you practice mindfulness and Zen meditation, the mental and physical illusions that have been right in front of you would be naturally revealed. This, in turn, would free you from any desires for material things that you may have.

Now, you have to take note that there is nothing wrong with wanting more for your life. You can desire a better job, a bigger house, a newer car, or more money, especially if your reasons are justifiable, such as wanting a much better life for your family. Then again, even though this is the case, you still have to remember that true happiness and peace will not stem from material things.

The Buddhist practice states that one must be aware of the illusions that are present around him. He must see reality as it is. Likewise, he must see the illusion as it is. This is primarily referred to as mental illusions in Buddhism.

There isn't a separation. The physical things in your life exist because you found them necessary to be there. The moment you realize that an idea is merely an illusion, you will be able to set yourself free from it.

Seeing clarity is a good natural byproduct of Zen Buddhism, and it is something that everyone can benefit from, especially today. Then again, you must keep in mind that it is only possible to properly understand Zen through direct experiences.

You can read all the books you want, watch every video online, or take tons of classes, but it is only when you have had a direct experience that you would truly understand Zen.

Key Points

- If you want to make significant changes in your life, you must learn to practice Zen Buddhism.
- Clarity is a natural byproduct of Zen Buddhism that many people can benefit from.
- It is only through direct experiences that you can truly understand Zen.
- Zen Buddhism focuses on gaining insights and direct experiences, not merely trying to understand its concept.
- As a human being, you have both a "small self" and a "big self" that you need to fully understand in order to get to know yourself.
- The actual path of Zen Buddhism is much more important than its concept.

Chapter Eight
Zen Is for Everybody

It Can Be Practiced by Both Beginners and Individuals Who Are Either Continuing With or Returning to Buddhism

"Zen is not some kind of excitement,

But concentration on our usual everyday routine."

-Shunryu Suzuki

Buddhism is a spiritual tradition that mainly focuses on spiritual growth and development. It also focuses on the attainment of a deeper insight into the real nature of life. According to Buddhist teachings, life is endless and filled with suffering, uncertainty, and impermanence.

Buddhism is regarded as an ancient Eastern religion by many people, specifically those who turn to it to help them deal with various mental health issues.

Now, even though a lot of people have already turned to Buddhism, there are still some who are still confused and skeptical about it. They want to find out why it is preferred by many and whether or not it is worth practicing.

Before we discuss this topic further, let us first have an overview of why Buddhism is ideal for beginners, including Westerners, and why many people are into it.

Why Do People Like Buddhism?

First of all, it is important to note that Buddhists are generally not aggressive at seeking out converts. Unlike other religious groups, they do not give out brochures or stand on the streets to prompt strangers to adopt their beliefs. They usually go about on their own until others seek their help for conversion or assistance.

Buddhism is also not dogmatic. This means that it does not believe in demons or devils. Buddhists do not believe in dogma, so they have the freedom to study and examine the doctrine of Buddhism. They are not prevented by lies and fears to think outside of their beliefs.

Likewise, Buddhists do not believe in a god or deity the way Christians do. They do not believe that there is a "God" who sits on a throne in heaven and watches everything that man does. Instead, they believe that nothing is permanent or fixed in the world, and that change is always a possibility.

With this being said, Buddhists do not live in fear of suffering for eternity if they do something that does not please "God." The belief that there is permanence is a cause for suffering.

According to Buddhist teachings, there is no state of good or bad that lasts forever. Everything is impermanent, and that the path towards enlightenment is through the development and practice of morality, wisdom, and meditation.

These are the primary reasons why more and more people are turning to Buddhism. Even those who have left to explore other religious practices have come back due to the numerous benefits the Buddhist philosophy gives them.

In addition, a lot of people do not like the conservativeness of certain religions, such as Judaism and Christianity. They also do not appreciate being told to do a certain thing or have a particular belief to be "saved." They prefer to live with an open mind and a conscience, but without the dogma.

Buddhism helps people achieve enlightenment and inner calm. It encourages them to look inwards as well as develop compassion, which is the way to overcoming fear and suffering. So, when you practice Buddhism, you would need to master yourself rather than solely believe and rely on a god.

Why Do People Turn to Spirituality and Religion?

There are various reasons why people turn to spirituality and religion. For instance, anxiety, deprivation, fear, and frustration can be factors in driving a person towards prayer and faith.

When people experience grief, hopelessness, or fear, they may look for an outlet or external source that they believe might save or help them. Both positive and negative experiences and emotions can drive people towards spirituality and religion.

This is why most people pray when they feel hopeless and desperate. They pray that their loved one be healed from a sickness, their relationship is fixed, or their financial status gets better. It is not surprising to find churches filled with devotees who pray to their chosen deity or saint for divine assistance.

Conversely, people also pray when they are overjoyed and grateful. They pray to give thanks for the blessings they have, such as getting a new job or winning a competition. Published studies by Saroglou, Buxant, and Tilquin have explored the causal relationship between spirituality and religion and positive emotions.

Also, self-growth motives can lead people towards spirituality and religion. Aside from the compensation needs in the cognitive and affective sphere, spirituality and religion can also be characterized by the motivations that denote self-development and self-realization.

Furthermore, spirituality and religion can play a crucial role in mental health. Sadly, many people who suffer from mental disorders do not have enough money for therapy. This is why they enroll in meditation classes, which are far less expensive. These classes help alleviate the stress and anxiety that they feel.

According to a Pew Research Center study done in 2012, about eighty percent of Americans claim that they practice spirituality and religiosity. About twenty percent, on the other hand, claim that they do not believe in religion.

It was found that many people generally turn to faith as a form of support and solace, especially during stressful situations. Certain groups, including minorities and seniors, also tend to turn to faith rather than family and friends.

Those who deal with major stressors in life, such as loss of a loved one, divorce, serious mental and physical illnesses, and natural diseases, tend to find spirituality and religion helpful in their coping. This is especially true for those who have limited resources in dealing with uncontrollable situations.

Key Points

- Buddhism is a spiritual tradition that focuses on spiritual growth and development.
- Buddhism is not dogmatic. Buddhists do not believe in deities.
- Buddhist teachings state that no state of good or bad lasts forever because nothing is permanent.
- People turn to spirituality and religion for a variety of purposes.

Chapter Nine
Center Your Life and Attain Inner Peace with Zen Buddhism

"Before enlightenment, chop wood and carry water.

After enlightenment, chop wood and carry water."

-Wu Li

For those who are not that familiar with Buddhism, the first noble truth may seem quite gloomy. Buddhists believe that life is filled with misery, pain, and suffering. You go through life experiencing stress, anxiety, natural disasters, family problems, broken relationships, physical and mental illnesses, and financial losses, among others. Then, you die.

Yes, you may experience happiness at certain points in your life. However, you still cannot deny the fact that there is suffering. Suffering is inevitable. Nobody can escape from it.

The Buddha believed that one's attitude towards life events is far more important than broken legs or thunderstorms. By nature, humans tend to consistently desire things that they do not have. Conversely, they tend to dislike the things that they do have. Such an attitude causes them to experience mental anguish.

According to Buddha, sufferings are mainly experienced due to the endless sense of lacking permanent and basic security. Life's happenstance just cannot provide it.

In addition, the Buddha claimed that there is a way beyond suffering, and it involves replacing ignorance with the wisdom of knowing. When you can possess this kind of wisdom, you will be able to forego suffering.

Essentially, you must practice being "right," which means being mindful. You need to be mindful of your speech and actions, for example, to live a good life or a life with the Zen spirit.

I believe that everyone holds a pearl of intuitive wisdom within themselves, and it is this wisdom that hits their interconnected and harmonious nature. Likewise, it is this wisdom that brings the world together in harmony and peace. This wisdom is the very spirit of Zen.

Zen Meditation and the Real Key to Happiness

Zen mainly emphasizes the practice of meditation. It emits an essence that directly speaks to those who practice it. Zen can be an antidote to a variety of problems in the modern world. You can read about this in the Introduction of the book Zen Keys by Thich Nhat Hanh. The Introduction was written by Philip Kapleau, an author and teacher of Zen.

Contrary to what most people believe, the real key to happiness is neither wealth nor fame. The real key to happiness cannot be found externally because it lies within yourself. Buddhism teaches people that the more you give, the more you gain. You must also be aware of interconnectedness as well as appreciate every little gift that life offers you.

The more your compassion and concern for other people grow, the more personal fulfillment you will achieve. Keep in mind that if you search for inner peace, you will not find it. You must learn how to give up the idea of this reward and focus on the happiness of other people to create lasting peace. This is the true Zen spiritual dimension.

Zen helps the mind achieve calmness. When you meditate, you allow yourself to reflect with improved creativity and focus. You are also able to improve your health. Some of the benefits you can get include lower levels of anxiety, stress, and blood pressure. You can also have a stronger immune system as well as sleep better.

So, what are the Zen meditation techniques that you have to learn? Well, you should take note of the following:

Breath Observation

When you meditate, you must be in a comfortable position. For example, you can choose from the Burmese, Seiza, or Half-Lotus poses during zazen. Ideally, you should sit on a cushion or padded mat. However, if you do not have any of these items or cannot sit on the ground, you may also sit on a chair.

You must direct your awareness towards a particular object and focus on your breathing. Notice the way your breath moves in and out of your system. Doing this would foster a sense of alertness and peace.

Quiet Awareness

When you practice quiet awareness, you do not repose on any focal point, such as your breath. Instead, you allow your thoughts to move through your mind without rejection, judgment, or grasping. This practice is known as "just sitting" or *Shikantaza* in Japanese. It is practiced without any object of meditation, content, or anchor.

There is no need for you to aim for anything when you practice this meditation technique. You just have to sit and allow your mind to move freely. Remember that zazen is the end and not a means towards it.

Intensive Group Meditation

If you are truly serious about meditating, you can go to a temple or meditation center. This practice is referred to as Sesshin by the Japanese. During this time, you practice intensive meditation through sitting meditation.

A session can last between thirty and fifty minutes. You can switch to walking meditation from time to time or take a short break. When it is time to eat your meal, you must be silent. You must also use an oryoki bowl if possible. Likewise, when it is time to do work, you must be mindful.

Of course, when you practice Zen meditation, see to it that you practice it with mindfulness energy. You must be completely aware of every moment. Meditate with single-pointed awareness.

For example, when you clean, you must be completely present for this act. When you are with your loved ones, you must be completely present for them. When you relax at home, you must be completely present for it. Do not allow anything to distract you. Refrain from occupying your mind with anxieties and worries.

You should also meditate naturally and simply. Understand that less is more. When you can accept this, your state of mind will improve. You must learn how to accept things as they come and go.

What's more, you have to be loving and compassionate. Be concerned not only for your well-being but for the well-being of other people as well. Keep in mind that everything and everyone in this world is interconnected.

Develop the habit of doing one thing at a time. Zen monks believe that it is much better to single-task than to multi-task. For example, when you have to pour water in your cup, you should pour water in your cup without doing anything else, such as listening to the morning news. Likewise, when you eat, you must focus on eating. Do not eat while watching TV or reading the newspaper.

Zen monks also do things deliberately and slowly. They do not rush their activities. You, too, should develop this habit. Rather than act randomly and rushed, you have to act in a deliberate matter.

Focus on a particular task. Refrain from moving on to another task without completing the current one. Then again, if there comes a time when you do not have any other option but to do something else, you should at least try to set aside your unfinished task and then clean up.

For example, when you make a sandwich, you should not begin eating until you have put away the bowls, spoons, bread knife, and ingredients that you have used. You should not begin enjoying your meal until you are done wiping your counter and washing the dishes. Once you are done cleaning up, then you can go ahead and enjoy your sandwich. Your first task, essentially, is cleaning up while your second task is eating.

As mentioned previously, doing less is doing more. Zen monks are not lazy, but they do believe in doing less and not rushing things. They wake up early in the morning and start doing their chores. Their days are filled with tasks, but they do not try to accomplish everything in a day if it means having to rush them. They do their chores slowly, deliberately, and completely. They focus intently on every task they do. Once they are truly done with a certain task, then that is the only time they move on to the next one.

You should also learn how to put a space between tasks. This is similar to doing more with less. It is a way on how to effectively manage your schedule so that you can have ample time to complete your tasks. As much as possible, you have to refrain from scheduling everything so close to one another. You must always leave room between them to take a short break and refresh your mind. Having a more relaxed schedule allows you to focus better on every task.

Do not forget to have your ritual. Zen monks, as you know, have rituals that guide them in everything they do, from meditating to eating to sleeping. Rituals give things a sense of importance. So, if a task is important enough for you to give it a ritual, then it is important enough to be completely focused upon. There is no need for you to follow the exact rituals of Zen monks. You can develop your own. Just make sure that you stick to it.

Of course, you also have to make time for everything that needs to be done. You need to allot a particular schedule for a particular task or activity. For example, you need to designate a specific hour for taking a shower, preparing a meal, eating, commuting to work, doing work, and meditating.

This practice helps you develop a habit so that you can do such activities regularly. When you have a habit, your mind and body automatically get into doing the task. Do not forget about it. Thus, you can successfully do it.

Devote some time to siting. Zen monks practice zazen or sitting meditation daily. They allocate a specific hour for this activity. Sitting meditation allows them to focus on the present moment. You, too, should practice sitting meditation to clear your mind and relax your body.

Besides practicing sitting meditation, cooking and cleaning are also regular parts of a Zen monk's day. These chores also allow them to practice mindfulness. You can have this ritual too. You can treat cooking and cleaning as forms of mindfulness meditation. Completely focus on these tasks as you do them slowly.

Furthermore, you have to live simply. Only use what is necessary. For example, rather than have a closet filled with shoes, you can give away the pairs that you do not use anymore and just keep the ones that you use. Likewise, you should get rid of the clothes that only serve as clutter in your closet. Refrain from buying new things, especially if you merely want to follow the latest trend in fashion.

Zen monks live simply. They only think of what is necessary. They do not buy trendy clothes, shoes, and bags. They are not fond of the latest gadgets. They do not even eat fancy foods. Most of the time, their diet consists of rice, soup, and vegetables. They only have the basics, but they are happy and content. This is what living a life of Zen is all about. You can be simply but still happy.

Key Points

- The noble truths of Buddhism are well understood by those who truly know Buddhism.
- Buddhists believe that attitude towards life is the most important of all.
- Practicing Zen meditation can lead you to the path of true happiness.
- There are various Zen meditation techniques that you have to learn in order for you to be able to practice Zen meditation properly.
- Following in the footsteps of Zen monks and living like the way they do can help you achieve true happiness and inner peace.

Chapter Ten
A Beginner's Guide to Daily Zen Mindfulness

"Mindfulness isn't difficult,

We just need to remember to do it."

-Sharon Salzberg

Developing the habit of meditation is among the best things you can do. Meditating is simple, yet a lot of people still fail to practice it regularly. It is easy to meditate anytime, anywhere.

You can enroll in a Zen center and receive guidance from a teacher, but you can also choose to practice Zen meditation on your own. You can meditate while sitting on a bus on your way to work or sitting in a coffee shop. You can simply pay attention to your breathing as you go through your day.

If you have a hectic schedule, don't worry because you can still practice Zen mindfulness. You may simplify the process by being mindful as you walk or take a shower. Being busy is not an excuse to avoid being mindful. If you are truly willing to do it, then you will surely find a way.

How to Practice Mindfulness on a Daily Basis

If you have never practiced mindfulness before, you might be wondering how to begin. Do not worry because this is a natural reaction of people who have never meditated in their lives. This chapter would help you get started as well as guide you towards finding your own mindfulness style.

Now, you must remember that there are numerous ways to meditate. However, your concern should not be to find the perfect form of meditation, but rather one that works best for you. This way, you would be able to practice mindfulness daily without feeling like it is a chore or burdensome task.

As a beginner, you can start with just a couple of minutes per day. Two minutes should not take up much of your schedule. After all, you probably spend a great deal of time procrastinating by watching TV shows, playing video games, scrolling your social media feed, or engaging in gossip.

Instead of wasting your precious time on these nonsensical activities, you should devote at least a couple of minutes to practicing mindfulness. If you think that you can devote more time to it, then you can start with five minutes.

The key is starting briefly. You should go from small to big if you want the new habit to stick. Once your mind and body get used to allotting two to five minutes for Zen mindfulness, then you can go ahead and add more time to your meditation session.

See to it that you choose a time as well as a trigger. It is up to you if you want the time to be specific or general. For example, you can choose to practice mindfulness meditation at 6 am every day before getting ready for work. Conversely, you can also choose to practice mindfulness meditation in the morning, regardless of what time it is. Go for whatever works best for you.

A lot of people find early morning and late evening best for mindfulness meditation. It is during these times when your mind is fresh and ready for being mindful. When you wake up in the morning, your mind is not yet bombarded with work or school issues. You have not yet faced anyone who may give you troublesome thoughts, such as your spouse, colleagues, or classmates.

Likewise, many people choose late evening for mindfulness meditation because they are finally able to relax their minds at this time. When you get home from work or school, you no longer have to deal with anyone who may cause you anxiety. You are already preparing to go to sleep. Thus, your mind is ready for relaxation.

Nevertheless, you may also choose to practice mindfulness meditation during other times, such as during your lunch break. If you have one or two hours of midday break, you can use this time to meditate. Close your office door, and do your best to relax. If you only have a cubicle, you can stay seated and close your eyes. Do your best to relax your mind and meditate, even for just a few minutes.

Once you have chosen a time, you should choose a trigger. It has to be something that you already do regularly. For example, it could be waking up in the morning and getting out of bed. The moment you get up and fix your bed, you should begin practicing mindfulness meditation immediately. You must do this activity before you do anything else, such as going to the bathroom to shower or going to the kitchen to eat breakfast.

Of course, you need peace and quiet to be able to meditate properly. Choose a quiet spot in your home. This can be a vacant room, for instance. It can also be your bedroom if you have nowhere else to go. Simply go to a corner or stay at the foot of your bed to meditate. See to it that you turn off anything that might cause unnecessary noise, such as your smartphone, alarm clock, TV, or radio.

Ideally, you should also talk to the people in your household if you do not live on your own. Inform them that you practice mindfulness meditation every morning, and you need to have some peace and quiet during this time. Ask them politely to avoid disturbing you when you meditate.

You may also go out to practice mindfulness meditation. Gardens, temples, parks, and beaches are great locations. If you like nature, you will find peace and solace in these areas. Just make sure that you also come prepared for possible external distractors, such as bad weather, animals and insects, or other people in the vicinity. You can bring sunscreen and an umbrella. Ensure that you are also dressed properly to keep you warm in cold weather and cool in hot weather.

Proper posture is very important as well. You can meditate while sitting or lying down, although sitting is more ideal since you might fall asleep if you lay down. Also, sitting is more practical in settings such as your office or outdoors.

You can try the half-lotus or full-lotus positions. They are highly recommended for meditation. Then again, you can still sit the way you want, depending on your comfort level. You can sit cross-legged or with your back against the wall. You can use a yoga mat or add some pillows or cushions if you are meditating on the floor. You can also sit on a stool, a bench, a couch, or your office chair, but make sure you are comfortable enough. Your comfort level is important so that you can refrain from fidgeting and being distracted.

When everything is ready, you may begin your mindfulness meditation session. Meditate for just two minutes. You can use an alarm clock or a timer to help you keep track of time.

Take note that this is crucial. A lot of people think that they can handle long hours of meditation when they are not. This is especially true for beginners. A lot of them tend to overestimate their capacity.

As a beginner, two minutes is already enough. Five minutes is plenty. Do not attempt to go beyond this because you may not be able to handle it. You might only exhaust yourself or lose focus. Fifteen to thirty minutes of meditation for beginners is not advisable.

Then again, once you get used to practicing mindfulness meditation, you can increase your time limit. Just make sure that you do it gradually. Allow your body to get used to the activity. Soon enough, you will be able to practice mindfulness meditation for thirty minutes to an hour.

The practice of mindfulness meditation is not a competition. There is no need for you to compete with other people or even yourself concerning how long you can meditate. You are not undergoing a test of how long you can stay seated on the floor with your eyes closed, and your mind focused on being mindful.

You are adjusting your time limit because you want to develop a long-lasting habit. In order to do this, you need to start small. You need to start with just a couple of minutes and then gradually increase your time limit.

For example, you can practice mindfulness meditation for just two minutes for one week. Then, you can increase your time limit to five minutes for the next week. You can increase it even further to seven minutes for another week. An interval of two minutes should allow your mind and body to adjust to the change.

You can then go for ten minutes for another week or two. Fourteen straight days of ten-minute mindfulness meditation can prepare your body for an even longer period of meditation. When you become successful in this, you can add five more minutes to your session. This becomes fifteen minutes of mindfulness meditation for three weeks.

If you think you can handle more time, you can move on to twenty minutes and stick to this time limit for four weeks or one month. It is up to you when you want to move on to thirty minutes to an hour. Again, there is no competition in meditation. You have to meditate based on your preference and comfort level. The key is having the self-discipline, determination, and willingness to stick to your new habit.

Keep in mind that it is necessary to focus on your breath. Always notice the way you breathe in and breathe out. When you inhale, observe the way the air goes into your nose and your throat. Then, follow its movement into your lungs and belly. Observe it as you exhale and let it out of your mouth.

As a beginner, you may have a bit of a hard time doing this. So, you may count with every breath to help you stay on track. Do not worry if you ever lose track. You can always start over.

You should also pay close attention to your thoughts. If you find yourself having unnecessary thoughts, gently bring your focus back to the present moment. It is common for beginners' minds to wander during meditation. Just do your best to stay focused. As you continue to practice mindfulness meditation, your mind would get used to it and no longer wander around.

How to Expand Your Practice

Once you have devoted an entire month to practicing mindfulness meditation, you may try expanding your practice. Here's how you can do this:

Sit and pay attention to your breath

Believe it or not, this simple act is already mindful practice. It is a way to train yourself to stay focused. You must sit in a quiet location for an adequate period of time. Do this on a regular basis until you get used to it.

Whenever you are stressed out, you must stop for a minute and pay attention to your breath. When the minute has passed, you can bring your mind back to the present moment.

You can also try to take a walk to clear your mind. Rather than worry about the things that you have to do for the day, you should pay attention to the sensations of your body and your breath. You should also observe your surroundings as you walk.

Each time you have a meal, you should focus on eating. Observe your food, its taste, appearance, and smell. Observe the way the food makes you feel. Focus on your feelings and sensations as you eat.

Tea is well-known worldwide to produce a calming effect. So, you can also drink tea as a mindfulness ritual. Keep your attention focused on your movements as you prepare and drink the tea. Observe the way the tea smells, tastes, and feels against your mouth. Stay focused on your breath throughout this ritual.

Furthermore, you can practice mindfulness as you do household chores. When you sweep the floors or wash dishes, you can stay focused and mindful. Pay attention to the activity alone. Refrain from thinking of or doing other things as you complete the task.

The Five Precepts of Buddhism

Those who are serious about adopting the Buddhist lifestyle tend to live with the five precepts. They have a shared objective, which is to achieve a state of enlightenment or nirvana. They do their best to become the best versions of themselves. They also believe that following these precepts will increase their likelihood of having a better life in their next rebirth.

So, what are these five precepts exactly? It is important to take note that these precepts are not rules, unlike the Ten Commandments of Christians, but rather lifelong undertakings that you must live by if you wish to become a better person.

1. **Do not kill**

    It applies to everything and everyone. So, you should not kill people, animals, and even insects. It is because of this particular precept that highly devout Buddhists stay vegan or vegetarian.

2. **Do not steal**

    It means that you should not take anything that does not belong to you. Some examples are money, food, and clothing. You should also refrain from hoarding items. In case other people need help, you should also be willing to extend a helping hand.

3. **Do not exploit or abuse**

    You should not exploit or abuse anything or anyone physically, mentally, emotionally, and sexually. Highly devout Buddhists live a life that does not include sexual activities. Then again, you can still practice Buddhism even if you do not practice abstinence. Just make sure that your partner is also an adult who gives you consent. Moreover, you have to learn to be content with what you have.

4. **Do not lie**

    Buddhists greatly value the truth. This is why you must never lie. Likewise, you must not keep secrets or hide vital information, especially if they would benefit the public. You have to stay clear and open.

5. **Do not use drugs**

    It means that you should not use recreational drugs, psychoactive substances, and hallucinogens. Avoid anything that can change your state of mind for the worse, as this can inhibit your ability to be mindful. As you know, practicing mindfulness is a critical element of Buddhism.

Alan Watts and Zen Mindfulness

Most of those who practice Buddhism and mindfulness know Alan Wilson Watts, more popularly known as Alan Watts. If you have never heard of him before, he was a British speaker and writer who popularized Buddhism in the West. He moved to the United States in the 1980s to study Zen.

However, Watts had quite an unconventional point of view with regard to Zen, mindfulness, and Buddhism. According to him, Zen was a worldlier version of Buddhism. He claimed that Zen Buddhism was practiced by the Chinese because they did not like to sit around for hours and are interested in a philosophy that incorporates sex, work, and everyday life.

Watts believed in thinking for yourself and not following any pre-existing beliefs or established rules when practicing Buddhism. He also believed that Buddhism was an early form of psychotherapy.

Then again, instead of saying that depressed individuals tend to suffer from belief systems that are harmful and inaccurate, he said that humans, in general, suffer from belief systems that are harmful and inaccurate. In other words, everyone is somehow crazy. Hence, everyone can benefit from practicing Buddhism, not just those who are depressed.

Most people identify Zen Buddhism with an ascetic lifestyle that typically involves shaven heads and robes. They also believe that it includes vegetarianism and pacifism, with a major emphasis on sitting meditation or zazen. What's more, they think that they have to have a strict spiritual practice in order to achieve enlightenment.

Watts believed otherwise. He was a known adulterer, sensualist, alcoholic, epicurean, and smoker during his lifetime. He had a bohemian and joyful approach to the practice of Buddhism. He did not believe in following a specific lifestyle to reap its rewards.

With this being said, you can choose to follow Watts' approach if you do not feel comfortable following the conventions of Buddhism and Zen mindfulness. Zenism does not make any prescription on how you must behave. There is no need for you to chant, wear orange, be a vegetarian, or even believe in peace. You just have to see straight and directly, with a mind that is not blocked.

For Watts, Buddhism does not have a specific moral code. He did not encourage anyone to behave in a certain way. He simply advised people to cultivate a particular condition of the mind, and that is a liberated mind. After all, it is not likely that you would want to do any harm. So, if you are liberated from the requirement to be good, then you may be good. Then again, it should also be noted that living a life of "sin," such as one that involves drugs or crime, cannot help achieve liberation.

Watts also said that there is no need to practice meditation. He claimed that zazen was unnecessary. This is such a huge contrast to the typical notion of Buddhism. How else can you practice Zen Buddhism without meditation? Indeed, Watts' point of view became highly controversial and led to many attacks from the Buddhist community.

It was widely believed that the main objective of Buddhism was enlightenment or samsara. It involved floating above worldly concerns and not suffering from attachment anymore. It was about being detached.

However, Watts did not agree with this concept. For him, trying to be "above it all" and detached was being "drunk on Zen." Being detached does not mean being perfect. You can be detached and still experience problems, desires, and frustrations.

In order to free your mind, you have to detach from a particular set of ideas. More often than not, people become too attached to their family, friends, pets, job, and material possessions. They fail to realize that the more ordinary life is, the more Zen it is.

Watts taught his followers that Zen is merely an attitude or a life orientation. Likewise, he claimed that detachment does not involve inoculation from emotions. It is not necessary to waste emotions attempting to accomplish the impossible.

Conventional Buddhist philosophy involves the Four Noble Truths, which were discussed earlier in this book. Watts, however, had a different definition of such precepts. He was not interested in following any instructions for living. This was probably why he skimmed over the Eight Noble Truths or the Noble Eightfold Path, which were often viewed as invocations, suggestions, or instructions.

Instead, Watts concentrated on the spirit of marga, which was about the middle way or the balanced life. Incidentally, it did not mean "moderation in all things." The Middle Way should be distinguished carefully from mere moderation or compromise. In essence, it is the first life principle since everything, and everyone who is born comes from the union of two opposites. It refers to a balanced life.

If you do an in-depth study of Watts' concept of the Noble Eightfold Path, you would realize that it does not have a dictionary definition. The truth is that Watts' understanding of Buddhism was generally about being in tune with oneself and not having any desire to do wrong. It was as simple as this.

Key Points

- Zen Buddhism and mindfulness can either be practiced conventionally or unconventionally.
- It is up to you if you will follow the way of the Zen monks or the philosophy of Alan Watts.
- Buddhism involves precepts that help guide those who wish to practice it. However, these precepts are not like the Ten Commandments of the Holy Bible in the sense that they are not specific rules to be followed but rather lifelong undertakings that can help you become a much better person.
- As long as you can achieve your goal with Zen Buddhism and mindfulness, you are doing all right.

Conclusion

"When we get too caught up in the busyness of the world,
We lose connection with one another – and ourselves."
-Jack Kornfield

The quote shown above was from Jack Kornfield, an author and mindfulness teacher who co-founded the Insight Meditation Society with Tara Bach and Sharon Salzberg. He also played a significant role in introducing mindfulness as well as mindfulness meditation to the West.

What he said is true. Throughout this book, you have learned about Buddhism, Zen, and mindfulness. You have read about their history, evolution, and benefits. You have also learned how you can effectively practice mindfulness in order to reap its rewards.

It is through mindfulness that you can free yourself from your chaotic mind. It is through Zen that you can finally be at peace. Whether you follow the traditional Buddhist teachings or not, Buddhism will still have a positive impact on the different aspects of your life if you take it seriously.

Allowing yourself to relax and let go is good for both your mind and body. You can be free from stress, anxiety, and even reduce your risk of physical ailments such as heart disease and high blood pressure.

When you practice mindfulness on a regular basis, your mind and body will get used to doing it. Eventually, you will form a habit, and you will notice your life becoming more peaceful than before.

On the other hand, if you allow yourself to get caught up in the hustle and bustle of everyday life, you will lose yourself. You will always be stressed and problematic, and your relationship with other people may get affected. This, in turn, can hurt your career, family life, and personal goals. Even worse, you can lose touch with yourself.

So, what should you do?

You need to practice Zen mindfulness. However, you should do it at your own pace and comfort level. This way, you will not be pressured to follow certain teachings or conduct yourself in a certain way.

At first, you may feel restless and uncomfortable. It is normal to assume that practicing meditation instantaneously results in inner peace. However, this may not be the case if it is your first time to meditate. Trying to be at peace may make you feel more chaotic than before.

You might constantly feel anxious about not doing it the right way, or you might worry about other people suddenly coming in and needing something from you. You might also be worried that your electronic devices would ring or give notifications; thus, disturbing your meditation session.

It is also natural to be anxious about missing out on something while you meditate. Someone might be texting an important message, for example. If you keep thinking about these things, then your mind will not concentrate on being mindful.

This is why you should not push yourself too hard. Do not force yourself to feel peaceful right away. Just let things be. Allow yourself to be at peace naturally, without pressure or force.

Once you get the hang of it, you will be able to improve. You will be able to sleep better and wake up more refreshed. If at first, your mind tends to wander during meditation or you usually feel sleepy afterward, things would get better on your second to the third week of practice. You will feel more alert and focused, even if you do not drink a cup of coffee beforehand.

Your mind and body will eventually get used to the peace and quiet that surround you. They will no longer give off the signal that it is time to fall asleep. Hence, your meditation session will not be interrupted. You will be able to complete every session without dozing off.

Then, when nighttime comes, you will be able to fall asleep faster, regardless of whether or not you meditated right before going to bed. You can meditate in the morning or afternoon and still get the same reward. As long as you meditated in the day, you will be able to have a relaxing sleep.

Other perks of meditation include feeling more confident and less rushed. Within a month of mindfulness meditation, you will notice that you are much less anxious yet much more productive. You will be able to do your work, but this time with more focus and grit. Since you no longer feel rushed or pressured, you can see the details more clearly and deliver more accurate results.

When you become more confident in yourself and your skills, you will get more things done. This, in turn, would give you an amazing feeling that would last for a long time.

Furthermore, your patience and mood levels will significantly improve. You will be much less moody than when you first started meditating. This would be evident in your daily life. You may no longer get cranky during traffic or while waiting in line. You may be more patient with colleagues, family members, and clients at work.

Through Zen mindfulness, you will achieve a sense of detachment. You will no longer have so many expectations; thus, preventing you from getting hurt easily. You will also be much kinder to yourself. The benefits of mindfulness meditation are truly satisfying.

So, if you want to attain peace of mind and be a better person in general, you should have an in-depth understanding of Zen, mindfulness, and Buddhism. This book is what you need to accomplish such personal goals.

See to it that you read each chapter carefully and internalize what you have learned. Share your newfound knowledge with other people so that they can also achieve genuine happiness and peace. Be an instrument to help people attain enlightenment.

I wish you the best of luck!

Thank you

Before you go, I just wanted to say thank you for purchasing my book. I poured a ton of time into this book and shared a lot of my personal experiences and those of people I spoke to when compiling the book to show you that you're not alone in this, and a beautiful and fulfilling life where you can feel safe and free from abuse is within your grasp.

You just need to reach out and make it happen. Every journey, even one along the road to recovery, starts with a single step. This is your permission to take yours.

It's also a fantastic thought to me that you could have picked from dozens of other books on the same topic, but you took a chance and chose this one.

So, a HUGE thanks to you for getting this book and for reading all the way to the end.

Now I wanted to ask you for a small favor. Could you please consider posting a review on the platform? Your reviews are one of the easiest ways to support the work of independent authors, and it's incredible to go online and see all the amazing support this work has received. I love hearing from you, and hearing your feedback inspires me to write more in the future and helps me to identify what to do better and how to be the best writer I can.

This feedback will help me continue to write the type of books that will help you get the results you want. So if you enjoyed it, please let me know.

www.ingramcontent.com/pod-product-compliance
Lightning Source LLC
Chambersburg PA
CBHW051803100526
44592CB00016B/2539